Encyclopedia of Math Topics and References

A Resource for Projects and Explorations (Grades 6–12)

Compiled by Dale Seymour

Dale Seymour Publications®

Dedicated to Jolene Schadler, for 25 years of outstanding service to the staffs at Creative Publications and Dale Seymour Publications.

Research Assistants: Tim Dolan, John Bennett, and David Patrick Marin
Project Editor: Joan Gideon
Production/Manufacturing Coordinator: Barbara Atmore
Art: Rachel Gage and Carl Yoshihara
Text design: Lisa Raine
Cover design: David Woods

Published by Dale Seymour Publications®, an imprint of the Alternative Publishing Group of Addison-Wesley Publishing Company.

Order Number DS21339
ISBN 0-86651-835-5

DALE
SEYMOUR
PUBLICATIONS
P.O. BOX 10888
PALO ALTO, CA 94303

3 4 5 6 7 8 9 10-MA-99 98 97

Contents

Preface

Although mathematics is an incredibly broad subject with widespread applications, the average secondary student is exposed to only a minute fraction of these applications. Teaching reforms, such as the NCTM *Curriculum and Evaluation Standards for School Mathematics,* propose that mathematics teachers spend more classroom time with their students exploring and investigating mathematics applications. In addition, they recommend that students learn to value the cultural, historic, and scientific evolution of the subject.

An effective way to involve students in these pursuits is through personal investigation of a specific topic of their choice. Teachers who make student projects a part of their curriculum often report positive changes in students' attitudes toward math class. Encouraging students to explore a math topic in depth helps them see the useful aspects of the topic and provides them an opportunity to be an "expert" in at least one area of mathematics.

Both the compiler of this encyclopedia and the author of the companion volume, *Math Projects: Organization, Implementation, and Assessment,* have experienced the advantages of student projects in their math classes; Seymour at the junior-high level and DeMeulemeester in her senior-high classes. The experience for them as teachers and for their students was enriching.

To produce successful projects, students need ideas for good project topics, and they need to know where to find information on those topics. This book provides both. The few previous books that list resources have been designed for the academically talented. We have suggested topics and resources for students of various levels of academic achievement. Of course, even in a comprehensive listing such as this, many other topics and references could have been included; add to these lists as you use them.

We hope you and your students enjoy learning more about the beautiful subject of mathematics.

Dale Seymour

How to Use This Book

The *Encyclopedia of Math Topics and References* is a time-saving resource to help teachers and students with math projects. All students, regardless of their interest in or knowledge of mathematics, can use this book to select and research topics about mathematics history, concepts, and applications. This book contains two types of information—topics to give students ideas of interesting mathematics projects and references to resources on those topics.

A companion publication, *Math Projects: Organization, Implementation, and Assessment,* tells teachers how to successfully use these projects. In addition, a data-base software version of the *Encyclopedia* and forms from *Math Projects* is available from the publisher. Students can use this software to select and print out information from the data base. Students and teachers are encouraged to make additions or deletions in the data base to keep the references current. The compiler welcomes your suggestions for additional references to be included in revisions.

Levels

The level ratings, indicated for each topic and reference, will help students choose projects and resources appropriate for their grade and ability level. Level 1 references and topics are appropriate for middle-school or junior-high students, Level 2 for high-school students, and Level 3 for students taking advanced courses. Some topics and references have a broad appeal and can be studied at several levels; they are consequently rated Level 1–3.

Topics for Math Projects

For each of over 250 topics, the alphabetical listing of topics with references includes a brief description of the topic, its level of difficulty, the identifying numbers of books or magazines containing information on that topic, pages in those resources, and the level of difficulty for each reference. Students can see, at a glance, the level of the topic and some possible references. By referring to the numerical list of books and magazines, students can identify the specific reference.

Concepts covered in the standard 7–12 curriculum, except those with interesting project extensions, are not included in the topic list. Certain areas, such as problem solving, are extremely important classroom experiences,

but are not included because these topics do not lend themselves to projects. Some general topics, such as computers, have been included. Students can narrow the topic once they begin their research.

The list of math project topics without descriptions and references can be easily copied and given to students searching for a project topic. Once they have chosen possible topics, they can look at the topics listed with the references.

References for Math Projects

References are listed alphabetically by title as well as by number. The numbers, used in the topic list in place of the full reference, were assigned arbitrarily. Book references begin at one; magazine references begin at eight hundred. Numbers between 676 and 799 have not been assigned. (Those using the data-base software can use those numbers for added book references.) References listed in this book are in bibliographic style, those in the software are in data-base records.

The only references included with copyrights before 1960 are classic references. Many libraries have mathematics books with copyrights older than 25 years. We have also included some references that are out of print, but still available in many libraries. Often a book that is referenced will include additional references on that topic. These bibliographies are often helpful, but they may contain references that are out of print or difficult to locate.

For most of the references listed with the math topics, page numbers are given in parentheses after the book or magazine number. If the pages are not indicated, it is because references to the topic are scattered throughout the book, most of the book is on that topic, or the page reference was not available.

Students need access to both math dictionaries and encyclopedias in their classrooms and to additional resources in libraries. If your school has only a few math resources, use your ingenuity to find ways to add to the math collections in your classroom and in the school and local libraries. Librarians usually welcome suggestions of good books to order for reference and enrichment. If funds are limited, solicit the PTA or find other ways to build adequate mathematics libraries.

Topics for Math Projects

Project Topics

Abacus

Abundant and Deficient Numbers

Algebra, History of

Algorithms

Alphametrics or Crypt Arithmetic

Amicable Numbers

Analyzing Data

Anamorphic Art

Ancient Asian Mathematics

Ancient Babylonian Mathematics

Ancient Egyptian Mathematics

Ancient Greek Mathematics

Angle-Trisection Problem

Annuities and Interest

Apollonius (255–170 B.C.)

Apportionment and Fair Division

Arabian and Persian Mathematics

Arabic Numeration

Archimedes (ca. 287– ca. 212 B.C.)

Archimedian Polyhedra

Architecture

Area Formulas and Calculations

Area vs. Perimeter

Aristotle (384–322 B.C.)

Arithmetic Progressions

Art and Geometry

Astronomy and Mathematics

Atoms and Molecules

Averages

Babbage, Charles (1792–1871)

Banneker, Benjamin (1731–1806)

Bernoulli

Billiards and Pool

Binary Number System

Binomial Theorem and Distribution

Birthday Problem

Book Reports

Boolean Algebra

Bridges

Buffon's Needle Problem

Calculating Devices

Calculating Prodigies

Calculation Shortcuts

Calculus

Calendars and Time

Calligraphy and Typography

Cantor, Georg (1845–1918)

Card and Number Tricks

Cartography and Maps

Casting Out Nines

Catenary Curves

Cayley, Arthur (1821–1895)

Celtic Design

Central Tendency Measures

Chaos

Chinese Mathematics

Circuits

Clock Arithmetic

Collecting Data

Combinations and Permutations

Complex Numbers

Compound Polyhedra

Computers

Conflict

Conics

Constructions

Constructions, Unusual

Consumer Math

Continued Fractions

Crypt Arithmetic

Cryptography and Cryptanalysis

Crystallography

Crystallography Patterns

Cube Root Algorithm

Curve Stitching

Curves

Data Analysis

Decision Making

Deduction vs. Induction

Deficient Numbers

Density of Numbers

Descartes, René (1596–1650)

Design

Designs from Many Cultures

Determinants

Difference Equations

Dimensions

Dissections

Divisibility Rules

Domes

Drawing Devices

Dürer, Albrecht (1471–1528)

e

Earth Measurement

Earthquakes and Logarithms

Egyptian Numeration

Einstein, Albert (1879–1955)

Elections and Social Choices

Ellipses

Eratosthenes of Alexandria (ca. 276–ca. 194 B.C.)

Escher, M. C. (1898–1972)

Euclid (ca. 300 B.C.)

Euclid's *Elements*

Euler, Leonard (1707–1783)

Euler's Formula

Fair Divisions

Famous Mathematicians

Fermat, Pierre de (1601–1665)

Fermat's Last Theorem

Fibonacci, Leonardo de Pisa (ca. 1170–ca. 1250)

Fibonacci Numbers

Fields and Groups

Figurate Numbers

Finger Reckoning

Finite Differences

Flexagons

Four-Color Problem

Fourth Dimension and Higher

Fractals
Fractions, History of
Frieze Patterns
Fuller, Buckminister
    (1895–1983)
Functions

Galilei, Galileo
    (1564–1642)
Galton's Board (Quincunx)
Gambling
Game Theory
Gauss, Karl Fredrich
    (1777–1855)
Gears, Ratios, and the
    Bicycle
Genetics
Geodesic Domes
Geometric Constructions
Geometric Design
Geometric
    Transformations
Geometry, History of
Germain, Sophie
    (1776–1831)
Goldbach's Conjecture
Golden Section
Graph Theory
Graphing Calculators
Graphing Data
Gravitation
Greek Numeration
Groups and Fields
Growth Models

Handicraft Designs
Harmonic Mean
Harmonic Sequences

Hebrew Numeration
Hexaflexagons
Hindu-Arabic Numeration
Hypatia (370–415)
Hyperbolas
Hypercubes

Imaginary Numbers
Indian Numeration
Induction
Infinity
Instruments in Geometry
Interest and Annuities
Irrational Numbers
Islamic Art
Iteration and Recursion

Kaleidoscopes
Kepler, Johann
    (1571–1630)
Kepler-Poinsot Polyhedra
Kites
Knots
Königsberg Bridge
    Problem
Kovalevsky, Sonya
    Kovalevskaya (1850–1891)

Lagrange, Joseph
    (1736–1813)
Land Measure
Laplace, Pierre
    (1749–1827)
Latitude and Longitude
Leibnitz, Gottfried
    Wilhelm (1646–1716)
Leonardo de Pisa
Life, Conway's Game of

Linear Programming
Line Designs
Line Groups
Logarithms
Logic
Logo Computer Language
Logos
Longitude and Latitude
Lovelace, Ada Byron
    (1815–1852)

Magic
Magic Squares and Cubes
Maps and Cartography
Map Coloring
Math Models
Math Theory of Elections
Mathematical Induction
Mathematician
Mathematics
Matrices
Mayan Numeration
Measurement
Measures of Central
    Tendency
Mental Calculating
    Shortcuts
Metric System
Minimal Surfaces
Mira Constructions
Möbius Strip
Modeling and Decision
    Making
Modern Mathematicians
Modular Arithmetic
Moiré Patterns
Molecules and Atoms
Monte Carlo Methods

Motion
Music and Mathematics
Mysticism in Math

Napier, John (1550–1617)
Napier's Rods
Nature
Navigation
Networks and Circuits
Newton, Isaac
    (1642–1727)
Nine-Point Circle
Noether, Amalie Emmy
    (1882–1935)
Non-Euclidean
    Geometries
Normal Distribution
    Curve
Numeration
Number Theory
Number Tricks
Numerology

Odds
Operations Algorithms
Operations Research
Optical Illusions
Optics
Origami

Packing Problems
Palindromes
Pantographs
Paper Airplanes and
    Boomerangs
Paper Engineering and
    Pop-Ups
Paper Folding and
    Origami

Papyrus Rhind

Parabolas

Paradoxes

Pascal, Blaise (1623–1662)

Pascal's Triangle

Pattern

Penrose Tiles

Perfect Numbers

Perimeter vs. Area

Permutations and
    Combinations

Perspective

Photography

Pi (π)

Plane Groups

Platonic Solids

Pólya, George
    (1887–1985)

Polygonal Numbers

Polyhedra

Polyominoes

Pool and Billiards

Population and Food

Powers and Roots

Primes and Composites

Probability Theory

Prodigies

Projective Geometry

Proof

Puzzles

Pyramids of Egypt

Pythagoras
    (ca. 580–ca. 500 B.C.)

Pythagoreans

Pythagorean Theorem

Pythagorean Triples

Quadratic Equations

Quadratic Formula

Ramanujan, Srinivasa
    (1887–1920)

Random Numbers

Rate and Ratio

Rational Numbers

Real Numbers

Recursion

Regular Polyhedra

Relativity Theory

Repeating Decimals

Rhind Papyrus

Riemann, Georg Fredrich
    Bernhard (1826–1866)

Roman Numerals

Roots and Powers

Scaling and Similarity

Scheduling and Planning

Semiregular Polyhedra

Semiregular Tessellation

Series and Sequences

Set Theory

Sierpiński Triangle

Sieve of Eratosthenes

Simulations

Slide Rule

Soap Film and Minimal
    Surfaces

Social Choices

Somerville, Mary Fairfax
    (1780–1872)

Space Program

Speed

Sphere Packing

Spirals

Spirographs®

Spirolaterals and
    Worm Paths

Sports

Square Root Algorithms

Squaring the Circle

Star Polygons

Statistical Inference

Statistics

Strip Groups

Sun Dials

Surveying

Symbolic Logic

Symmetry

Symmetry Groups

Symmetry in Design

Symmetry in Logos

Symmetry in Nature

Tangrams

Tensegrity

Tessellations and Tiling

Tessellations, Space

Thales (640–550 B.C.)

Time and Calendars

Topology

Transfinite Numbers

Transformations

Triangular Numbers

Trigonometry

Trisection of an Angle

Unsolved Problems

Vectors

Velocity and Speed

Volume Problems

Wallpaper Patterns

Weights and Measures

Western European
    Mathematics

Women

Zero

Project Topics and References

Abacus   [Level 1–2]

This counting frame, used to record numbers and to calculate, has many different forms and has been used by many cultures.

References: 15 (156–196) [L 1–2]; 16 (199–201) [L 2]; 290 (1–22) [L 1–2]; 343 (94–108) [L 1–2]; 501 [L 2]; 512 [L 2]; 523 [L 1–2]; 536 [L 1–2]; 537 [L 1–2]; 538 [L 2]; 581 (159–61) [L 2]; 675 (117–20) [L 1–2].

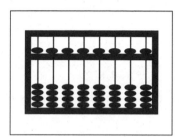

Abacus

Abundant and Deficient Numbers   [Level 1–3]

An abundant number is a positive integer whose proper divisors add to a number greater than itself. A deficient number is a positive integer whose proper divisors add to a number less than itself. Positive integers are either abundant, deficient, or perfect.

See also **Perfect Numbers.**

References: 62 (32–4) [L 1–2]; 79 (91–5) [L 2–3]; 81 (1–194) [L 1–2]; 472 (1–168) [L 1–2]; 675 (59–61) [L 1–2]; 1143 (692–6) [L 1–2].

Algebra, History of   [Level 1–3]

Algebra, the generalization of arithmetic, was primarily the science of equations until the middle of the nineteenth century.

References: 12 (68–9) [L 2]; 13 (102–3, 239–43) [L 2]; 15 (395–530) [L 1–3]; 16 (575–598) [L 3]; 100 (1–74) [L 1–2]; 594 [L 3]; 675 (233–332) [L 1–2].

Algorithms   [Level 1–3]

An algorithm is a process for solving a problem. Algorithms for computation were often done differently in different cultures (examples: division algorithms and square root algorithms).

References: 12 (68, 81) [L 1–2]; 15 (88–155) [L 1–2]; 53 (523–38) [L 2–3]; 77 (89–115) [L 1–2]; 381 (195–206) [L 2–3]; 391 (291–9) [L 3]; 471 (43–6) [L 1–2]; 498 (85–125) [L 1–2]; 557 (11–23) [L 2];

880 (209–12) [L 1–2]; 957 (554–8) [L 2–3]; 995 (430–5) [L 1–2]; 1168 (96–110) [L 2]; 1175 (60–9) [L 2–3].

Alphametrics or Crypt Arithmetic   [Level 1–2]

In these problems or puzzles, the numerical digits have been replaced by alphabet letters. Solutions require logic and trial-and-error.

References: 295 (25–39) [L 1–2]; 353 (90–5) [L 1–2]; 354 (22–6) [L 1–2]; 362 (1–72) [L 1–2]; 413 (78–81) [L 1–2]; 471 (94–6) [L 1–2]; 502 [L 1–2].

Alphametrics

Amicable Numbers   [Level 1–2]

If the sum of the proper divisors of each of a pair of numbers equals the other number, the numbers are amicable.

References: 15 (23–4) [L 2]; 79 (104–17) [L 1–2]; 81 (1–194) [L 1–2]; 349 (160–71) [L 1–2]; 413 (35–7) [L 1–2]; 471 (53–4) [L 1–2]; 675 (58–9) [L 1–2]; 1211 [L 2].

Amicable Numbers

Analyzing Data

See **Data Analysis.**

Anamorphic Art   [Level 1–3]

Anamorphic art is distorted artwork that looks normal when reflected in a curved mirror.

References: 10 (100–1) [L 1–2]; 187 (223–6) [L 1–2]; 253 (1–24) [L 1–3]; 254 (1–34) [L 1–2]; 347 (97–109) [L 2]; 502 [L 2]; 504 [L 2]; 1210 (176–87) [L 2–3].

Ancient Asian Mathematics   [Level 1–2]

Did mathematics develop independently in different parts of the world? Which concepts were similar in different continents?

References: 12 (65–75) [L 1–2]; 13 (8–10) [L 1–2]; 14 (138–176, 266–91) [L 1–2]; 16 (195–224) [L 1]; 89 (181–98) [L 2]; 287 (130–214) [L 2]; 469 (146–167) [L 1–2]; 559 (27–37) [L 1]; 560 [L 1]; 561 (139–48) [L 1–2]; 617 [L 2–3]; 1029 (72–9) [L 1–2]; 1233 (424–32) [L 1–2].

Ancient Babylonian Mathematics   [Level 1–2]

Around 2000 B.C., the Babylonians developed a base-sixty numeration system. What were its advantages and disadvantages?

References: 15 (36–9) [L 1–2]; 48 (8–14) [L 1–2]; 50 (5–29) [L 1–2]; 77 (33–7) [L 1–2]; 87 (29–37) [L 1–2]; 287 (91–129) [L 2]; 413 (64–72) [L 2–3]; 675 (36–7) [L 1–2]; 1021 (295–8) [L 1–2].

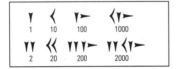

Babylonian Numerals

Ancient Egyptian Mathematics   [Level 1–2]

The history of mathematics as an organized discipline begins with the Ionian Greeks, but they were indebted to the Egyptians and Phoenicians for many discoveries in arithmetic and geometry earlier than 600 B.C.

References: 13 (1–8) [L 1–2]; 14 (41–53) [L 1–2]; 89 (29–43) [L 2]; 287 (57–90) [L 2]; 469 (50–73) [L 1–2]; 556 (520–2) [L 2]; 558 (24–38) [L 1]; 559 [L 1]; 578 (1–160) [L 1–2]; 1055 (133–171) [L 1–2] 1234 (630–4) [L 1–2].

Ancient Greek Mathematics   [Level 1–2]

The period from 600 B.C. to A.D. 640 is considered the beginning of the history of mathematics.

References: 10 (38–50) [L 1–2]; 12 (37–63) [L 1–2]; 13 (11–128) [L 1–2]; 14 (54–137) [L 1–2]; 16 (43–194) [L 2–3]; 89 (52–165) [L 2]; 469 (74–97) [L 1–2]; 556 (1–519) [L 2]; 557 (1–250) [L 2]; 674 [L 1–2]; 1055 (133–71) [L 1–2].

Angle-Trisection Problem   [Level 2–3]

This classic problem is to divide an angle into three equal parts using only compass and straightedge.

References: 15 (297–302) [L 2–3]; 16 (126–8) [L 2–3]; 120 [L 2–3]; 127 (9–12) [L 1–2]; 132 (58–63) [L 3]; 344 (255–65) [L 2]; 410 (73–80) [L 2–3]; 506 [L 2–3]; 507 [L 2–3]; 508 [L 2–3]; 675 (199–201) [L 2–3]; 993 (220–22) [L 1–2]; 1035 (319–21) [L 1–2]; 1045 (290–3) [L 2].

Annuities and Interest

See Interest and Annuities.

Apollonius (255–170 B.C.)   [Level 1–2]

This Greek geometer posed several interesting and classic problems.

References: 11 (97–105) [L 1–2]; 13 (77–83) [L 1–2]; 14 (116–7) [L 1–2]; 16 (140–57) [L 2–3]; 17 [L 1–2]; 20 (34–47) [L 1–2]; 48 (56–182) [L 2].

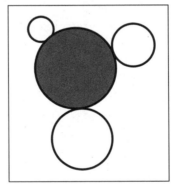

Apollonius' Problem

Apportionment and Fair Division   [Level 1–3]

Apportionment is the division of the population for fair representation in our government. Alexander Hamilton suggested one system to determine the number of representatives from each state.

See also Elections.

References: 53 (297–319) [L 2–3]; 271 (22–3) [L 1–2]; 276 (1–51) [L 1–2]; 277 (1–40) [L 1–2]; 828 (89–91) [L 1–2]; 858 (523–5) [L 1–2]; 1058 (20–5) [L 1–2].

Arabian and Persian Mathematics   [Level 1–2]

Arabian mathematics based mainly on Hindu sources, drew also from the Greeks. Before the end of the ninth century the Arabs had translations of the works of Euclid, Archimedes, Apollonius, and others.

References: 11 (113–4) [L 1–2]; 13 (144–63) [L 1–2]; 14 [L 1–2]; 16 (225–45) [L 1–2]; 287 (301–48) [L 2].

Arabic Numeration   [Level 1–2]

The Hindu-Arabic numeration system prevailed over others. Why? When did it begin?

References: 13 (184–8) [L 1–2]; 15 (42–3, 69–71) [L 1–2]; 16 (253–4) [L 1–2]; 48 (56–182) [L 2]; 77 (79–90) [L 1–2]; 87 (137–56) [L 1–2]; 413 (64) [L 1–2]; 675 (46–9) [L 1–2]; 827 (58–60) [L 2].

Archimedes (ca. 287–212 B.C.)   [Level 1–2]

This famous Greek scholar was one of the greatest geometers and physicists of all time.

References: 11 (97–105) [L 1–2]; 13 (64–77) [L 1–2]; 14 (111–6) [L 1–2]; 16 (120–39) [L 2–3]; 17 (28–34) [L 1–2]; 19 (19–27) [L 1]; 20 (34–47) [L 1–2]; 21 (4–7) [L 1–2]; 23 [L 1]; 50 (73–100) [L 1–2]; 420 (57–9) [L 1–2]; 621 [L 2–3]; 833 (204–6) [L 2]; 981 (378–85) [L 1–2].

Archimedes. From Susan and John Edeen. *Portraits, Mathematicians Book 1.* Dale Seymour Publications, 1988.

Archimedian Polyhedra   [Level 1–3]

Also known as semiregular polyhedra, these shapes are formed from combinations of regular polygons. All vertices are identical.

References: 199 [L 2–3]; 200 (15–44) [L 1–2]; 201 (55–67) [L 1–2]; 202 (40–58) [L 1–2]; 203 (120–33) [L 1–2]; 209 (20–33) [L 1–2]; 210 (100–28) [L 1–2]; 219 (72–97) [L 3]; 493 (327–31) [L 2–3]; 601 [L 2–3]; 819 (689–93) [L 2–3]; 924 (371–6) [L 1–2]; 1061 (577–81) [L 1–2].

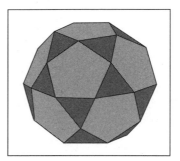

Icosidodecahedron

Architecture   [Level 1–3]

What kinds of mathematics do architects use in their work? What major geometric properties or concepts are illustrated in well–known structures?

References: 109 (103–10) [L 1–2]; 125 (102–23) [L 2–3]; 130 (1–326) [L 2–3]; 135 (98–105) [L 2–3]; 159 (1–84) [L 1–2]; 264 (1–182) [L 1–2]; 265 (20–232) [L 1–2]; 423 (1–34) [L 2]; 488 (1–303) [L 1–2]; 489 (1–143) [L 1–2]; 490 (1–191) [L 1–2]; 491 (1–303) [L 1–2]; 492 (1–288) [L 1–2]; 1105 (104–9) [L 2–3]; 1106 (66–76) [L 2–3]; 1163 (162–73) [L 2–3]; 1173 (132–45) [L 2–3]; 1174 (176–85) [L 2–3]; 1198 (160–75) [L 2–3].

Area Formulas and Calculations   [Level 1–3]

How did the basic area formulas evolve? What are some unusual formulas for simple shapes?

References: 131 (116–34) [L 2–3]; 802 (273–4) [L 1–2]; 814 (258–9) [L 2–3]; 829 (92–3) [L 2–3]; 984 (294–6) [L 2–3]; 1012 (738–40) [L 2]; 1142 (420–3) [L 2–3].

Area vs. Perimeter   [Level 1–2]

What shapes give the largest area for the smallest perimeter?

References: 652 (142–6) [L 2]; 835 (222–3) [L 1–2]; 992 (65–70) [L 1–2]; 1065 (360–3) [L 1–2]; 1078 (342–4) [L 1–2]; 1090 (218–21, 231–2) [L 1–2]; 1226 (659–60) [L 1–2]; 1229 (157–9) [L 1–2].

Aristotle (384–322 B.C.)   [Level 1–2]

This great Greek philosopher and mathematician was the author of many books.

References: 11 [L 1–2]; 13 (48–9) [L 1–2]; 14 (93–4) [L 1]; 16 (97–9) [L 1–2]; 17 [L 1–2]; 23 [L 1]; 468 (9–28) [L 1–2]; 990 (507) [L 2].

Aristotle. From Susan and John Edeen. *Portraits, Mathematicians Book 1.* Dale Seymour Publications, 1988.

Arithmetic Progressions

See Series and Sequences.

Art and Geometry   [Level 1–2]

Art, design, and mathematics, especially geometry, have many interesting connections. Many famous artists have used mathematical principles in their work.

References: 72 [L 2–3]; 118 (1–40) [L 1–2]; 126 (1–113) [L 1–2]; 130 (1–326) [L 2–3]; 187 (1–293) [L 1–2]; 222 (1–13) [L 1–2]; 236 (1–153) [L 1–2]; 237 (1–100) [L 1–2]; 238 (1–469) [L 1–2]; 240 (1–173) [L 1–2]; 241 (151–73) [L 1–2]; 244 (1–48 & software) [L 1–2]; 245 (1–228) [L 1–2]; 251 (1–154) [L 1–2]; 252 (1–38) [L 1–2]; 423 (1–32) [L 2]; 498 (142–74) [L 1–2]; 524 (39–56) [L 2–3]; 570 (1–64) [L 1–2]; 651 [L 2]; 967 (133) [L 1–2]; 1032 (298–308) [L 1–2]; 1206 (278–82) [L 1–2].

Art and Geometry. From Mabel Sykes. *Source Book of Problems for Geometry.* Dale Seymour Publications, 1994.

Astronomy and Mathematics   [Level 1–3]

What role does mathematics play in the study of outer space, the planets, and stars?

References: 11 [L 2]; 32 (51–85) [L 1–2]; 53 (433–75) [L 1–3]; 330 (7–10) [L 1–2]; 391 (192–207) [L 3]; 466 (91–2) [L 2–3]; 484 (1–330) [L 1–2]; 654 (1–172) [L 2–3]; 1140 (122–6) [L 2–3].

Atoms and Molecules

See Molecules and Atoms.

Averages   [Level 1–2]

Averages are measures of central tendency. What are they, how are they calculated, and how are they used in our daily lives?

References: 323 (1–128) [L 2]; 324 (1–110) [L 1–2]; 534 (1–33) [L 1]; 937 (744–6) [L 2]; 1005 (24) [L 1–2]; 1076 (250–3) [L 1–2].

Babbage, Charles (1792–1871)   [Level 1–2]

This English statistician and inventor envisioned the modern digit computing machine long before its time.

References: 22 (73–80) [L 1]; 52 (176–7) [L 1–2]; 87 (191–208) [L 1–2]; 442 [L 1–2]; 443 [L 2]; 444 [L 1–2]; 445 [L 1–2]; 446 [L 2]; 447 (1–265) [L 1–2]; 970 (366–72) [L 2–3].

Banneker, Benjamin (1731–1806)   [Level 1–2]

An African-American farmer, Banneker studied mathematics and astronomy on his own and used his knowledge to create accurate ephemerides for almanacs.

References: 22 (63–72) [L 1]; 675 [L 1–2]; 1020 (155–60) [L 1–2].

Bernoulli   [Level 1–3]

More than a dozen members of this Swiss family contributed to mathematical developments in the period 1650–1850.

References: 11 (140–4) [L 1–2]; 12 (118–20) [L 1–2]; 13 (366–9) [L 1–2]; 14 (426–33) [L 1–2]; 16 (415–38) [L 3]; 17 (131–8) [L 2–3]; 20 (107–13) [L 1–2]; 21 (8–9) [L 1–2]; 24 [L 1]; 55 (184–206) [L 2–3].

Billiards and Pool   [Level 1–2]

Playing pool or billiards requires application of geometric principles.

References: 52 (42) [L 1–2]; 241 (45–51) [L 1–2]; 539

(51–8) [L 1]; 540 (31–72) [L 1]; 553 (71–80) [L 1–2]; 907 (60–4) [L 1–2]; 968 (429–30) [L 2]; 1004 (456–60) [L 2–3]; 1031 (154–63) [L 1–2]; 1158 (124–35) [L 2].

Binary Number System   [Level 1–2]

The binary number system uses base 2 instead of base 10. This system has been used extensively in computers and electrical engineering.

References: 76 (42–4) [L 1–2]; 82 (1–75) [L 1–2]; 330 (23–8) [L 1–2]; 343 (11–27) [L 1–2]; 415 (28–40) [L 1–2]; 511 [L 1–2]; 583 (16–29) [L 2].

1 = 1	100 = 6
10 = 2	111 = 7
11 = 3	1000 = 8
100 = 4	1001 = 9
101 = 5	⋮

Binary Numerals

Binomial Theorem and Distribution   [Level 1–3]

The rule for the expansion of any power of a binomial has many applications and connections.

See also **Normal Distribution Curve.**

References: 16 (393–4) [L 3]; 35 (190–225) [L 1–2]; 55 (165–74) [L 2–3]; 100 (6–8) [L 1–2]; 411 (67–85) [L 2–3]; 675 (264–6) [L 2]; 842 (698–701) [L 2–3].

Birthday Problem   [Level 1–2]

How many people need to be in a room to have a 50/50 chance of two of them having the same birthday? How is this figured?

References: 997 (769–75) [L 2]; 1033 (348–53) [L 1–2]; 1093 (373–7) [L 1–2]; 1216 (322–5) [L 1–2].

Book Reports

Several books dealing with mathematics, mathematicians, or math concepts—both fiction and non-fiction—have been written in the past half century. These books are interesting reading for reports and discussion.

References: 29 (1–430) [L 2–3]; 30 (1–500) [L 3]; 40 (1–166) [L 1–3]; 54 (1–230) [L 2–3]; 55 (1–300) [L 2–3]; 59 [L 1–2]; 60 [L 1–2]; 114 (1–135) [L 1–2]; 115 (1–239) [L 1–2]; 194 (1–153) [L 1–3];

340 (1–229) [L 3]; 420 (1–300) [L 2]; 421 (1–227) [L 1–2]; 422 (1–204) [L 3]; 441 [L 3].

Boolean Algebra   [Level 2–3]

This type of algebra deals with logical properties of statements (propositions).

References: 17 (433–47) [L 2–3]; 87 (209–26) [L 2]; 100 (26–9) [L 2]; 415 [L 2–3]; 509 [L 2–3]; 542 [L 2]; 624 [L 2–3]; 675 (284–7) [L 2–3]; 883 (602–5) [L 2].

Bridges   [Level 1–3]

What are the main types of bridges? What are the advantages and disadvantages of each? Could you build a model of a bridge?

References: 487 (1–28) [L 1–2]; 488 (144–78) [L 1–2]; 1102 (66–73) [L 3].

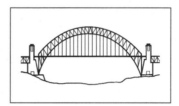

Arch Bridge. From Jeanne Pollard. *Building Toothpick Bridges.* Dale Seymour Publications, 1985.

Buffon's Needle Problem   [Level 2–3]

This fascinating experiment was designed by Georges Buffon (1707–1788) to approximate the value of π.

References: 5 (574–5) [L 2–3]; 16 (455, 493) [L 1–2]; 844 (638–40) [L 2–3]; 1228 (183–6) [L 2].

Calculating Devices   [Level 1–3]

For centuries people have created many devices to help perform arithmetic computations. Today we have electronic calculators. What were some of the earlier devices?

See also **Abacus, Napier's Bones.**

References: 5 (732–44) [L 3]; 6 (73–97) [L 2–3]; 10 (20–37) [L 1–2]; 77 (56–78) [L 1–2]; 87 (217–26) [L 1–2]; 514 [L 1–2]; 553 (16–25) [L 1–3]; 1009 (59–64) [L 1–2].

Calculating Prodigies   [Level 1–2]

Many people have demonstrated the ability to perform rapid and complex computations in their heads. Fascinating and unbelievable accounts are recorded.

References: 11 (455–76) [L 1–2]; 17 (484–9) [L 1–2];

304 [L 1–2]; 344 (66–88) [L 1–2]; 351 (360–87) [L 1–2]; 515 [L 1–2]; 516 [L 1–2]; 669 (1–365) [L 1–2]; 675 (159–60) [L 1–2].

✓ Calculation Shortcuts   [Level 1–2]

Many shortcuts to standard algorithms enable people to perform difficult arithmetic computations in their heads. What are some of these? Why do they work?

See also **Card and Number Tricks.**

References: 304 (1–218) [L 1–2]; 305 (1–350) [L 1–2]; 306 (1–39) [L 1–2]; 309 (1–112) [L 1–2]; 376 [L 1–2]; 377 [L 1–2]; 378 [L 1–2]; 379 [L 1]; 380 (1–229) [L 1–2]; 425 [L 1–2]; 582 [L 2]; 585 [L 1–2]; 628 [L 1–2]; 826 (20–1) [L 2].

Calculus   [Level 3]

This field of mathematics studies change using the infinitesimal. Its tools are differentiation and integration of functions.

References: 15 (676–702) [L 3]; 34 (120–170) [L 2–3]; 48 (342–435) [L 3]; 49 (125–50) [L 2]; 396 (1–680) [L 2–3]; 397 (1–267) [L 3]; 398 (1–211) [L 2–3]; 399 (1–112) [L 2–3]; 400 (1–120) [L 2–3]; 407 (1–118) [L 2–3]; 463 (454–520) [L 2–3]; 497 [L 3]; 544 (1–427) [L 3]; 545 (1–262) [L 3]; 546 (1–206) [L 3]; 547 (1–165) [L 3]; 548 (1–196) [L 3]; 675 (376–459) [L 3]; 955 (377–85) [L 3].

Calendars and Time

See **Time.**

Calligraphy and Typography   [Level 1–3]

Calligraphy is the art of writing beautifully. Typography is the art or process of printing with type. These two fields apply math concepts such as measurement, proportion, and symmetry.

References: 52 (16) [L 1–2]; 177 (1–125) [L 1–2]; 231 (129–34) [L 1–2]; 234 (70–160) [L 1–2]; 235 (527–42) [L 1–2]; 583 (139–52) [L 2].

Calligraphy. From Dan Pedoe. *Geometry and the Visual Arts.* New York: Dover Publications, 1976.

Cantor, Georg (1845–1918)   [Level 1–3]

Cantor was a German mathematician who made many contributions to set theory.

References: 12 (162–3) [L 1–2]; 16 (563–70) [L 3]; 17 (555–79) [L 2–3]; 30 (77–86) [L 2–3]; 55 (267–83) [L 2–3]; 517 [L 2–3]; 518 [L 2–3]; 1183 (122) [L 3].

Card and Number Tricks   [Level 1–3]

Many card and number tricks have algebraic solutions. Being a good magician requires both slight-of-hand talent and mathematical knowledge.

References: 307 (1–41) [L 1–2]; 345 (206–13) [L 1–2]; 347 (71–84) [L 1–2]; 349 (94–104) [L 1–2]; 521 (1–84) [L 1–2]; 805 (326–8) [L 1–2]; 826 (20–1) [L 2]; 857 (568–70) [L 1–2]; 903 (100–3) [L 2]; 959 (618–9) [L 2–3]; 1184 (19–33) [L 2].

Cartography and Maps

See **Maps and Cartography.**

Casting Out Nines   [Level 1–3]

This method is used to check multiplication and division. What is it, and why does it work?

References: 15 (151–4) [L 1–2]; 97 (94–102) [L 2–3]; 470 (25–9) [L 1–2]; 675 (140–1) [L 1–2]; 846 (661–5) [L 2–3]; 1100 (85–93) [L 2–3].

Catenary Curves

See **Curves.**

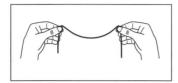

Catenary Curve

Cayley, Arthur (1821–1895) [Level 1–2]

Cayley was an English algebraist, geometer, and analyst who made many contributions to higher algebra.

References: 12 (166–73) [L 1–2]; 14 (465–7) [L 1–2]; 16 (587–91) [L 2]; 17 (378–405) [L 2]; 20 (134–5) [L 1–2]; 340 (167–8) [L 2].

Celtic Design [Level 1–2]

The Celtic artists developed techniques to produce beautiful designs, decorations, and patterns. Many of these were very mathematical.

References: 233 (1–159) [L 1–2]; 234 (1–160) [L 1–2]; 649 (25–96) [L 1–2]; 650 (1–160) [L 2].

Central Tendency Measures

See Averages.

Chaos [Level 2–3]

Systems governed by physical laws undergo transitions to highly irregular forms of behavior. Chaos involves tracking the behavior of mathematical models to study phenomena in nature.

References: 340 (144–73) [L 3]; 341 (222–38) [L 3]; 451 (1–178) [L 3]; 452 (1–317) [L 3]; 453 (1–390) [L 3]; 454 (1–218) [L 3]; 455 (1–128) [L 2–3]; 459 (1–183) [L 2–3]; 460 (1–203) [L 2–3]; 551 (75–99) [L 2–3]; 553 (93–108) [L 2–3]; 571 [L 3]; 1130 (42–9) [L 2–3].

Chinese Mathematics [Level 1–2]

Did other cultures influence the Chinese system? What similarities existed? Compare Chinese and Hindu-Arabic numeration systems.

References: 15 (39–42) [L 1–2]; 16 (198) [L 2–3]; 77 (40–2) [L 1–2]; 87 (53–72) [L 1–2]; 287 (130–214) [L 2]; 469 (146–67) [L 1–2]; 561 (139–41) [L 1–2]; 617 [L 2]; 675 (43–4) [L 1–2]; 1029 (72–9) [L 1–2]; 1233 (424–32) [L 1–2].

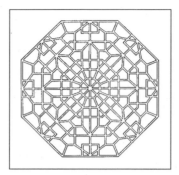

Chinese Lattice Design. From Daniel S. Dye. *Chinese Lattice Designs.* New York: Dover, 1974.

Circuits

See Networks and Circuits.

Clock Arithmetic

See Modular Arithmetic.

Collecting Data

See Data Analysis.

Combinations and Permutations [Level 1–3]

A combination of a set of things is a selection of those things without regard to order. Permutations take order into account. Combinations and permutations are used in the study of probability.

References: 14 (524–30) [L 2–3]; 79 (19–56) [L 1–2]; 381 (59–66) [L 1–2]; 848 (269–73) [L 1–2]; 854 (183–7) [L 1–2]; 873 (50–1) [L 1–2]; 1006 (263–6) [L 1–2].

Complex Numbers [Level 2–3]

Complex numbers include all numbers real and imaginary. The general form for a complex number is $a + bi$, where a and b are real numbers and $i^2 = {}^-1$.

References: 5 (77–9) [L 2]; 15 (261–8) [L 3]; 76 (19–23) [L 2]; 100 (32–6) [L 2]; 598 (142–53) [L 2–3]; 849 (278–82) [L 2–3]; 895 (589–97) [L 3]; 991 (583–92) [L 2–3].

Compound Polyhedra [Level 2–3]

A compound polyhedra is the combination of two or more polyhedra, such as five interlocking cubes.

References: 200 (84–99) [L 2]; 202 (34–9) [L 2–3]; 209 (34–45) [L 2]; 210 (129–42) [L 2]; 213 [L 2–3]; 227 [L 1–2].

Compound of Two Tetrahedra

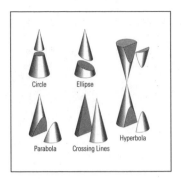

Conic Sections

Computers [Level 1–3]

A computer is any instrument that performs mathematical operations. This broad topic could be explored from a number of different points of view (such as history, type, or applications).

References: 5 (745–56) [L 3]; 10 (18–37) [L 1–2]; 11 (2043–2108) [L 2]; 53 (521–84) [L 1–3]; 87 (227–44) [L 1–2]; 267 (1–96) [L 1–2]; 269 (1–145) [L 1–2]; 395 (1–118) [L 2–3]; 466 (42–54) [L 2–3]; 496 [L 1–3]; 500 (88–102) [L 2–3]; 553 (7–56) [L 1–3]; 646 [L 2–3]; 647 [L 2–3]; 648 [L 2–3]; 655 [L 2–3]; 675 (161–4) [L 1–2]; 1124 (44–51) [L 2–3]; 1137 (120–3) [L 2–3]; 1156 (136–47) [L 2]; 1176 (188–99) [L 2–3]; 1200 (94–106) [L 2–3].

Conflict

See **Game Theory.**

Conics [Level 1–3]

Conic curves are the lines of intersection of a plane and a cone. The circle, ellipse, parabola, and hyperbola are conics.

References: 5 (302–19) [L 3]; 16 (144–56, 343–4) [L 2–3]; 33 (125–30) [L 2]; 52 (196–7) [L 2]; 103 (1–108) [L 2–3]; 350 (205–18) [L 2]; 409 (138–44) [L 2–3]; 414 (99–103) [L 3]; 426 (1–100) [L 2–3]; 427 (36–64) [L 3]; 429 (1–33) [L 3]; 438 (29–57) [L 1–2]; 573 (1–16) [L 2–3]; 803 (190–3) [L 3]; 851 (363–8) [L 2–3]; 892 (414–7) [L 2–3]; 973 (294–6) [L 3]; 976 (361–3) [L 2–3]; 1145 (102–10) [L 2–3]; 1164 (16–27) [L 2].

Constructions [Level 1–3]

Geometric constructions are drawn, using only a compass and straightedge, to satisfy given conditions.

References: 30 (140–57) [L 3]; 50 (54–6) [L 2]; 127 (5–19) [L 1–2]; 129 (1–170) [L 2–3]; 161 (1–64) [L 1–2]; 162 (1–123) [L 1–2]; 163 (1–102) [L 2–3]; 164 (1–87) [L 2]; 165 (1–172) [L 1–2]; 186 (1–25) L 1–3; 259 (79–88) [L 1–3]; 330 (141–54) [L 1–2]; 675 (192–6) [L 1–2]; 820 (288–90) [L 2]; 823 (32–4) [L 1–2]; 954 (361–5) [L 3].

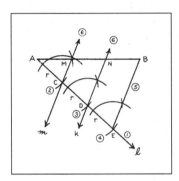

Geometric Constructions. From Posamentier and Wernick. *Advanced Geometric Constructions.* Dale Seymour Publications, 1988.

Constructions, Unusual [Level 1–3]

Unusual geometric constructions are drawn with tools other than compass and straightedge.

References: 30 (146–57, 196) [L 3]; 50 (54–6) [L 2]; 164 (1–87) [L 2]; 165 (1–172) [L 2]; 852 (291–5) [L 2]; 888 (380–6) [L 3]; 893 (296–301) [L 1–2]; 1050 (361–4) [L 2]; 1088 (166–7) [L 1–2].

Consumer Math [Level 1–2]

Mathematics used for purchasing, selling, and investing is consumer or business math.

See also **Interest and Annuities.**

References: 70 (45–88) [L 1–2]; 918 (610–3) [L 2–3]; 966 (562–7) [L 2]; 1000 (299–300) [L 2]; 1042 (134–6) [L 1–2]; 1053 (184–6, 238) [L 1–2]; 1062 (124–7) [L 1–2]; 1086 (62–3) [L 1–2].

Continued Fractions   [Level 2–3]

A continued fraction is a number plus a fraction whose denominator is a number plus a fraction, whose denominator is a number plus a fraction, and so on. It may have a finite or infinite number of terms.

References: 15 (418–21) [L 2–3]; 100 (9–13) [L 1–2]; 102 (56–8) [L 2]; 104 (1–162) [L 2–3]; 135 (137–40) [L 2]; 675 (264–71) [L 2]; 867 (424–8) [L 2–3].

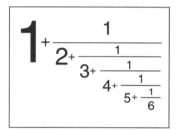

Finite Continued Fraction

Crypt Arithmetic

See **Alphametrics.**

Cryptography and Cryptanalysis   [Level 1–3]

Both terms refer to the science of translating or interpreting secret codes, which often use mathematical methods.

References: 110 (62–8) [L 2]; 291 [L 2–3]; 293 (1–241) [L 1–2]; 330 (90–135) [L 1–2]; 340 (38–43) [L 3]; 351 (388–418) [L 2]; 403 (1–222) [L 3]; 424 [L 1–3]; 493 (48–78) [L 2]; 816 (18–26) [L 3]; 853 (249–51) [L 2–3]; 891 (547–53) [L 2–3]; 922 (34–62) [L 2–3]; 952 (676–80) [L 2–3]; 1114 (50–7) [L 3]; 1147 (146–57) [L 3]; 1204 (228–30) [L 2]; 1241 [L 2–3].

Crystallography   [Level 1–3]

This science involves the study of the forms and structures of shapes. Identifiable patterns in crystals have applications to the study of polyhedra and tessellations.

References: 11 (857–66) [L 1–2]; 37 (74–97) [L 2–3]; 52 (38–39) [L 1–2]; 53 (81) [L 2]; 146 (1–226) [L 1–2]; 348 (91–101) [L 1–2]; 438 (181–5) [L 2–3]; 466 (47–8) [L 2–3]; 524 (1–199) [L 2–3]; 855 (377–88) [L 1–2]; 887 (454–61) [L 2–3]; 1103 (44–53) [L 3]; 1115 (48–55) [L 3]; 1123 (120–3) [L 2–3].

Crystallography Patterns   [Level 2–3]

These patterns define the properties of the 7 line patterns and 17 plane patterns as well as three-dimensional patterns.

References: 53 (492–4) [L 2]; 185 (37–56) [L 2–3]; 187 (54–77) [L 2]; 193 (23–52) [L 3]; 223 (1–400) [L 2–3]; 224 (127–298) [L 2–3]; 467 (122–9) [L 2–3].

Cube Root Algorithm   [Level 2–3]

What algorithms have been devised to compute cube root?

References: 15 (144–51) [L 2–3]; 307 (156–8) [L 1–2]; 1022 (402–3) [L 1–2]; 1046 (448–9) [L 2–3]; 1236 (175–6) [L 1–2].

Curve Stitching

See **Line Designs.**

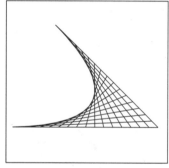

Curve Stitching. From Dale Seymour. *Introduction to Line Designs.* Dale Seymour Publications, 1992.

Curves   [Level 2–3]

What are some classifications of curves? How do curves compare? Which curves can be represented algebraically?

See also **Conics, Spirals.**

References: 58 (608) [L 2]; 102 (21–2) [L 2]; 125 (196–255) [L 3]; 427 (1–238) [L 3]; 428 (1–464) [L 2–3]; 429 (1–190) [L 3]; 467 (164–74) [L 2–3]; 550 (343–55) [L 2]; 598 (56–80) [L 2]; 1223 (239–42) [L 2–3].

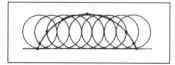

Cycloid

Data Analysis [Level 1–3]

Data analysis involves working with information; calculating statistics, such as measures of central tendency, on that data; and compiling it in a form, often a chart or graph, that can be easily understood.

References: 53 (151–82) [L 1–3]; 54 (95–113) [L 1–2]; 90 (213–40) [L 2–3]; 289 (1–25) [L 2–3]; 320 (1–161) [L 1–2]; 323 [L 1–3]; 332 (13–56) [L 1–2]; 382 (1–49) [L 1–2]; 1001 (90–3) [L 1–2]; 1201 (163–74) [L 3]; 1079 (392) [L 1–2].

Decision Making

See Modeling and Decision Making.

Deduction vs. Induction [Level 2–3]

These are two approaches to mathematical investigation and proof. In what type of problems would you use one and not the other? How is mathematical induction different from induction?

See also Proof.

References: 100 (55–8) [L 3]; 381 (171–7) [L 2–3]; 435 (192–3) [L 2–3]; 495 [L 2–3]; 527 (79–93) [L 2–3]; 574 (1–90) [L 2–3]; 595 (121–3) [L 2]; 675 (313–6) [L 2–3]; 1209 (408–17) [L 3].

Deficient Numbers

See Abundant and Deficient Numbers.

Density of Numbers [Level 1–3]

Is there always another number of the same type between any two whole numbers? rational numbers? real numbers?

References: 30 (68–72) [L 2–3]; 52 (108–9) [L 1–2]; 406 (88–125) [L 2]; 415 (144–53) [L 1–2]; 467 (35) [L 1–2]; 859 (547–8) [L 1–2].

Descartes, René (1596–1650) [Level 1–2]

This European mathematician, along with Fermat, founded analytic geometry. He is considered one of the first modern mathematicians.

References: 11 (124–35, 235–48) [L 1–2]; 13 (268–78) [L 1–2]; 14 (371–7) [L 1–2]; 16 (333–67) [L 2]; 17 (35–55) [L 1–2]; 20 (79–96) [L 1–2]; 21 (20–3) [L 1–2]; 22 (35–44) [L 1]; 24 [L 1]; 449 [L 2]; 865 (706–9) [L 1–2].

René Descartes. From John and Susan Edeen. *Portraits, Mathematicians Book 2*, Dale Seymour Publications, 1988.

Design [Level 1–3]

Geometric patterns and structures provide the basis for many types of design. Nearly every culture has developed special designs that are used extensively.

See also **Celtic Design, Crystallography Patterns, Design from Many Cultures, Frieze Patterns, Islamic Art, Line Designs, Logos, Moiré Patterns, Penrose Tiles, Tessellations.**

References: 117 (1–60) [L 1–2]; 118 (1–40) [L 1–2]; 130 (1–326) [L 2–3]; 162 (1–123) [L 1–2]; 176 (1–40) [L 1–2]; 178 (1–216) [L 1–2]; 187 (1–293) [L 1–2]; 221 (1–64) [L 1–2]; 223 (1–400) [L 2–3]; 224 (1–298) [L 1–3]; 230 (1–200) [L 1–2]; 231 (1–151) [L 1–2]; 232 (1–192) [L 2–3]; 233 (1–159) [L 1–2]; 234 (1–160) [L 1–2]; 238 (1–469) [L 1–2]; 239 (1–93) [L 1–2]; 240 (1–173) [L 1–2]; 265 (1–235) [L 1–2]; 285 (1–40) [L 1–2].

Geometric Design. From Dale Seymour. *Geometric Design.* Dale Seymour Publications, 1988.

Designs from Many Cultures [Level 1–2]

How have geometric concepts influenced the design of handicrafts and ornaments in various cultures? Which cultures have developed their designs to the greatest level of sophistication?

References: 12 (9–22) [L 1–2]; 130 (1–326) [L 2]; 224 (1–281) [L 1–2]; 233 (1–159) [L 1–2]; 235 (1–542) [L 1–2]; 236 (1–153) [L 1–2]; 237 (1–100) [L 1–2]; 238 (1–467) [L 1–2]; 239 (1–93) [L 1–2]; 300 (1–44) [L 2]; 512 (1–170) [L 1–2]; 948 (138–43) [L 2].

Steel Ceiling Design. From Mabel Sykes. *Source Book of Problems for Geometry.* Dale Seymour Publications, 1994.

Determinants [Level 2–3]

A determinant is a square array, or matrix, of numbers or variables used, for example, in the solution of simultaneous equations.

See also Matrices.

References: 5 (359–61) [L 3]; 15 (475–7) [L 2–3]; 16 (470–1) [L 3]; 28 (125–42) [L 3]; 48 (795–811) [L 2–3]; 100 (23–6) [L 2]; 675 (281–4) [L 2–3].

Difference Equations

See Finite Differences.

Dimensions

See Fourth Dimension and Higher.

Dissections [Level 2–3]

Polygons can be broken up into smaller polygons with specific characteristics. This process of geometric dissection produces interesting and challenging problems.

References: 52 (9, 35) [L 2]; 133 (1–184) [L 2]; 185 (91–8) [L 2–3]; 210 (17–27) [L 2]; 295 (110–3) [L 2]; 350 (165–81) [L 2]; 467 (88–99) [L 2]; 942 (302–8) [L 2].

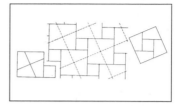

Geometric Dissection. From Harry Lindgren. *Recreational Problems in Geometric Dissections and How to Solve Them.* New York: Dover, 1972.

Divisibility Rules [Level 1–3]

Rules to test whether or not a given whole number is divisible by 2, 3, 5, and 10 are commonly known. What about tests for divisibility by 4, 6, 7, 8, 9, 11, and other numbers?

References: 79 (104–17) [L 1–2]; 306 (143–56) [L 1–2]; 471 (70–1) [L 1–2]; 800 (542–6) [L 1–2]; 806 (223–5) [L 2]; 1024 (670–4) [L 2–3]; 1025 (667–8) [L 2–3].

Domes

See Geodesic Domes.

Drawing Devices

See Instruments in Geometry.

Dürer, Albrecht (1471–1528) [Level 1–2]

This German artist and mathematician explored geometric properties and artistic perspective, and he often depicted mathematical objects in his woodcuts.

References: 11 (591–612) [L 1–2]; 125 (44–81) [L 2]; 448 (61–70) [L 2]; 569 [L 1–2]; 1206 (278–82) [L 1–2].

Albrecht Dürer

e [Level 2–3]

The irrational number *e* is the base of the natural system of logarithms. Its numerical value is approximately 2.7182818284. . . .

References: 98 (92–105) [L 2–3]; 102 (19, 28–9, 34) [L 2]; 415 (154–73) [L 3]; 550 (80–9) [L 2–3]; 595 (62–5) [L 2]; 675 (154) [L 3].

Earth Measurement [Level 1–3]

Pythagoras (ca. 540 B.C.) was possibly the first to teach that the earth was a sphere. The Greeks were interested in calculating the circumference and density of the earth. How did they arrive at these numbers? How accurate were their early calculations?

References: 15 (368–76) [L 1–2]; 53 (410–65) [L 2–3]; 69 (129–60) [L 2]; 70 (37–42) [L 2]; 80 (1–144) [L 1–2]; 280 (1–58) [L 2–3]; 469 (124–45) [L 1–2]; 480 (1–54) [L 1–2]; 484 (1–330) [L 1–2]; 1112 (54–61) [L 3]; 1037 (400–4); [L 2–3]; 1150 (172–82) [L 2].

Earthquakes and Logarithms [Level 1–3]

The Richter scale for measuring the strength of an earthquake was devised in 1935 by Charles Richter. The scale is logarithmic.

References: 52 (20–1) [L 2]; 328 (249–60) [L 1–2]; 485 [L 1–2]; 486 (1–87) [L 1–2]; 1152 (152–9) [L 2].

Egyptian Numeration [Level 1–2]

What was this system? When was it developed? Is there any carryover to our current numeration system?

References: 15 (45–7) [L 1–2]; 48 (15–23) [L 1–2]; 87 (39–52) [L 1–2]; 675 (38–40) [L 1–2].

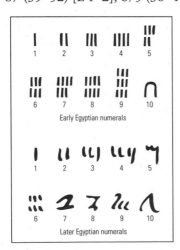

Egyptian Numerals

Einstein, Albert (1879–1955) [Level 1–2]

Einstein was a theoretical physicist and a mathematical genius who revolutionized thinking about time, space, mass, light, motion, and gravitation.

References: 11 [L 1–2]; 17 [L 1–2]; 18 [L 1–2]; 21 (24–7) [L 1–2]; 22 (119–26) [L 1]; 109 [L 1–2]; 340 (87, 142) [L 1–2]; 468 (229–48) [L 1–2]; 531 (1–298) [L 1–2]; 676 (1–697) [L 1–2].

Elections and Social Choices [Level 1–3]

Mathematicians have looked for a perfect voting system for centuries. The analysis of elections has been explored extensively by mathematicians.

References: 53 (237–319) [L 2–3]; 271 (1–28) [L 2]; 328 (79–150) [L 1–2]; 683 (1–697) [L 1–2]; 828 (89–91) [L 1–2]; 912 (520–1) [L 2]; 971 (493–501) [L 1–2]; 994 (605–8) [L 1–2]; 1051 (635) [L 1–2]; 1125 (44–53) [L 2–3]; 1157 (88–95) [L 2–3]; 1159 (16–26) [L 2–3].

Ellipses

See **Conics.**

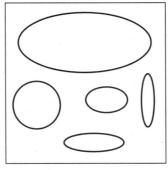

Ellipses

Eratosthenes of Alexandria (ca. 276–ca. 194 B.C.) [Level 1–2]

The Greek mathematician was also an astronomer, geographer, and philosopher. He developed the first systematic method for determining prime numbers.

See also Sieve of **Eratosthenes.**

References: 13 (83–4) [L 1–2]; 14 (108–11) [L 1–2]; 46 (69–72) [L 1–2]; 466 (23–4) [L 2]; 675 (72–4) [L 1–2]; 981 (378–85) [L 1–2].

Escher, M. C. (1898–1972) [Level 1–3]

This Dutch graphic artist was the first to depict

animated figures that tessellate (tile) the plane. He corresponded with mathematicians who influenced his work, such as Pólya and Coxeter.

References: 181 (184–236) [L 1–2]; 183 (1–195) [L 1–2]; 189 (1–111) [L 1–2]; 190 (1–100) [L 1–2]; 191 (1–263) [L 1–2]; 192 (1–402) [L 1–3]; 193 (1–354) [L 2–3]; 194 (1–153) [L 1–2]; 195 (1–276) [L 1–2]; 344 (89–102) [L 1–2]; 898 (307–10) [L 1–2]; 910 (299–306) [L 1–2].

Escher Drawing. © 1994 M.C. Escher/Cordon Art—Baarn—Holland. All rights reserved.

Euclid (ca. 300 B.C.) [Level 1–2]

This Greek geometer compiled all the information known about geometry in *Elements*.

References: 11 (97–105) [L 1–2]; 13 (52–62) [L 1–2]; 14 (103–8) [L 1–2]; 16 (100–19) [L 2]; 20 (34–47) [L 1–2]; 21 (28–9) [L 1–2]; 22 (1–8) [L 1]; 23 [L 1]; 48 (56–182) [L 2]; 50 (37–72) [L 1–2]; 450 [L 2]; 865 (706–9) [L 1–2]; 866 (16–7) [L 2]; 1080 (460–3) [L 1–2].

Euclid. From John and Susan Edeen. *Portraits, Mathematicians Book 1,* Dale Seymour Publications, 1988.

Euclid's *Elements* [Level 1–3]

This famous work of 13 books contains 465 propositions about plane geometry and presents a deductive theory of geometry.

References: 16 (100–19) [L 1–2]; 125 (140–72) [L 2–3]; 391 (47–68) [L 1–2]; 450 [L 2–3]; 596 (40–59) [L 2–3].

Euler, Leonard (1707–1783) [Level 1–2]

Sometimes referred to as the most prolific mathematician in history, Euler was the first to discover many important relationships and formulas.

References: 11 (140–4, 173–81) [L 1–2]; 12 (120–5) [L 1–2]; 13 (393–400) [L-2]; 14 (520–5) [L 1–2]; 16 (439–65) [L 2]; 17 (139–52) [L 1–2]; 19 (73–81) [L 1]; 20 (107–13) [L 1–2]; 24 [L 1]; 55 (223–44) [L 2]; 867 (424–8) [L 2].

Euler. From John and Susan Edeen. *Portraits, Mathematicians Book 2.* Dale Seymour Publications, 1988.

Euler's Formula [Level 1–3]

This formula states the relationship between the numbers of vertices, edges, and faces in any simple polyhedron. Explore the relationship on your own before you read the formula.

References: 30 (236–40) [L 2]; 64 (52–8) [L 1–2]; 102 (30–3) [L 2]; 381 (96–103) [L 1–3]; 392 (33–9) [L 2–3]; 393 (1–66) [L 2–3]; 436 (10–19) [L 1–2].

Fair Divisions

See **Apportionment and Fair Division.**

Famous Mathematicians

See Apollonius, Archimedes, Aristotle, Babbage, Banneker, Bernoulli, Cantor, Cayley, Descartes, Dürer, Einstein, Eratosthenes, Euclid, Euler, Fermat, Fibonacci, Fuller, Galileo, Gauss, Germain, Hypatia, Kepler, Kovalevsky, Lagrange, Laplace, Leibnitz, Lovelace, Napier, Newton, Noether, Pascal, Pólya, Pythagoras, Ramanujan, Riemann, Thales, Modern Mathematicians.

Math Hall of Fame

Fermat, Pierre de (1601–1665)   [Level 1–2]

A brilliant French mathematician, Fermat was cofounder of both probability theory and analytic geometry.

References: 13 (293–301) [L 1–2]; 14 (377–8) [L 1–2]; 16 (333–67) [L 2–3]; 17 (56–72) [L 1–2]; 22 (45–52) [L 1]; 24 [L 1]; 55 (223–41) [L 2–3]; 623 [L 1–2].

Fermat's Last Theorem   [Level 2–3]

This famous theorem state that $x^n + y^n = z^n$, where n is greater than 2, has no solution in positive integers.

References: 132 (277–303) [L 2–3]; 345 (10–19) [L 3]; 415 (65–70) [L 2]; 551 (177–200) [L 2–3]; 563 (1–80) [L 3]; 564 [L 3]; 565 [L 3]; 566 [L 3]; 595 (75–7) [L 2]; 675 (79–80) [L 2]; 815 (389–90) [L 2]; 875 (637–40) [L 2–3]; 1180 (104–22) [L 2–3].

Fibonacci, Leonardo de Pisa (ca. 1170–ca. 1250) [Level 1–2]

In 1202 Fibonacci published a work known as Liber Abaci where he explained the advantages of the Arabic system of numeration over the Roman system.

References: 13 (167–70) [L 1–2]; 14 (214–8) [L 1–2]; 22 (17–24) [L 1]; 23 [L 1]; 102 (75–79) [L 2]; 562 [L 2]; 629 [L 3].

Fibonacci Numbers   [Level 1–3]

In the Fibonacci sequence 1, 1, 2, 3, 5, 8, 13, 21, 34, . . . each number is the sum of the two previous numbers.

References: 9 (1–9) [L 2–3]; 52 (28–9) [L 1–2]; 76 (61–7) [L 1–2]; 81 (1–194) [L 1–2]; 91 (1–96) [L 1–2]; 102 (75–79) [L 2]; 135 (141–78) [L 2–3]; 288 [L 2–3]; 430 (1–255) [L 1–2]; 461 (3–18) [L 1–2]; 470 (53–8) [L 1–2]; 471 (47–52) [L 1–2]; 562 [L 2–3]; 628 [L 3]; 629 [L 3]; 675 (77–9) [L 1–2]; 927 (314–6) [L 1–2]; 972 (357–8) [L 3]; 976 (361–3) [L 2–3].

$$
\begin{array}{rcl}
& & 1 \\
1 & = & 1 \\
1 + 1 & = & 2 \\
1 + 2 & = & 3 \\
2 + 3 & = & 5 \\
3 + 5 & = & 8 \\
5 + 8 & = & 13 \\
8 + 13 & = & 21 \\
& \vdots &
\end{array}
$$

Fibonacci Numbers

Fields and Groups

See Groups and Fields.

Figurate Numbers   [Level 1–2]

Also known as polygonal numbers, these can be represented by points (or pebbles) in the form of a polygon or polyhedron—for example, square numbers, triangular numbers, rectangular numbers, cubic numbers.

References: 15 (24–6) [L 1–2]; 33 (53–72) [L 1–2]; 61 (1–30) [L 1–2]; 81 (1–194) [L 1–2]; 95 (159–201) [L 2]; 111 (1–115) [L 1–2]; 242 (1–102) [L 1–2]; 347 (15–25) [L 2]; 415 (71–82) [L 2]; 471 (55–8) [L 1–2]; 675 (53–8) [L 1–2]; 936 (555–62) [L 1–2]; 1066 (624–5) [L 1–2].

Pentagonal Numbers

Finger Reckoning [Level 1–2]

Most early cultures had systems for representing natural numbers with their fingers; some developed forms of finger computation.

References: 15 (196–202) [L 1–2]; 77 (26–8) [L 1–2]; 316 (136–42) [L 1]; 349 (105–22) [L 1–2]; 675 (120–3) [L 1–2].

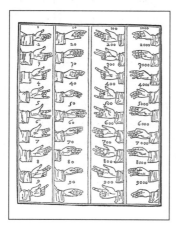

Finger Reckoning

Finite Differences [Level 2–3]

A method of determining generalizations from number sequences by subtracting consecutive numbers in the sequence, then subtracting the consecutive differences until all differences are the same.

References: 15 (512–3) [L 2–3]; 64 (1–108) [L 2–3]; 111 (1–113) [L 1–2]; 474 (1–107) [L 2–3]; 645 [L 3]; 970 (366–72) [L 2–3]; 982 (466–70) [L 2–3].

Flexagons [Level 1–2]

Flexagons are paper models folded from a colored equilateral triangular grid to make a hexagon shape. The hexagon shape can then be flexed to make new hexagons, which have different color combinations.

References: 52 (107) [L 1–2]; 152 (16–7) [L 1–2]; 198 (1–40) [L 1–2]; 207 (bk 1) [L 1–2]; 286 (1–8) [L 1–2]; 461 (87–96) [L 1–2]; 618 [L 1–3].

Four-Color Problem

See **Map Coloring.**

Fourth Dimension and Higher [Level 2–3]

Fourth-dimensional space can be defined algebraically and represented geometrically with a model called a hypercube. Higher dimensions are explored by physi-cists, mathematicians, and other research scientists.

References: 54 (39–59) [L 2–3]; 71 [L 3]; 72 [L 2–3]; 109 (61–70) [L 2–3]; 340 (62–98) [L 3]; 344 (41–54) [L 2]; 348 (151–63) [L 2–3]; 410 [L 2–3]; 411 [L 3]; 499 (351–413) [L 2]; 524 (1–199) [L 2–3]; 528 (1–227) [L 1–2]; 582 [L 3]; 597 (400–7) [L 2–3]; 599 (81–92) [L 3]; 633 [L 3]; 675 (211–4) [L 2]; 1118 (14–23) [L 3].

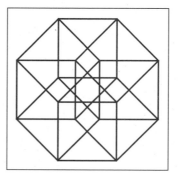

Model of the Fourth Dimension

Fractals [Level 1–3]

Fractals are geometric objects whose growth exponents are not whole numbers. Find out how fractal images are created on a computer.

References: 33 (161–83) [L 2–3]; 109 (112–33) [L 2–3]; 187 (170–201) [L 1–2]; 340 (114–42) [L 3]; 341 (239–53) [L 3]; 350 (31–48) [L 2–3]; 451 (1–178) [L 3]; 453 (1–390) [L 3]; 454 (1–218) [L 3]; 455 (1–128) [L 2–3]; 457 (1–465) [L 3]; 459 (1–183) [L 2–3]; 460 (1–203) [L 2–3]; 553 (109–28) [L 2–3]; 804 (265–75) [L 2–3]; 872 (179–85) [L 2–3]; 879 (178–85) [L 2–3]; 1130 (42–9) [L 2–3]; 1131 (60–7) [L 2–3].

Mandelbrot Set

Fractions, History of [Level 1–2]

When were fractions first used? How were they represented?

References: 15 (208–50) [L 1–2]; 16 [L 1–2]; 77 (99–105) [L 1–2]; 675 (135–9) [L 1–2]; 1055 (133–71) [L 1–2].

Frieze Patterns   [Level 1–3]

These are linear patterns formed by repeating a unit design through slides, flips, and turns that can be classified into one of seven symmetry groups, also known as strip groups or line groups.

References: 11 (218–50) [L 2]; 36 (88–90) [L 1–2]; 53 (485–94) [L 1–2]; 175 (26–30) [L 1–2]; 185 (37–56) [L 2–3]; 187 (52–3) [L 1–2]; 223 (94–165) [L 1–2]; 224 (81–125) [L 2–3]; 467 (120–1) [L 2]; 1028 (55–8) [L 1–3].

Fuller, Buckminister (1895–1983)   [Level 1–3]

Fuller, a designer, engineer, and architect, invented the geodesic dome and energetic geometry. Many of his structures used the idea that the basic energy patterns in nature can be expressed by families of geometric solids created from regular tetrahedra.

See also **Geodesic Domes, Polyhedra.**

References: 216 (1–234) [L 2]; 217 (1–876) [L 2–3]; 284 (1–63) [L 1–2]; 1079 (568–77) [L 1–2]; 1107 (24) [L 3].

Functions   [Level 1–3]

Functions are relations where one object is associated with each object from another set. The area of a square is a function of the length of its side.

References: 5 (110–38) [L 2]; 16 [L 1–3]; 98 (1–144) [L 2–3]; 100 (54–5) [L 2]; 337 (1–32) [L 2–3]; 595 (87–90) [L 2]; 598 (102–18) [L 2]; 970 (366–72) [L 2–3].

Galilei, Galileo (1564–1642)   [Level 1–2]

Galileo was instrumental in the founding of modern physics. His experiments on falling bodies from the leaning tower of Pisa established the first principles of dynamics.

References: 11 (715–57) [L 2]; 13 (247–51) [L 1–2]; 14 (363–6) [L 1–2]; 16 (319, 326) [L 2]; 19 (45–51) [L 1]; 21 (34–5) [L 1–2]; 23 [L 1]; 468 (29–48) [L 1–2]; 1192 (133–43) [L 2]; 1193 (150–7) [L 2].

Galton's Board (Quincunx)   [Level 1–3]

Galton's board, the Quincunx, is used to simulate a normal distribution curve. Nails or pegs are positioned in a board, and balls are funneled from the top through the pegs to land in bins at the bottom. As a ball falls between two pegs, it hits the peg below and has a 50/50 chance of falling to the left or right.

References: 52 (184–5) [L 1–2]; 210 (217–8) [L 1–2]; 332 (82–6) [L 1–2]; 830 (571–3) [L 2–3].

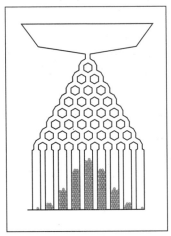

Galton's Board

Gambling   [Level 1–3]

Games of chance each have their own mathematical expectations. Probability tells us what the mathematical expectations are for a given game.

References: 109 (238–44) [L 1–2]; 303 (51–157) [L 1–2]; 310 (1–178) [L 1–2]; 311 (1–161) [L 1–2]; 312 (1–134) [L 1–3]; 313 (1–236) [L 1–2]; 344 (123–38) [L 1–2]; 389 (312–15) [L 2–3]; 411 (1–134) [L 2–3]; 847 (121–3) [L 2–3]; 869 (136–41) [L 1–2]; 881 (139–43) [L 1–2]; 882 (138–42) [L 3]; 958 (394–9) [L 3]; 1011 (726–31) [L 1–2]; 1041 (458–61) [L 1–2]; 1016 (13–7) [L 1–2]; 1038 (766–71) [L 1–2]; 1068 (35–6) [L 1–2]; 1185 (144–51) [L 2].

Probability Models

Game Theory   [Level 2–3]

Game theory is a mathematical theory of optimal behavior in situations involving competition or conflict; it can be applied to economics and military strategies as well as to games.

References: 5 (723–9) [L 3]; 53 (320–344) [L 2–3]; 273 (1–30) [L 2–3]; 314 (1–113) [L 2–3]; 381 (214–27) [L 2]; 389 (1–65) [L 3]; 411 (86–115) [L 2–3]; 466 (53–4) [L 2–3]; 640 [L 3]; 653 (1–198) [L 2–3]; 882 (138–42) [L 3]; 1108 (126–8) [L 2–3]; 1187 (18–28) [L 2]; 1208 (328–31) [L 2–3].

Gauss, Karl Fredrich (1777–1855)   [Level 1–3]

Gauss, one of the greatest mathematicians of all times, made important contributions to most major branches of mathematics known at his time.

References: 11 (149–56, 291–332) [L 1–2]; 12 (142–6) [L 1–2]; 13 (447–54) [L 1–2]; 14 (502–4) [L 1–2]; 16 (497–511) [L 2–3]; 17 (218–69) [L 1–2]; 19 (99–105) [L 1]; 20 (122–33) [L 1–2]; 21 (38–43) [L 1–2]; 24 [L 1]; 422 (1–204) [L 3]; 860 (288–93) [L 2–3]; 1162 (17–20) [L 2].

Gauss. From Susan and John Edeen. *Portraits, Mathematicians Book 2.* Dale Seymour Publications, 1988.

Gears, Ratios, and the Bicycle

See **Motion.**

Genetics   [Level 2–3]

Genetics, the study of the biological basis of inheritance, employs systematic counting and probability.

References: 68 (91–110) [L 1–2]; 466 (15–7) [L 2–3]; 980 (685–90) [L 2–3].

Geodesic Domes   [Level 1–3]

A spherelike structure formed by a grid of support materials parallel to one of three great circles is known as a geodesic dome. The dome has equilateral triangular faces and possesses amazing strength and efficiency for its size.

References: 200 (56–74, 100–7) [L 1–3]; 215 (1–172) [L 3]; 216 (1–234) [L 2]; 217 (1–876) [L 3]; 488 (225–46) [L 1–2]; 886 (582) [L 1–2]; 960 (227–8) [L 2–3]; 1030 (117–24) [L 2–3]; 1107 (24) [L 3].

Geometric Constructions

See **Constructions.**

Geometric Design

See **Design, Designs from Many Cultures.**

Geometric Transformations   [Level 1–3]

These occur with a movement or change in a geometric figure involving a slide (translation), turn (rotation), flip (reflection), scaling (shrinking or enlarging), or combinations of these.

References: 28 (183–200) [L 3]; 35 (279–96) [L 1–2]; 98 (106–12) [L 2–3]; 121 (207–30) [L 2]; 165 (1–172) [L 2]; 166 (1–192) [L 2]; 244 (1–48 & sftwr) [L 1–2]; 259 (147–68) [L 2–3]; 274 (1–36) [L 2–3]; 409 (80–102) [L 2–3]; 414 (104–31) [L 3]; 423 (383–404) [L 3]; 636 [L 3]; 637 [L 3]; 879 (178–85) [L 2–3]; 907 (60–4) [L 1–2]; 1197 (206–30) [L 3].

Geometry

See **Non-Euclidean Geometry, Projective Geometry.**

Geometry, History of   [Level 1–2]

The ancient Greeks were fascinated with geometry. Men such as Thales, Pythagoras, Hippocrates, Plato, Aristotle, Euclid, and Archimedes made major contributions to its development.

References: 14 [L 1–2]; 16 (6–7) [L 2–3]; 533 [L 2–3]; 674 [L 1–2]; 675 (165–231) [L 1–2]; 1080 (460–3) [L 1–2].

Germain, Sophie (1776–1831)   [Level 1–3]

A French mathematician who was interested in number theory and analysis, Germain won the grand prize from the French academy in 1816 for her work on the law of vibrating elastic surfaces.

References: 16 (503) [L 1–2]; 17 [L 1–2]; 19 (91–7)

[L 1]; 20 (63–82) [L 1–2]; 21 (44–5) [L 1–2]; 25
[L 1]; 26 (63–82) [L 1–3].

Sophie Germain. From John and Susan Edeen. *Portraits, Women Mathematicians.*
Dale Seymour Publications, 1990.

Goldbach's Conjecture   [Level 1–3]

The conjecture (unproven idea) states every even
number, except 2, is equal to the sum of two prime
numbers (such as, 8 = 5 + 3, 10 = 7 + 3, 12 = 7 + 5).
Christian Goldbach made this conjecture in the early
1700s.

References: 16 (457–8) [L 1–2]; 81 (70–1) [L 1–2];
84 (96–101) [L 2–3]; 85 (153–6) [L 3]; 340 (26–7)
[L 1–2].

Golden Section   [Level 1–3]

The division of a line into two parts such that the
larger compares to the smaller in the same ratio that
the whole line compares to the larger. The golden
section has many applications in mathematics, art,
music, and nature.

References: 16 (73–4) [L 2–3]; 52 [L 1–2]; 53
(479–82) [L 1–2]; 76 (36–40) [L 1–2]; 91 (1–96)
[L 1–2]; 102 (53–71) [L 2]; 134 (1–167) [L 2]; 135
(1–117) [L 2]; 186 (27–198) [L 1–2]; 412 (75–95)
[L 2–3]; 423 (75–103) [L 2]; 428 (461–9) [L 2–3];
430 (1–255) [L 1–2]; 461 (19–36) [L 1–2]; 470
(53–8) [L 1–2]; 493 (75–104) [L 2–3]; 675 (204–7)
[L 1–2]; 972 (357–8) [L 3]; 975 (554–7) [L 2]; 976
(361–3) [L 2–3].

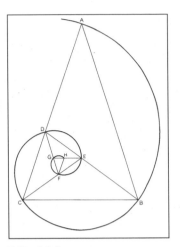

Golden Spiral

Graph Theory   [Level 2–3]

Graph Theory is the study of the combinatorial
structure of two- and three-dimensional structures; it
involves networks and is used to analyze and optimize
the progress of complicated processes, such as the
erection of large buildings.

References: 5 (688–90) [L 3]; 51 (58–70) [L 1–2]; 98
(1–144) [L 2–3]; 103 (1–108) [L 2–3]; 108 (1–139)
[L 2]; 275 (1–31) [L 2–3]; 381 (87–95) [L 2–3]; 384
(1–72) [L 2–3]; 392 (1–82) [L 2–3]; 393 (1–66)
[L 2–3]; 401 (1–145) [L 2–3]; 404 (90–135) [L 3];
423 (105–66) [L 2]; 461 (19–36) [L 1–2]; 493
(105–66) [L 2–3]; 499 (414–63) [L 2]; 581 (1–78)
[L 2–3]; 603 [L 2]; 619 [L 3].

Graphing Calculators   [Level 2–3]

Graphing calculators enable one to visualize equations,
relationships, and data for better understanding.

References: 99 (1–84) [L 2–3]; 315 (1–78) [L 2–3];
335 (1–32) [L 2–3]; 336 (1–120) [L 2–3]; 337 (1–32)
[L 2–3]; 338 (1–32) [L 2–3]; 397 (1–267) [L 3]; 1205
(240–3) [L 2–3].

Graphing Data

See **Data Analysis.**

Gravitation [Level 2–3]

The gravitational force of the attraction between two masses varies directly as the product of their masses and varies inversely as the square of the distance between them. The concept was formulated by Newton in his law of attraction.

References: 32 (107–25) [L 2–3]; 330 (109–18) [L 2–3]; 432 [L 2–3]; 433 [L 3]; 434 [L 2–3]; 878 (601–4) [L 2–3]; 1161 (166–81) [L 2].

Greek Numeration [Level 1–2]

What symbols were used? How were larger numbers written? How did their system compare to the Romans? Could they use the system for computation?

References: 15 (47–53) [L 1–2]; 48 (24–55) [L 1–2]; 50 (35–72) [L 1–2]; 77 (44–6) [L 1–2]; 87 (73–92) [L 1–2]; 415 [L 1–2]; 675 (42–3) [L 1–2].

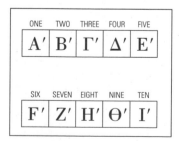

ONE	TWO	THREE	FOUR	FIVE
A′	B′	Γ′	Δ′	E′

SIX	SEVEN	EIGHT	NINE	TEN
F′	Z′	H′	Θ′	I′

Greek Numerals

Groups and Fields [Level 2–3]

A group is a set of elements and an operation to combine the elements of the set having specified properties; a field has two operations to combine the elements of the set. They are algebraic ways of identifying the structure of sets.

References: 5 (343–56) [L 3]; 9 (22–9) [L 3]; 11 (1509–47) [L 3]; 28 (201–17) [L 3]; 499 (298–350) [L 2]; 500 (25–47) [L 2–3]; 644 [L 3]; 1190 (136–49) [L 2–3]; 1219 (525–8) [L 2–3].

Growth Models [Level 2–3]

The growth rate or patterns of many things can be calculated using mathematical formulas. Population growth, bacterial growth, financial investments, and predator and prey counts are applications of growth models.

See also **Population and Food.**

References: 37 (16–24) [L 2–3]; 53 (347–409) [L 2–3]; 98 (55–75) [L 2–3]; 102 (23–4) [L 2]; 109 (140–50) [L 2]; 414 (25–75) [L 3]; 423 (238–43) [L 2–3]; 466 (10–3) [L 2–3]; 595 (71–4) [L 2]; 1117 (40–7) [L 3]; 1134 (58–69) [L 3]; 1136 (98–103) [L 3].

Handicraft Design

See **Designs from Many Cultures.**

Quilt Pattern

Harmonic Mean [Level 1–3]

The harmonic mean is an average computed by taking the reciprocal of the arithmetic mean of the reciprocals of the numbers.

References: 16 [L 1–2]; 55 (196–206) [L 2–3]; 63 (3–5) [L 2–3]; 823 (32–4) [L 1–2]; 977 (146–8) [L 1–2]; 1026 (20–5) [L 2–3]; 1027 (30–4) [L 2–3].

Harmonic Sequences [Level 1–3]

The reciprocals of a harmonic sequence form an arithmetic sequence. For example, $\{1, \frac{1}{2}, \frac{1}{3}, \frac{1}{4}, \ldots, \frac{1}{n}\}$ is a harmonic sequence. Harmonic tones in music are produced on strings whose proportions are in harmonic sequence.

References: 16 [L 1–2]; 55 (196–206) [L 2–3]; 63 (3–5) [L 2–3]; 999 (238–44) [L 1–3]; 1064 (178–9) [L 2–3].

Hebrew Numeration [Level 1–2]

Much like the Greeks, the Hebrews used letters of the alphabet for their numeration system.

References: 11 (442) [L 1–2]; 15 (53) [L 1–2]; 87 (93–114) [L 1–2].

Hexaflexagons

See **Flexagons.**

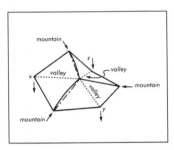

Hexaflexagon. From *Build Your Own Polyhedra* by Peter Hilton and Jean Pedersen. Copyright ©1988 by Addison-Wesley Publishing.

Hindu-Arabic Numeration

See **Arabic Numeration.**

Hypatia (370–415) [Level 1–2]

As a brilliant Greek scholar and mathematician, she built scientific instruments and advanced the study of algebra.

References: 13 (111–2) [L 1–2]; 14 (137) [L 1–2]; 16 (190–2) [L 1–2]; 19 (29–35) [L 1]; 21 (52–3) [L 1–2]; 23 [L 1]; 25 [L 1]; 26 (9–28) [L 1–2]; 46 (77–80) [L 1–2]; 663 [L 1–2].

Hypatia

Hyperbolas

See **Conics.**

Hypercubes

See **Fourth Dimension and Higher.**

Imaginary Numbers [Level 1–3]

Imaginary numbers have $\sqrt{-1}$, i, as a factor. A complex number, $a + bi$, has a real part, a, and an imaginary part, bi.

See also **Complex Numbers.**

References: 16 [L 1–2]; 340 (155–7) [L 2]; 391 (155–61) [L 3]; 451 (251–70) [L 1–2]; 550 (80–104) [L 2–3]; 583 (97–108) [L 2]; 1149 (18–24) [L 2–3].

Indian Numeration [Level 1–2]

The Indian numeration system was far superior to the Egyptian, Babylonian, or Greek.

References: 16 (206–24) [L 1–2]; 77 (42–4) [L 1–2]; 87 (115–24) [L 1–2]; 287 (215–300) [L 2].

Induction

See **Deduction vs. Induction.**

Infinity [Level 1–3]

Infinity is the assumed limit of a sequence, series, or something that increases forever. The finite has a boundary; the infinite has no boundary.

References: 9 (30–8) [L 2]; 33 (253–314) [L 2–3]; 55 (254–83) [L 2–3]; 296 (1–151) [L 2–3]; 406 (1–265) [L 2–3]; 412 (1–149) [L 2–3]; 587 (183–200) [L 2]; 597 (152–7) [L 2–3]; 902 (284–92) [L 2–3]; 1111 (144–7) [L 3]; 1112 (54–61) [L 3].

Instruments in Geometry [Level 1–3]

Geometers have devised many interesting instruments to make different kinds of measurements.

References: 15 (344–68) [L 1–2]; 53 (433–65) [L 2–3]; 160 (1–55) [L 2–3]; 570 (1–64) [L 1–2]; 469 [L 1–2]; 911 (129–38) [L 1–2]; 1088 (166–7) [L 1–2]; 1206 (278–82) [L 1–2].

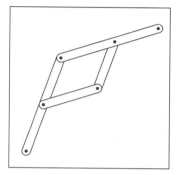

Pantograph

Interest and Annuities [Level 1–2]

Interest is money paid on an investment or loan. An annuity is a guaranteed regular payment in return for an investment.

References: 15 (559–67) [L 1–2]; 36 (98–124) [L 1–2]; 69 (91–126) [L 2]; 70 (67–88) [L 2]; 100 (67–8) [L 1–2]; 675 (325–6) [L 1–2]; 824 (126–7) [L 2–3]; 876 (624–30) [L 1–2]; 890 (703–5) [L 2–3]; 918 (610–3) [L 2–3]; 946 (376–9) [L 1–2]; 987 (450–3) [L 1–2]; 1000 (299–300) [L 2].

Irrational Numbers [Level 1–3]

Irrational numbers cannot be expressed as an integer or the quotient of two integers. Pi (π) and $\sqrt{2}$ are examples of irrational numbers.

References: 15 (251–60) [L 1–2]; 16 [L 1–2]; 30 (58–71) [L 2–3]; 410 (52–64) [L 2–3]; 467 (130–41) [L 2]; 499 (265–87) [L 2]; 595 (205–8) [L 2]; 652 (22–6) [L 2–3]; 675 (70–2) [L 1–2]; 947 (195–6) [L 1–2]; 956 (258–61) [L 2].

Islamic Art [Level 1–2]

This highly developed art form was limited to geometric patterns and calligraphy because of religious limitations on what artists could and could not draw.

References: 188 (1–110) [L 1–2]; 230 (1–200) [L 1–2]; 231 (1–151) [L 1–2]; 232 (1–192) [L 2–3]; 243 [L 2–3]; 285 (1–40) [L 1–2]; 423 (200–7) [L 2]; 493 (200–8) [L 1–2].

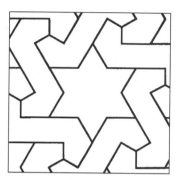

Islamic Pattern. From Dale Seymour. *Tessellation Teaching Masters.* Dale Seymour Publications, 1989.

Iteration and Recursion [Level 2–3]

Iteration describes the repetition of a process. For example, long division is an iterative method. A recursive relation is a formula that states each number of a sequence in terms of the preceding numbers.

References: 272 (1–24) [L 2–3]; 292 (60–98) [L 2–3]; 340 [L 2–3]; 381 (149–83) [L 2–3]; 1047 (685–9) [L 2–3]; 1056 (19–28) [L 2–3]; 1081 (571–2, 576) [L 2–3]; 1087 (150–6) [L 2–3]; 1091 (233–9) [L 2–3]; 1095 (676–80) [L 2]; 1097 [L 2–3]; 1221 (61–7) [L 2–3].

Kaleidoscopes [Level 1–2]

This optical device shows continually changing symmetrical designs as it is rotated. How are they built?

References: 118 (1–40) [L 1–2]; 144 (1–160) [L 1–2]; 1172 (182–8) [L 2]; 1196 (576–9) [L 1–2].

Kaleidoscope Design

Kepler, Johann (1571–1630) [Level 1–2]

Kepler was a European astronomer and mathematician who studied planetary motion. Kepler's discoveries influenced Newton's laws of motion.

References: 11 (113–23, 215–29) [L 1–2]; 13 (254–7) [L 1–2]; 16 (323–6) [L 2]; 20 (61–78) [L 1–2]; 21 (56–7) [L 1–2]; 24 [L 1]; 53 (443–6) [L 2]; 200 (84–99) [L 2–3]; 209 [L 2].

Kepler-Poinsot Polyhedra   [Level 2–3]

These four star-shaped polyhedra are formed by extending the planes of the faces of dodecahedra or icosohedra until they intersect. Kepler described two of these in his book *Harmonices Mundi*. Louis Poinsot discovered the other two.

References: 52 (113) [L 1–2]; 200 (84–99) [L 3]; 201 (70–2) [L 2]; 202 (66–239) [L 2]; 209 [L 2–3]; 210 (89–99) [L 2]; 213 (96–111, 263–5) [L 2]; 467 (4–5) [L 2].

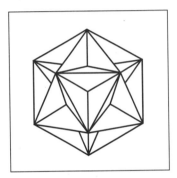

Kepler-Poinsot Polyhedron

Kites   [Level 1–2]

Mathematicians, scientists, and engineers are interested in kites. Alexander Graham Bell was one of the inventors who built huge kites in attempts to develop manned flight.

References: 503 (1–96) [L 1–2]; 510 (1–136) [L 1–2]; 670 (1–64) [L 1–2]; 1171 (156–61) [L 2]; 1240 (382–6) [L 1–2].

Knots   [Level 1–3]

A knot can be thought of as a simple closed curve in three-dimensional space. The study and classification of knots is part of the branch of mathematics called topology.

References: 109 (52–61) [L 1–2]; 210 (56–9) [L 2]; 340 (70–80) [L 3]; 341 (130–45, 267–90) [L 3]; 363 (1–395) [L 1–2]; 551 (229–61) [L 2–3]; 552 (252–81) [L 2]; 1182 (18–28) [L 2–3].

Königsberg Bridge Problem   [Level 1–2]

This famous problem influenced the development of topology. The city of Königsberg contained two islands joined by seven bridges. The problem was to cross each of the bridges once without crossing any twice.

References: 11 (561–71) [L 1–2]; 52 (124–7) [L 1–2]; 64 (25–65) [L 1–2]; 391 (130–1) [L 1–2]; 392 (23–5) [L 2–3]; 406 (34–6) [L 1–2]; 581 [L 2–3].

Kovalevsky, Sonya Kovalevskaya (1850–1891)   [Level 1–2]

Kovalevsky was a Russian mathematician known for her contribution to improved methods of mathematical research and for her research on infinite series.

References: 16 (518, 560) [L 1–2]; 21 [L 1–2]; 22 (109–18) [L 1]; 25 [L 1]; 26 (127–48) [L 1–2]; 42 [L 1–2].

Sonya Kovalevsky. From John and Susan Edeen. *Portraits, Women Mathematicians.* Dale Seymour Publications, 1990.

Lagrange, Joseph (1736–1813)   [Level 1–2]

Lagrange was a French mathematician who contributed to many different branches of mathematics.

References: 11 (144–9) [L 1–2]; 13 (401–12) [L 1–2]; 14 (482–6) [L 1–2]; 16 (470–1) [L 3]; 17 (153–71) [L 2]; 19 (83–9) [L 1]; 20 (114–21) [L 1–2]; 24 [L 1].

Land Measure

See **Earth Measurement.**

Laplace, Pierre (1749–1827)   [Level 1–3]

This French mathematician is best known for his contributions to probability theory and mechanics.

References: 13 (412–21) [L 1–2]; 14 (486–7) [L 1–2];

16 (491–3) [L 3]; 17 (172–82) [L 2–3]; 21 (60–3)
[L 1–2]; 24 [L 1].

Latitude and Longitude

See Earth Measurement.

Leibnitz, Gottfried Wilhelm (1646–1716) [Level 1–2]

Leibnitz was a German mathematician who invented
calculus independent of Newton.

References: 13 (353–67) [L 1–2]; 14 (417–21)
[L 1–2]; 16 (391–414) [L 3]; 17 (117–30) [L 2–3];
21 (64–5) [L 1–2]; 24 [L 1]; 1149 (20–34) [L 2].

Gottfried Leibnitz. From John and Susan Edeen. *Portraits, Mathematicians Book 2.*
Dale Seymour Publications, 1988.

Leonardo de Pisa

See Fibonacci.

Life, Conway's Game of [Level 2–3]

In this solitaire game invented by Princeton
mathematician John Conway, "living" and "dead" cells
appear on a square grid. Patterns emerge as "living"
cells reproduce or die according to a given rule.

Source: 33 (111–8) [L 1–2]; 340 (176–200) [L 3];
345 (214–57) [L 2–3]; 1238 (496–502) [L 2].

Linear Programming   [Level 3]

This technique is used to optimize productivity by
allocating resources in a problem situation and looking
at the minimum and maximum values of related
functions.

References: 37 (52–6) [L 2–3]; 53 (94–119) [L 2–3];
70 (117–34) [L 3]; 340 (107–12) [L 2–3]; 390 (1–66)
[L 3]; 466 (36–8) [L 2–3]; 1067 (664–6) [L 1–2].

Line Designs   [Level 1–3]

A pattern of straight line segments can produce an
apparent curve. Some properties of curves can be
understood from an advanced analysis of line designs.

References: 167 (1–80) [L 1–2]; 168 (1–291) [L 1–2];
169 (1–68) [L 1–2]; 170 (1–96) [L 2–3]; 171 (1–68)
[L 1–2]; 172 (1–64) [L 1–2]; 173 (1–84) [L 1–2]; 210
(44–6) [L 1–2]; 553 (222–30) [L 1–2]; 856 (726–32)
[L 2–3].

Line Design. From Dale Seymour. *Introduction to Line Designs.*
Dale Seymour Publications, 1992.

Line Groups

See Frieze Patterns.

Logarithms   [Level 2–3]

In the equation $10^2 = 100$, 2 is the logarithm of 100
to the base 10. Since $10^3 = 1000$, $10^{2.536}$ equals some
number between 100 and 1000.

See also Earthquakes and Logarithms.

References: 5 (57–67) [L 2]; 15 (513–23) [L 3]; 16
(312–3) [L 2–3]; 463 (402–53) [L 2–3]; 675 (142–5)
[L 2]; 1002 (250–3) [L 2–3].

Number		Logarithm
$\frac{1}{1000}$	$= 10^{-3}$	-3
$\frac{1}{100}$	$= 10^{-2}$	-2
$\frac{1}{10}$	$= 10^{-1}$	-1
1	$= 10^0$	0
10	$= 10^1$	1
100	$= 10^2$	2
1000	$= 10^3$	3

Logarithm

Logic [Level 1–3]

Logic, the science of reasoning or argumentation, is used in mathematics and studied as a branch of mathematics.

See also **Symbolic Logic.**

References: 33 (201–47) [L 2–3]; 330 (70–85) [L 1–2]; 346 (51–64) [L 1–2]; 350 (281–92) [L 1–2]; 416 (1–153) [L 1–2]; 417 (1–463) [L 1–2]; 418 (1–197) [L 3]; 419 (1–284) [L 1–3]; 499 (465–84) [L 2]; 542 [L 2]; 543 [L 3]; 553 (16–25) [L 1–3]; 598 (81–102) [L 2]; 638 [L 3]; 639 [L 3].

Logo Computer Language [Level 1–2]

This simple computer language uses instructions based on geometric transformations in a plane, to make drawings on a computer screen.

References: 184 (1–90) [L 1–2]; 267 (45–7) [L 1–2]; 269 (1–145) [L 1–2]; 270 (1–400) [L 2–3]; 1072 (424–8) [L 1–2]; 1178 (14–20) [L 2–3].

Logos [Level 1–2]

Logos are graphic trademarks used to identify a product or company. Many logos are geometric designs that contain one or more symmetries.

References: 179 (1–216) [L 1–2]; 180 (1–149) [L 1–2]; 223 [L 1–2]; 914 (437–9) [L 1–2].

Logo. Courtesy of Stanford Shopping Center, Palo Alto, CA.

Longitude and Latitude

See **Earth Measurement.**

Lovelace, Ada Byron (1815–1852) [Level 1–2]

Lady Lovelace was the British mathematician who invented computer programming.

References: 22 (101–8) [L 1]; 25 [L 1]; 26 (101–26) [L 1–2]; 442 [L 1–2]; 443 [L 1–2]; 444 [L 1–2].

Ada Byron Lovelace. From John and Susan Edeen. *Portraits, Women Mathematicians.* Dale Seymour Publications, 1990.

Magic

See **Calculation Shortcuts, Card and Number Tricks.**

Magic Squares and Cubes [Level 1–3]

A magic square is an array of numbers where the sum of the numbers in each row, column, and diagonal, totals the same number.

References: 13 (118–20) [L 1–2]; 15 (591–8) [L 2–3]; 16 (197) [L 2–3]; 52 (80–7) [L 1–2]; 241 (1–20) [L 1–2]; 347 (211–25) [L 2–3]; 351 (193–221) [L 3]; 353 (23–34) [L 2–3]; 356 (1–414) [L 1–3]; 357 (1–186) [L 2–3]; 358 (1–223) [L 1–2]; 461 (127–42) [L 1–2]; 470 (1–16) [L 1–2]; 471 (1–13) [L 1–2]; 675 (80–2) [L 1–2]; 850 (471–6) [L 2–3]; 885 (216–21) [L 2–3]; 908 (464–72) [L 1–2]; 909 (674–8) [L 1]; 920 (50–6) [L 1–2].

10	18	1	14	22
11	24	7	20	3
17	5	13	21	9
23	6	19	2	15
4	12	25	8	16

Magic Square

Maps and Cartography [Level 1–3]

Producing maps uses mathematical principles including projection, scaling, and construction.

References: 16 (299–301) [L 2–3]; 69 (129–60) [L 1–2]; 216 (57–8, 148–63) [L 2–3]; 263 (1–32) [L 1–2]; 347 (189–203) [L 2–3]; 469 (124–45) [L 1–2]; 478 (85–96) [L 1–2]; 533 (85–96) [L 1–2]; 1037 (400–4) [L 2–3]; 1101 (120–1) [L 1–3]; 1116 (134) [L 2–3].

Map Coloring   [Level 1–3]

This investigation in topology requires a map to be colored using the smallest number of colors.

References: 52 (152–3) [L 1–2]; 64 (34–41) [L 1–2]; 90 (153–80) [L 2–3]; 132 (226–42) [L 2–3]; 281 (1–43) [L 1–2]; 295 (16–20) [L 1–2]; 340 (1–9) [L 3]; 351 (222–42) [L 3]; 374 (1–20) [L 3]; 391 (146–54) [L 2–3]; 393 (1–66) [L 2–3]; 401 (125–35) [L 3]; 436 (108–19) [L 1–2]; 467 (80–1) [L 1–2]; 551 (148–76) [L 2–3]; 617 [L 2–3]; 808 (759–63) [L 1–2]; 1154 (14–19) [L 2].

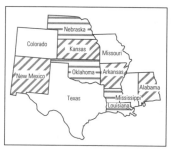

Map Coloring

Math Models

See **Modeling and Decision Making.**

Math Theory of Elections

See **Elections and Social Choices.**

Mathematical Induction

See **Deduction vs. Induction.**

Mathematician   [Level 1–3]

Mathematicians are employed to do many different jobs. What kinds of jobs do they have? What training do they need? How well are they paid?

References: 18 [L 2–3]; 28 [L 3]; 31 (1–403) [L 2–3]; 51 [L 1–3]; 56 (1–119) [L 1–2]; 462 (73–93) [L 2–3]; 554 (1–410) [L 2–3]; 555 [L 2–3]; 575 (1–21) [L 1–2]; 669 (1–365) [L 1–2].

Mathematics   [Level 1–3]

Mathematics is a very broad subject. It involves more than computation, manipulating symbols, and studying shapes. What do mathematicians and mathematics educators say about what math really is?

References: 29 (6–31) [L 1–2]; 30 [L 2–3]; 33 [L 1–3]; 34 [L 1–2]; 381 [L 2–3]; 391 (9–20) [L 2].

Matrices   [Level 2–3]

A matrix is a rectangular array of numbers or variables used to study simultaneous linear equations and other relationships.

See also **Determinants.**

References: 5 (373–7) [L 3]; 28 (103–124) [L 3]; 37 (57–64) [L 2–3]; 48 (795–811) [L 2–3]; 100 (23–6) [L 2]; 381 (104–14) [L 2–3]; 388 (1–65) [L 2–3]; 392 (13–22) [L 2–3]; 402 (1–115) [L 3]; 414 (104–31) [L 3]; 595 (136–40) [L 2]; 675 (281–4) [L 2–3]; 1194 (20–4) [L 2].

$$\begin{bmatrix} 3 & 7 & -1 \\ 4 & 1 & -5 \\ -2 & 3 & 1 \end{bmatrix}$$

Matrix

Mayan Numeration   [Level 1–2]

The Mayan culture, unlike most other cultures, was not influenced by the outside world. Investigate the system they developed to work with numbers.

References: 15 (44–5) [L 1–2]; 16 (213) [L 2]; 87 (125–36) [L 1–2]; 675 (45–6) [L 1–2]; 1018 (249–55) [L 1–2]; 1235 (762–8) [L 1–2].

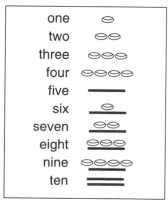

Mayan Numerals

Measurement [Level 1–3]

Did each culture have its own measurement system? Why did England choose to have a system which was not based on base 10? How did the metric system evolve?

References: 11 (1471–821) [L 3]; 15 (634–74) [L 1–2]; 16 (471–2) [L 2–3]; 53 (410–32) [L 1–2]; 478 (1–143) [L 1–2]; 479 (1–240) [L 1–2]; 480 (1–54) [L 1–2]; 481 (1–270) [L 1–2]; 482 (1–51) [L 1–2]; 494 (1–199) [L 1–2]; 532 [L 1–2]; 906 (51–3) [L 1–2]; 1133 (68–74) [L 2–3]; 1141 (122–7) [L 1–3].

Measures of Central Tendency

See Averages.

Mental Calculating Shortcuts

See Number Tricks, Calculation Shortcuts.

Metric System [Level 1–2]

The decimal system of weights and measures is now used almost everywhere. The United States is one of the few countries that has not yet adopted this system. Why? Will we ever adopt it?

References: 15 (648–50) [L 1–2]; 330 (18–23) [L 1–2]; 478 (1–143) [L 1–2]; 481 (1–270) [L 1–2]; 482 (1–51) [L 1–2]; 494 (1–199) [L 1–2]; 533 (1–143) [L 1–2]; 1225 (581–5) [L 1–2]; 1232 (297–302) [L 1–2].

Minimal Surfaces

See Soap Film and Minimal Surfaces.

Mira Constructions [Level 1–2]

The Mira is a geometrical construction device used to study reflections of lines and shapes. Most constructions, normally produced with a compass and straightedge, can be performed with a Mira.

References: 164 (1–87) [L 2]; 165 (1–172) [L 2]; 1036 (394–9) [L 1–2]; 1044 (204–8) [L 2].

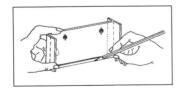

Mira

Möbius Strip [Level 1–2]

This one-sided surface is created by joining the two ends of a long strip of paper after making a half twist at one end.

References: 51 (55–8) [L 1–2]; 52 (3) [L 1–2]; 152 (20–1) [L 1–2]; 340 [L 1–2]; 349 (123–36) [L 1–2]; 436 (24–61) [L 1–2]; 493 (110–24) [L 2]; 595 (144–6) [L 2]; 1170 (18–25) [L 2].

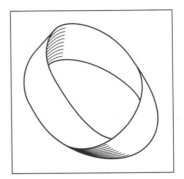

Möbius Strip

Modeling and Decision Making [Level 2–3]

To make the best decisions, business and industry are constantly evaluating alternatives. Modeling these alternatives uses mathematical procedures.

See also **Scheduling and Planning.**

References: 36 (217–26) [L 2–3]; 53 [L 2–3]; 282 (1–50) [L 2–3]; 340 [L 2–3]; 383 (1–41) [L 2]; 465 (1–205) [L 2–3]; 641 [L 2–3]; 642 [L 3]; 643 [L 3]; 912 (520–1) [L 2]; 1082 (516–9) [L 2]; 1083 (770–3) [L 2]; 1085 (722–6) [L 2–3]; 1096 (628–33) [L 2].

Modern Mathematicians [Level 1–3]

Who are some of the mathematicians who have made major contributions or discoveries in the past 100 years?

References: 18 (1–372) [L 1–2]; 22 (1–138) [L 1]; 31 (1–403) [L 2–3]; 39 [L 1–2]; 40 (1–160) [L 1–2]; 340 (1–230) [L 1–2]; 505 (1–363) [L 1–2]; 675 [L 1–2].

See also **Cantor, Einstein, Noether, Pólya, Ramanujan.**

Modular Arithmetic [Level 1–2]

The arithmetic on a finite set of whole numbers, sometimes called clock arithmetic. For example, in modulus 4: $1 + 1 = 2$, $1 + 2 = 3$, $1 + 3 = 0$, $2 + 3 = 1$.

References: 37 (46–7) [L 1–2]; 79 (156–71) [L 1–2]; 330 (118–25) [L 1–2]; 340 (17–43) [L 2]; 953

(312–6) [L 2]; 1162 (17–20) [L 2]; 1215 (645–7)
[L 2]; 1218 (207–9) [L 1–2]; 1219 (525–8) [L 2];
1237 (385–91) [L 2].

Moiré Patterns   [Level 1–3]

A wavelike moiré pattern of parallel lines, concentric circles, or dots can be created with transparent grids. The mathematics of moiré patterns can be studied using trigonometry.

References: 251 (1–160) [L 1–2]; 255 (1–55) [L 1–2]; 256 (1–73) [L 1–2]; 257 (1–32) [L 1–2]; 258 (1–40) [L 2–3]; 1172 (182–8) [L 2].

Moiré Pattern. From Dale Seymour. *Introduction to Line Designs.* Dale Seymour Publications, 1992.

Molecules and Atoms   [Level 2–3]

The complex structure of atoms that make up molecules are often three-dimensional, polyhedral shapes.

See also **Crystallography Patterns.**

References: 37 (74–97) [L 2–3]; 175 (51–70) [L 2–3]; 192 (297–313) [L 3]; 348 (103–50) [L 2–3]; 441 (514–48) [L 3]; 1139 (40–7) [L 3].

Monte Carlo Methods   [Level 2–3]

These methods use statistical sampling to give probabilistic approximations to a strategy.

References: 919 (335–9) [L 2–3]; 983 (327–34) [L 2–3]; 1054 (340–1) [L 2–3]; 1227 (458–60) [L 2–3].

Motion   [Level 1–3]

Since the time of Galileo, scientists have applied mathematics to their study of velocity, acceleration, gravity, light waves, and other motion.

See also **Velocity and Speed.**

References: 11 (715–57) [L 2]; 37 (25–35) [L 2–3];

340 [L 2–3]; 396 (1–680) [L 2–3]; 414 (169–98)
[L 3]; 431 (1–124) [L 2–3]; 432 (1–142) [L 2–3]; 433
(1–107) [L 3]; 434 [L 1–2]; 884 (466–8) [L 1–2];
1181 (163) [L 2]; 1195 (154–65) [L 2–3].

Music and Mathematics   [Level 1–3]

The Greeks thought of music as mathematics. String length ratios and piano keys are based on harmonic divisions and Fibonacci numbers.

References: 11 (2251–85) [L 2]; 14 (75–6) [L 1–2]; 36 (126–36) [L 1–2]; 37 (44–8) [L 2–3]; 52 (142–5) [L 1–2]; 91 (33–40) [L 1–2]; 102 (85–101) [L 2]; 423 (97–103) [L 1–2]; 441 (1–742) [L 3]; 458 (1–23) [L 2–3]; 466 (2–4) [L 2–3]; 553 (179–98) [L 2–3]; 596 (287–303) [L 2–3]; 999 (238–44) [L 1–3]; 1040 (414–22) [L 1–2]; 1104 (110–5) [L 2–3]; 1121 (126–33) [L 2–3]; 1124 (44–51) [L 2–3]; 1166 (171–86) [L 2–3].

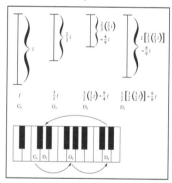

Music and Mathematics. From Garland and Kahn. *Math and Music: Harmonious Connections.* Dale Seymour Publications, 1995.

Mysticism in Math   [Level 1–2]

The Pythagoreans' concept of the universe was "All is Number." They ascribed many properties to numbers including the theory that even numbers were female, and odd numbers were male.

References: 33 (50–72) [L 1–2]; 110 (48–57) [L 1–2]; 308 (1–288) [L 1–2]; 463 (167–204) [L 1–2]; 557 (237–9) [L 2]; 581 (272–7) [L 2]; 596 (257–71) [L 2–3]; 597 (108–12) [L 2–3].

Napier, John (1550–1617)   [Level 1–2]

The Scottish mathematician who invented logarithms is also known for inventing multiplication aids.

References: 11 (113–23) [L 1–2]; 13 (235–6) [L 1–2]; 14 (389–91) [L 1–2]; 16 (311–3) [L 2]; 19 (37–43)

[L 1]; 20 (61–78) [L 1–2]; 23 [L 1]; 87 (165–74) [L 1–2]; 343 (94–108) [L 1–2]; 448 (71–88) [L 2].

Napier's Rods   [Level 1–2]

Ten rectangular rods can be combined to find solutions to mathematical operations such as multiplication, division, exponents, and roots. Each rod was a list of the multiples of the number on the top.

References: 13 (235–6) [L 1–2]; 15 (202–4) [L 1–2]; 52 (64–5) [L 1–2]; 343 (85–93) [L 1–2]; 448 (82–4) [L 2]; 581 (161–2) [L 2]; 675 (141–2) [L 1–2].

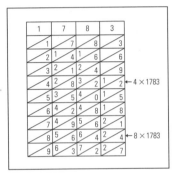

Napier's Bones

Nature   [Level 1–3]

Mathematical patterns and properties occur frequently in natural forms such as flowers, growth patterns, and shapes.

References: 109 (111–39) [L 1–2]; 146 (1–226) [L 1–2]; 175 (41–70) [L 2–3]; 178 (1–100) [L 1–2]; 187 (39–77) [L 1–2]; 220 (1–239) [L 3]; 265 (1–232) [L 1–2]; 341 (189–207) [L 3]; 464 (1–464) [L 2–3]; 466 (14) [L 2–3]; 1120 (52–75) [L 2–3]; 1127 (68–77) [L 2–3]; 1138 [L 2–3]; 1167 (231–8) [L 2]; 1203 (64–83) [L 2–3].

A Marine Protozoa. From Ernst Haeckel. *Art Forms in Nature.* New York: Dover, 1974.

Navigation   [Level 1–3]

The process of directing a ship or airplane requires the use of angles, vectors, speeds, and other mathematical concepts.

References: 69 (129–59) [L 1–2]; 70 (32–6) [L 2]; 463 (294–342) [L 1–3]; 483 [L 1]; 1063 (165–8) [L 2–3].

Networks and Circuits   [Level 1–3]

Networks and circuits, used to determine the most efficient way of managing a complex activity, can be used to schedule such things as airline or parking meter routes.

References: 53 (5–65) [L 1–2]; 64 (1–87) [L 1–3]; 68 (56–9) [L 1–2]; 69 (1–22) [L 1–2]; 220 (50–239) [L 3]; 275 (1–31) [L 2–3]; 344 (3–11) [L 3]; 350 (231–47) [L 3]; 392 (1–82) [L 2–3]; 393 (1–66) [L 2–3]; 401 (1–145) [L 2–3]; 423 (209–53) [L 2]; 436 (120–35) [L 1–2]; 475 (1–87) [L 1–2]; 493 (360–70) [L 2–3]; 1109 (72–85) [L 2–3]; 1113 (118–20) [L 2–3]; 1191 (24–38) [L 2–3].

Newton, Isaac (1642–1727)   [Level 1–2]

Newton, along with Gauss and Aristotle, is considered one of the three greatest mathematicians of all time. He invented calculus independently of Leibniz.

References: 11 (135–40, 249–80) [L 1–2]; 13 (319–35) [L 1–2]; 14 (398–404) [L 1–2]; 16 (391–414) [L 2]; 17 (90–116) [L 2–3]; 19 (63–71) [L 1]; 20 (97–106) [L 1–2]; 21 (68–9) [L 1–2]; 24 [L 1]; 55 (155–83) [L 2–3]; 87 (175–90) [L 1–2]; 396 (1–680) [L 2–3]; 622 [L 1–2]; 901 (711–4) [L 1–2]; 1161 (166–81) [L 2]; 1193 (150–7) [L 2].

Nine-Point Circle   [Level 2–3]

For every triangle there is a circle which passes through nine points related to that triangle.

References: 21 (141) [L 2]; 129 (124–35) [L 2–3]; 259 (55–61) [L 2]; 409 (20–2) [L 2]; 675 (230–1) [L 2]; 899 (389–93) [L 2]; 1239 (141–4) [L 2–3].

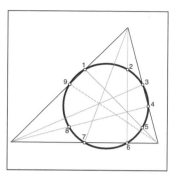

Nine-Point Circle

Noether, Amalie Emmy (1882–1935) [Level 1–2]

As a mathematician who contributed to many branches of mathematics, Noether was a pioneer in establishing a place for women in mathematics.

References: 16 [L 1–2]; 19 (115–21) [L 1]; 25 [L 1]; 26 (173–94) [L 1–2]; 626 [L 1–2]; 863 (246–9) [L 1–2].

Emmy Noether. From John and Susan Edeen. *Portraits, Women Mathematicians.* Dale Seymour Publications, 1990.

Non-Euclidean Geometries [Level 2–3]

Geometries not based on the postulates of Euclid.

See also **Riemann.**

References: 9 (76–85) [L 2]; 13 (485–9) [L 2]; 15 (335–8) [L 2]; 16 (519–22) [L 3]; 28 (65–88) [L 3]; 48 (861–81) [L 2–3]; 52 (90–2) [L 2]; 72 [L 2–3]; 127 (44–58) [L 2–3]; 410 (178–98) [L 2–3]; 461 (49–60) [L 2]; 466 (86–8) [L 2–3]; 499 (90–9) [L 2]; 500 (9–24) [L 2–3]; 513 [L 2–3]; 533 (61–114) [L 2–3]; 596 (410–31) [L 2–3]; 597 (217–23) [L 2–3]; 599 (105–16) [L 3]; 620 [L 3]; 675 (207–10) [L 2].

Normal Distribution Curve [Level 2–3]

This symmetrical, bell-shaped curve shows the normal distribution as defined by probability functions.

See also **Binomial Theorem and Distribution.**

References: 317 (115–21) [L 2–3]; 318 (1–174) [L 2–3]; 319 (30–41) [L 2–3]; 334 (1–96) [L 2–3]; 830 (571–3) [L 2–3].

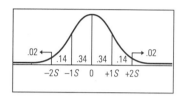

Normal Distribution Curve

Numeration [Level 1–3]

Numeration is the process of naming, writing, and expressing numbers and performing operations on those numbers. Compare the numeration systems of various cultures.

References: 5 (69–77) [L 2]; 10 (9–18) [L 1–2]; 11 (433–54) [L 1–2]; 12 (19–34) [L 1–2]; 13 (121–8) [L 1–2]; 14 (1–14) [L 1–2]; 15 (36–90) [L 1–2]; 16 (1–61) [L 2–3]; 33 (77–89) [L 1–2]; 52 (2–3) [L 1–2]; 54 (81–8) [L 2–3]; 77 (29–55) [L 1–2]; 87 (1–125) [L 1–2]; 110 (8–25) [L 1–2]; 413 (63–81) [L 1–2]; 469 (26–49) [L 1–2]; 581 [L 2]; 584 [L 1]; 604 [L 2–3]; 605 [L 2–3]; 675 (18–85) [L 1–2]; 896 (253–6) [L 1–2]; 1021 (295–8) [L 1–2]; 1075 (499–505) [L 1–2]; 1099 (263–72, 293–9) [L 1–2]; 1179 (110–9) [L 2–3]; 1224 (413–5) [L 2–3].

Number Theory [Level 2–3]

Euler, Goldbach, and Fermat were early pioneers in number theory, the study of integers and their relationship to each other.

References: 5 (669–75) [L 3]; 48 (813–33) [L 2–3]; 55 (223–44) [L 2–3]; 90 (37–64) [L 2–3]; 413 (1–123) [L 2–3]; 500 (59–71) [L 2–3]; 562 (1–310) [L 2–3]; 566 [L 2–3]; 586 [L 2]; 606 [L 2–3]; 607 [L 3]; 922 (34–62) [L 2–3]; 923 (20–2) [L 2]; 930 (294–8) [L 2].

Number Tricks

See Calculation Shortcuts, Card and Number Tricks.

Number Tricks

Numerology   [Level 1–2]

This is the study of the assumed relationship between numbers (such as the year, date, and time of birth) and events.

References: 16 (52–4) [L 2]; 33 (72–7) [L 1–2]; 308 (1–288) [L 1–2]; 344 (150–60) [L 1–2]; 412 (3–32) [L 2]; 463 (167–204) [L 1–2]; 675 (74–6) [L 1–2]; 920 (50–6) [L 1–2].

Odds

See Gambling.

Operations Algorithms

See Algorithms.

Operations Research

See Modeling and Decision Making.

Optical Illusions   [Level 1–2]

Optical illusions are graphics that deceive the eye.

See also Moiré Patterns.

References: 244 (1–48 & sftwr) [L 1–2]; 245 (1–228) [L 1–2]; 246 (1–95) [L 1–2]; 247 (1–239) [L 1–2]; 248 (1–252) [L 1–2]; 249 (1–32) [L 1–2]; 250 (1–27) [L 1–2]; 255 (1–55) [L 1–2]; 256 (1–52) [L 1–2]; 257 (1–32) [L 1–2]; 258 (1–40) [L 2]; 458 (76–87) [L 1–2]; 461 (61–86) [L 1–2].

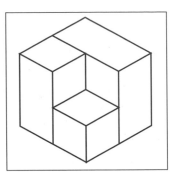

Optical Illusion

Optics   [Level 2–3]

Many of the principles of optics, the study of sight, involve properties of geometry.

References: 37 (36–43) [L 2–3]; 125 (234–39) [L 2–3]; 414 (75–103) [L 3]; 1057 (636–7) [L 2]; 1073 [L 2–3]; 1119 (112–8) [L 2–3].

Origami

See Paper Folding and Origami.

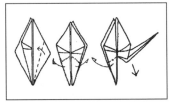

Origami Pattern

Packing Problems

See Sphere Packing.

Palindromes   [Level 1–2]

Number palindromes are numbers that contain the same order of digits if read left to right or right to left.

References: 81 (1–194) [L 1–2]; 350 (79–101) [L 1–2]; 355 (14–5) [L 1–2]; 470 (31–2) [L 1–2]; 471 (26–31) [L 1–2]; 845 (269–71) [L 1–2].

703828307

Number Palindrome

Pantographs

See Instruments in Geometry.

Paper Airplanes and Boomerangs [Level 1–2]

What are the factors to consider in designing a paper airplane? What is the effect of wing size? What role does balance play in creating a distance glider?

References: 152 (96–7) [L 1–2]; 155 (1–147) [L 1–2]; 156 (1–126) [L 1–2]; 1151 (162–72) [L 2].

Paper Engineering and Pop-Ups [Level 1–2]

How are pop-up designs created? Design a pop-up.

References: 157 (1–92) [L 1–2]; 158 (1–45) [L 1–2]; 159 (1–84) [L 1–2]; 226 (1–72) [L 1–2]; 228 (1–91) [L 1–2]; 525 (1–49) [L 1–2].

Paper Folding and Origami [Level 1–2]

The Japanese have perfected the art of paper folding in origami.

References: 52 (48–50) [L 1–2]; 147 (1–32) [L 1–2]; 148 (1–94) [L 1–2]; 149 (1–59) [L 2]; 150 (1–148) [L 2–3]; 151 (1–64) [L 1–2]; 152 (1–117) [L 1–2]; 153 (1–192) [L 1–2]; 154 (1–124) [L 1–2]; 225 (1–76) [L 1–3]; 226 (1–72) [L 1–2]; 227 (1–243) [L 1–3]; 229 (1–191) [L 1–2]; 345 (60–73) [L 1–2]; 461 (37–48) [L 1–2]; 568 (1–95) [L 1–2].

Papyrus Rhind [Level 1–2]

This collection of mathematical examples was copied by a scribe around 1650 B.C. It contains many interesting examples of early Egyptian mathematics.

References: 11 (161–71) [L 1–2]; 12 (22–6) [L 1–2]; 15 (123–7) [L 1–2]; 16 (11–14) [L 2]; 578 (1–160) [L 1–2].

Parabolas

See Conics.

Paradoxes [Level 1–3]

Problems or situations that seem to have two contradictory solutions are called *paradoxes*. Paradoxes occur in number theory, geometry, logic, and other branches of mathematics.

References: 11 (1905–46) [L 2–3]; 307 (115–55) [L 1–2]; 342 (1–159) [L 1–2]; 343 (162–75) [L 1–2]; 345 (40–50) [L 2–3]; 347 (55–69) [L 2–3]; 375 [L 2]; 580 [L 2–3]; 596 (395–409) [L 2–3]; 990 (507) [L 2]; 1076 (250–3) [L 1–2].

Pascal, Blaise (1623–1662) [Level 1–2]

This great French mathematician and philosopher founded probability and invented the first calculating machine.

References: 1 (124–35) [L 1–2]; 2 [L 1–2]; 13 (281–8) [L 1–2]; 14 (381–4) [L 1–2]; 16 (361–7) [L 2]; 17 (73–89) [L 1–2]; 19 (53–61) [L 1]; 20 (79–96) [L 1–2]; 21 (72–3) [L 1–2]; 448 (89–102) [L 2].

Blaise Pascal. From John and Susan Edeen. *Portraits, Mathematicians Book 2.* Dale Seymour Publications, 1988.

Pascal's Triangle [Level 1–3]

Pascal's triangle is a triangular array of numbers with ones along two sides. Each number is the sum of two numbers closest to it in the row above. Find out when the triangle was first known and how it can be used.

References: 9 (39–46) [L 2–3]; 15 (508–11) [L 1–2]; 16 (205–6) [L 2–3]; 52 [L 1–2]; 66 (1–91) [L 1–3]; 94 (1–138) [L 1–2]; 95 (1–273) [L 1–2]; 135 (131–7) [L 2]; 344 (194–207) [L 3]; 561 (146–7) [L 1–2]; 675 (156–8) [L 1–2]; 926 (505–10) [L 2–3]; 927 (314–6) [L 1–2]; 928 (449–50) [L 1–3]; 935 (532–5) [L 1–2].

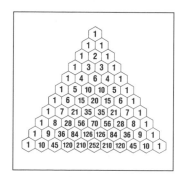

Pascal's Triangle

Pattern   [Level 1–3]

Mathematics is often defined as the study of pattern. Number theory, in particular, is filled with interesting patterns.

References: 33 (49–72) [L 1–2]; 53 (476–506) [L 1–3]; 54 (1–10) [L 1–2]; 64 (1–108) [L 2–3]; 65 (1–41) [L 1–2]; 66 (1–91) [L 1–3]; 68 (27–37) [L 1–2]; 76 (7–210) [L 1–2]; 78 (1–65) [L 1–2]; 83 (1–101) [L 1–2]; 135 (118–30) [L 1–2]; 185 (203–66) [L 2–3]; 188 (1–112) [L 2–3]; 221 (1–64) [L 1–2]; 223 (1–400) [L 2–3]; 224 (1–298) [L 1–3]; 232 (1–192) [L 2–3]; 234 (1–37) [L 1–2]; 240 (1–173) [L 1–2]; 242 (1–102) [L 1–2]; 470 (17–79) [L 1–2]; 471 (32–42) [L 1–2]; 499 (18–61) [L 2]; 930 (294–8) [L 1–2].

Penrose Tiles   [Level 1–3]

Invented by British scientist Roger Penrose in 1974, these two tiles combine to create many interesting patterns.

References: 33 (108–11) [L 1–2]; 53 (498–503) [L 2]; 109 (81, 86–92) [L 1–2]; 185 (531–49) [L 3]; 340 (200–12) [L 3]; 350 (1–29) [L 2–3]; 423 (243–51) [L 2].

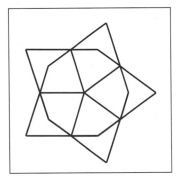

Penrose Tiles

Perfect Numbers   [Level 1–2]

A perfect number is an integer that is equal to the sum of all its proper factors. If a number is not perfect, it is either abundant or deficient.

References: 15 (20–3) [L 2–3]; 16 (115–6) [L 2–3]; 62 (1–169) [L 1–2]; 79 (84–103) [L 1–2]; 81 (1–194) [L 1–2]; 86 (1–28) [L 2–3]; 268 (39–42) [L 1–2]; 349 (160–71) [L 1–2]; 415 (83–90) [L 2]; 471 (53–4) [L 1–2]; 472 (1–168) [L 1–2]; 652 (129–34) [L 2–3]; 675 (59–61) [L 1–2]; 1023 (469–70) [L 2]; 1143 (692–6) [L 1–2].

Perimeter vs. Area

See **Area vs. Perimeter.**

Permutations and Combinations

See **Combinations and Permutations.**

Perspective   [Level 1–3]

Perspective drawing represents three-dimensional shapes on a two-dimensional surface so that they appear as our eye sees them.

References: 15 (338–44) [L 2]; 16 (295–8) [L 2–3]; 125 (44–81) [L 2–3]; 245 (1–228) [L 1–2]; 232 (1–64) [L 1–2]; 259 (79–88) [L 1–3]; 260 (1–90) [L 1–2]; 570 (1–64) [L 1–2]; 596 (126–43) [L 2–3]; 1032 (298–308) [L 1–2].

Photography   [Level 1–3]

Photography uses many concepts of geometry and optics.

References: 68 (65–92) [L 1–2]; 916 (657–62) [L 2–3]; 1052 (366–7, 398) [L 2].

Pi (π)   [Level 1–3]

The ratio of the circumference of a circle to its diameter is the irrational number π. Trace the history of approximations given π and methods of calculating π.

References: 15 (308–13) [L 2]; 76 (48–55) [L 1–2]; 85 (119–40) [L 2–3]; 97 (55–73) [L 2–3]; 105 [L 2–3]; 106 (1–113) [L 1–2]; 107 (1–30 & video) [L 1–2]; 109 (178–86) [L 2]; 127 (20–6) [L 1–2]; 268 (4–10) [L 1–2]; 414 (59–69) [L 3]; 550 (65–80) [L 1–2]; 675 (148–54) [L 1–2]; 818 (52, 47) [L 1–2]; 832 (121–4) [L 2–3]; 833 (204–6) [L 2]; 834 (208–10) [L 2–3]; 844 (638–40) [L 2–3]; 905 (154–9) [L 2–3]; 1128 (112–7) [L 2–3].

$$\pi = 3.14159265358979392\ldots$$

π

Plane Groups

See **Frieze Patterns, Crystallography Patterns.**

Platonic Solids   [Level 1–3]

There are five regular polyhedra having faces that are congruent regular polygons and dihedral (space) angles that are congruent. These five Platonic solids are the regular tetrahedron (triangular pyramid), the regular hexahedron (cube), the regular octahedron, the regular dodecahedron, and the regular icosohedron.

References: 175 (36–40) [L 1–2]; 198 (1–40) [L 1–2]; 199 [L 2–3]; 200 (1–14) [L 1–2]; 201 (22–43) [L 1–2]; 202 (1–39) [L 1–2]; 203 (1–119) [L 1–2]; 209 (14–9) [L 1–2]; 210 (83–8) [L 1–2]; 219 (63–7) [L 3]; 423 (255–345) [L 2–3]; 493 (255–94) [L 2–3]; 1015 (657–61) [L 1–2]; 1207 (312–8) [L 1–2].

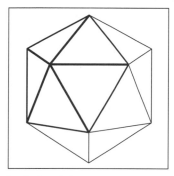

Regular Icosohedron

Pólya, George (1887–1985)   [Level 1–2]

Pólya, who wrote *How to Solve It,* has been called the father of heuristics (problem-solving techniques).

References: 18 (245–54) [L 1–2]; 22 (127–34) [L 1]; 29 (285–91) [L 2]; 39 [L 1–2]; 40 (1–160) [L 1–2]; 505 [L 1–2]; 1212 (598–9) [L 2].

George Pólya. Photo courtesy John Pólya.

Polygonal Numbers

See **Figurate Numbers.**

Polyhedra   [Level 1–3]

Polyhedra are solids bounded by plane polygons. These shapes are common in nature and in man-made objects.

See also **Archimedean Polyhedra, Compound Polyhedra, Platonic Solids, Kepler-Poinsot Polyhedra.**

References: 196 (1–30) [L 1–2]; 197 (1–30) [L 1–2]; 198 (1–175) [L 1–2]; 199 [L 2–3]; 200 (1–118) [L 1–2]; 201 (45–129) [L 1–2]; 202 (1–200) [L 1–2]; 204 (1–79 & video) [L 1–2]; 205 (1–64) [L 1–2]; 206 [L 1–2]; 207 [L 1–2]; 208 (1–190) [L 1–3]; 209 (1–205) [L 1–3]; 210 (76–157) [L 1–2]; 212 (1–144) [L 3]; 219 (54–103) [L 3]; 220 (32–7) [L 2–3]; 227 (1–243) [L 1–3]; 264 (150–71) [L 1–2]; 284 (1–63) [L 1–2]; 351 (128–61) [L 2–3]; 493 (255–382) [L 2–3]; 602 [L 2]; 836 (204–10) [L 1–2].

Polyominoes   [Level 1–3]

Polyominoes are shapes formed from congruent squares joined along an entire side. A monomino is one square; a domino is two squares; a tromino is three squares; a tetromino is four squares; and so forth.

References: 116 (1–154) [L 1–2]; 241 (74–94) [L 1–2]; 343 (28–54) [L 1–2]; 346 (19–31) [L 1–2]; 349 (146–59, 172–87) [L 1–2]; 353 (77–89) [L 1–2]; 359 (1–181) [L 1–2]; 361 (1–46) [L 1–2]; 600 (58–69) [L 3]; 933 (560–2) [L 1–2].

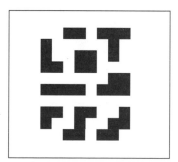

Polyominos

Pool and Billiards

See **Billiards and Pool.**

Population and Food   [Level 1–3]

What is the projected rate of population growth in the United States? What will this mean in 50 years in terms of population and food requirements?

See also **Growth Models.**

References: 11 (1167–74) [L 1–2]; 53 (379–409) [L 2–3]; 331 (111–28) [L 2–3]; 414 (45–58) [L 3]; 900 (92–4) [L 2–3]; 925 (605–8) [L 1–2]; 931 (283–91) [L 2–3]; 1129 (118–27) [L 2–3]; 1136 (98–103) [L 3]; 1153 (57–65) [L 3]; 1177 (138–47) [L 3]; 1199 (38–47) [L 3]; 1203 (64–83) [L 2–3]; 1238 (496–502) [L 2].

Powers and Roots

See **Roots and Powers.**

Primes and Composites   [Level 1–3]

Number theory explores patterns, properties, and relationships for both prime and composite numbers.

See also **Gambling, Statistics.**

References: 11 (491–9) [L 2]; 55 (61–83) [L 2–3]; 62 (24–44) [L 1–2]; 79 (40) [L 1–2]; 81 (1–194) [L 1–2]; 84 (1–101) [L 1–2]; 85 (1–235) [L 2–3]; 268 (39–42) [L 1–2]; 295 [L 1–2]; 325 (331–76) [L 2–3]; 340 (15–38) [L 3]; 413 (15–25) [L 1–2]; 415 (1–109) [L 2]; 470 (60–79) [L 1–2]; 471 (59–70) [L 1–2]; 472 (1–168) [L 1–2]; 499 (39–56) [L 2]; 562 (1–310) [L 2–3]; 675 (62–6) [L 1–2]; 866 (16–7) [L 2–3]; 881 (139–43) [L 1–2]; 938 (105–8) [L 1–2]; 939 (434–7) [L 2–3]; 1126 (120–3) [L 2–3]; 1156 (136–47) [L 2].

> **2, 3, 5, 7, 11, 13, 17, 19, 23, 29, 31, 37, 41, 43, 47, 53, 59, 61, 67, . . .**

Prime Numbers

Probability Theory   [Level 1–3]

The study of probability and its applications is becoming more important in the information age.

References: 5 (578–94) [L 3]; 11 (1301–90) [L 2–3]; 53 (183–209) [L 1–2]; 70 (91–116) [L 1–2]; 279 (1–21) [L 1–2]; 301 (1–61) [L 1–2]; 302 (1–169) [L 1–2]; 303 (1–229) [L 1–2]; 329 (1–145) [L 2–3]; 391 (1–58) [L 3]; 469 (250–71) [L 1–2]; 499 (122–58) [L 2]; 630 [L 2–3]; 631 [L 2–3]; 632 [L 2–3]; 633 [L 2–3]; 801 (623–30) [L 1–2]; 847 (121–3) [L 2–3]; 929 (337) [L 1–2]; 941 (446–9) [L 1]; 980 (685–90) [L 2–3]; 983 (327–34) [L 2–3]; 997 (769–75) [L 2]; 1007 (559–63) [L 1–3]; 1016 (13–7) [L 1–2].

Prodigies

See **Calculating Prodigies.**

Projective Geometry   [Level 2–3]

Projective geometry studies the properties of geometric figures that remain the same when the figure is projected.

References: 5 (547–56) [L 3]; 9 (10–21) [L 2–3]; 11 (613–31) [L 2]; 15 (331–5) [L 2]; 28 (143–66) [L 3]; 48 (285–301, 834–60) [L 2–3]; 52 (66–7) [L 2]; 125 (173–95) [L 2–3]; 409 (132–53) [L 2–3]; 533 (117–58) [L 2–3]; 596 (144–58) [L 2–3]; 654 (1–172) [L 2–3]; 1188 (136) [L 2–3].

Proof   [Level 2–3]

Proof is the logical process of establishing the validity of a statement. A direct proof begins with a postulate that leads logically to the conclusion. An indirect proof shows that assuming the conclusion is false leads to a contradiction.

References: 11 (1587–1724) [L 3]; 439 (1–261) [L 2–3]; 440 (1–250) [L 3]; 520 [L 3]; 527 (69–140) [L 2–3]; 597 (147–51) [L 2–3]; 639 [L 3].

Puzzles   [Level 1–3]

Often problems involving geometric figures can be considered puzzles to solve.

References: 208 (1–190) [L 1–3]; 293 [L 1–2]; 294 (1–160) [L 1–2]; 295 (1–157) [L 1–2]; 367 (1–64) [L 2–3]; 368 (1–34) [L 2–3]; 369 (1–120) [L 1–2]; 370 (1–100) [L 1–2]; 371 (1–25) [L 1–2]; 372 (1–237) [L 1–2]; 373 (1–20) [L 1–2]; 1077 (260–3) [L 1–2]; 1155 (16–31) [L 2]; 1160 (20–39) [L 2]; 1220 (131–5) [L 2]; 1231 (583–92) [L 1–3].

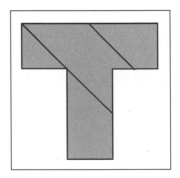

T Puzzle

Pyramids of Egypt [Level 1–3]

Building the Great Pyramid required transporting, preparing, and laying about 2,300,000 blocks, each of which weighed about $2\frac{1}{2}$ tons. The geometry used and measurements required made this construction a true wonder of the world.

References: 16 (18–20) [L 1–2]; 52 (36) [L 1–2]; 264 (139–47) [L 1–3]; 469 (65–71) [L 1–2]; 822 (124–7) [L 1–2]; 1089 (198–200) [L 2].

Pythagoras (ca. 580–ca. 500 B.C.) [Level 1–2]

This famous Greek mathematician and philosopher was an excellent teacher who developed a strong following of students.

References: 11 (77–87) [L 1–2]; 13 (19–28) [L 1–2]; 14 (69–77) [L 1–2]; 19 (9–17) [L 1]; 20 (6–17) [L 1–2]; 21 (80–1) [L 2]; 23 [L 1].

Pythagoras. From John and Susan Edeen. *Portraits, Mathematicians Book 1.* Dale Seymour Publications, 1988.

Pythagoreans [Level 1–3]

These 300 followers of Pythagoras developed a secret brotherhood with initiations and rites. Although women were not allowed to attend school, they were welcome to join the Pythagoreans.

References: 16 (43–54) [L 2–3]; 20 (6–17) [L 1–2]; 33 (50–3) [L 1–2]; 415 [L 1–2].

Pythagorean Theorem [Level 1–3]

This famous relationship in geometry states that in any right triangle, the square of the hypotenuse equals the sum of the squares of the other two sides.

References: 15 (288–91) [L 1–2]; 55 (48–60) [L 2–3];

127 (27–43) [L 1–2]; 131 (77–88) [L 2–3]; 136 (1–42) [L 1–2]; 137 (1–267) [L 2–3]; 138 (1–68) [L 2]; 139 (1–30) [L 1–2]; 140 (5–12) [L 3]; 413 (49–61) [L 2]; 675 (215–8) [L 1–2]; 821 (98–100) [L 2–3]; 942 (302–8) [L 1–2]; 985 (141–4) [L 1–2]; 998 (336–41) [L 2–3].

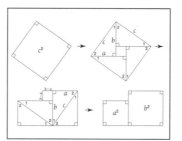

Therefore, $c^2 = a^2 + b^2$

Pythagorean Triples [Level 1–3]

A Pythagorean triple is a set of three integers that satisfy the Pythagorean theorem. The numbers 3, 4, and 5 are a Pythagorean triple.

References: 81 (1–194) [L 1–2]; 268 (32–3) [L 1–2]; 675 (66–8) [L 1–2]; 810 (103–8) [L 2–3]; 831 (611–3) [L 2–3]; 838 (540–4) [L 2]; 868 (48–51) [L 3]; 921 (724–5) [L 2–3]; 943 (652–5) [L 2]; 944 (346–8) [L 2–3].

Quadratic Equations [Level 2–3]

These are algebra equations whose highest exponent is two.

References: 15 (443–54) [L 2–3]; 817 (327–30) [L 2–3]; 825 (127–8) [L 1–2]; 841 (63–5) [L 2]; 878 (601–4) [L 2–3]; 892 (414–7) [L 2–3]; 947 (195–6) [L 1–2]; 965 (13–6) [L 1–2].

Quadratic Formula [Level 1–3]

This formula gives the roots (solutions) of any quadratic equation.

References: 94 (461–5) [L 2–3]; 268 (53–4) [L 2]; 986 (670) [L 2]; 1059 (146–52) [L 2–3]; 1217 (472–3) [L 2–3].

Ramanujan, Srinivasa (1887–1920) [Level 1–2]

This mathematician from India with very little formal education made remarkable discoveries in mathematics. Among his discoveries were formulas for approximating the value of π.

References: 11 (361–8) [L 1–2]; 19 (123–32) [L 1]; 20 [L 1–2]; 46 (139–42) [L 1–2]; 79 (54–5) [L 1–2]; 109 (171–8) [L 1–2]; 567 [L 2–3]; 579 [L 2–3].

Srinivasa Ramanujan

Random Numbers [Level 1–3]

Random numbers are digits that are distributed by chance. Lists of random numbers are used to test statistical data.

References: 109 (244–7) [L 1–2]; 268 (1–3) [L 1–2]; 329 (11–22) [L 2–3]; 344 (161–72) [L 1–2]; 917 (132–6) [L 2–3]; 1039 (772–4) [L 2–3]; 1069 (118–23) [L 1–2]; 1148 (20–34) [L 2]; 1213 (663–4) [L 2–3]; 1237 (385–91) [L 2–3].

Rate and Ratio [Level 1–2]

See also Interest, Velocity.

A rate is a quantity or amount of one thing considered in relation to a unit of another thing. Examples are 100 miles per hour, 29¢ a pound, and $8 per $100 borrowed.

References: 69 (91–128) [L 1–2]; 70 (71–89) [L 1–2]; 283 (1–40) [L 2]; 946 (376–9) [L 1–2]; 977 (146–8) [L 1–2]; 987 (450–3, 480) [L 1–2]; 1060 (595–7) [L 1–2].

Rational Numbers [Level 2–3]

A rational number can be expressed as an integer or as the quotient of two integers (the divisor may not be zero).

References: 5 (30–6) [L 2]; 30 (52–7) [L 2–3]; 96

(1–140) [L 2–3]; 410 (21–37) [L 2]; 499 (265–867) [L 2]; 467 (130–41) [L 2]; 996 (418–9) [L 2–3].

Real Numbers [Level 1–3]

A real number is any number that is either rational or irrational.

References: 5 (74–7) [L 2]; 48 (979–1004) [L 2–3]; 96 (1–140) [L 2–3]; 410 (38–51) [L 2]; 467 (130–41) [L 2]; 499 (265–87) [L 2]; 614 [L 2–3]; 870 (369–70) [L 1–3].

Recursion

See Iteration and Recursion.

Regular Polyhedra

See Platonic Solids.

Relativity Theory [Level 2–3]

This advanced theory in physics relates energy, mass, and the speed of light.

References: 11 (1083–1116) [L 3]; 16 [L 2]; 32 (148–80) [L 3]; 37 (65–73) [L 3]; 53 (460–4) [L 2–3]; 596 (432–52) [L 3].

Repeating Decimals [Level 1–2]

Fractions expressed in decimal form that do not terminate are repeating fractions. The number patterns in repeating decimals are interesting to investigate.

References: 83 (1–101) [L 1–2]; 268 (36–8) [L 1–2]; 351 (53–4) [L 1–2]; 880 (209–12) [L 1–2]; 932 (126–33) [L 1–2]; 949 (600–2) [L 1–2]; 963 (144–8) [L 2].

1/7 = 0.142857142857...

Repeating Decimals

Rhind Papyrus

See Papyrus Rhind.

Riemann, Georg Friedrich Bernhard (1826–1866) [Level 1–3]

This German mathematician made contributions to several branches of mathematics. Riemannian geometry is the foundation for modern relativity theory.

References: 12 (157–61) [L 1–2]; 13 (464) [L 1–2]; 16 (554–6) [L 3]; 17 (484–509) [L 2–3]; 29 [L 1–2]; 950 (675–81) [L 3].

Roman Numerals   [Level 1–2]

The Roman numeration system uses letters of the alphabet as symbols for key numbers. The letters, combined according to rules, can be used to express any natural number.

References: 15 (54–64) [L 1–2]; 77 (47–55) [L 1–2]; 675 (40–1) [L 1–2]; 1048 (108, 156) [L 1–2].

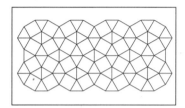

Roman Numerals

Roots and Powers   [Level 1–3]

The *n*th root of a number is a number which, when taken as a factor *n* times, produces the given number. The *n*th power of a number is the result when the number is used as a factor *n* times.

References: 5 (47–56) [L 2]; 15 (144–51) [L 1–2]; 675 (98–101) [L 1–2]; 870 (369–70) [L 2–3]; 895 (589–97) [L 3]; 930 (294–8) [L 1–2]; 996 (418–9) [L 2–3]; 1049 (218–21) [L 3]; 1098 [L 1–2].

Scaling and Similarity   [Level 1–2]

Scaling is the transformation of a figure by shrinking or enlarging. Scaled figures are the same shape—they are similar.

References: 70 (24–48) [L 2]; 80 (1–144) [L 1–2]; 119 (1–30 & video) [L 1–2]; 423 (1–73) [L 2]; 493 (35–74) [L 1–2]; 579 [L 1–2].

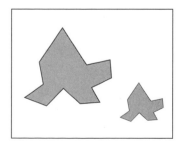

Similar Shapes

Scheduling and Planning   [Level 1–3]

Discrete mathematics can be applied to analysis of schedules or tasks.

See also **Modeling and Decision Making.**

References: 53 (66–81) [L 2–3]; 656 [L 3]; 951 (194–5) [L 2–3]; 964 (124–32) [L 2–3]; 969 (346–50) [L 2–3].

Semiregular Polyhedra

See **Archimedian Polyhedra.**

Semiregular Tessellation

See **Tessellations and Tiling.**

![Semiregular Tessellation]

Semiregular Tessellation. From Britton and Seymour. *Introduction to Tessellations.* Dale Seymour Publications, 1989.

Series and Sequences   [Level 1–3]

A sequence is a set of ordered numbers such as 5, 10, 15, 20, 25, . . . , 5*n*. A series is the sum of the numbers in a sequence, such as 5 + 10 + 15 + 20 + 25 + . . . + 5*n*.

References: 5 (381–96) [L 3]; 15 (494–513) [L 2–3]; 48 (436–67) [L 2–3]; 55 (207–222) [L 2–3]; 63 (1–46) [L 2–3]; 64 (1–108) [L 2–3]; 101 (51–6, 201–19) [L 2]; 108 (32–48) [L 2]; 111 (1–113) [L 1–2]; 272 (1–24) [L 2–3]; 330 (1–17) [L 2]; 425 (1–293) [L 3]; 473 (1–46) [L 1–2]; 474 (1–107) [L 1–2]; 562 (183–8) [L 2–3]; 608 [L 3]; 609 [L 2–3]; 867 (424–8) [L 2–3]; 889 (218–21) [L 2–3]; 894 (665–72) [L 2–3]; 950 (675–81) [L 3].

Set Theory

See **Logic.**

Sierpiński Triangle   [Level 1–3]

This equilateral triangle is repeatedly partitioned into smaller and smaller similar triangles. It was named after the Polish mathematician Waclaw Sierpiński. A Sierpiński triangle is a fractal.

See also **Fractals.**

References: 54 (25–6) [L 1–2]; 109 (122–3) [L 2]; 340 (120–1) [L 2–3]; 455 [L 2–3]; 457 [L 2–3]; 989 (617–21) [L 2–3].

Sierpiński Triangle

Sieve of Eratosthenes [Level 1–2]

This process will determine all of the primes not greater than a given number—write down all numbers up to that number and remove multiples of 2, 3, 5, 7, etc., up to the square root of the given number.

See also **Eratosthenes of Alexandria.**

References: 79 (68–72, 119, 121) [L 1–2]; 84 (57–60) [L 1–2]; 85 (12) [L 2]; 413 (23–5) [L 2]; 581 (127–8) [L 2]; 467 (32–3) [L 1–2].

Sieve of Eratosthenes

Simulations [Level 1–2]

A simulation is a procedure for answering questions about real problems by running experiments that closely resemble the real situation. There are several techniques for creating simulations including computer programs, random digits, and sampling.

References: 54 [L 1–2]; 322 (1–53) [L 1–2]; 1074 (726–31) [L 2]; 1084 (713) [L 2].

Slide Rule [Level 1–2]

Although the slide rule has been replaced by calculators and computers, understanding its design and rationale gives one a better understanding of logarithms.

References: 5 (66–9) [L 2]; 15 (205–6) [L 1–2]; 100 (13–5) [L 1–2]; 675 (271–3) [L 2]; 1214 (162–4) [L 2].

Soap Film and Minimal Surfaces [Level 1–3]

Mathematicians are interested in the minimal surfaces, which form the faces of 3-dimensional shapes. Experiments with soap film on networks often reveal the natural minimal surface area connecting vertices and edges in space.

References: 11 (867–95) [L 2–3]; 51 (110–2) [L 1–2]; 145 (1–192) [L 1–2]; 220 (9–239) [L 2–3]; 265 (68–9) [L 1–2]; 297 (1–188) [L 2–3]; 298 [L 2–3]; 299 (1–228) [L 1]; 340 (46–70) [L 3]; 438 (64–185) [L 2]; 493 (209–21) [L 2–3]; 552 (214–28) [L 2]; 955 (377–85) [L 3]; 1010 (146–52) [L 2–3]; 1122 (104–7) [L 2–3]; 1144 (82–93) [L 2–3].

Social Choices

See **Elections and Social Choices.**

Somerville, Mary Fairfax (1780–1872) [Level 1–2]

This mathematician and scientist from Scotland became famous for her book *Mechanism of the Heavens.*

References: 22 (81–90) [L 1]; 25 [L 1]; 26 (83–100) [L 2–3]; 44 (1–14) [L 1–2]; 45 (9–19) [L 1].

Mary Somerville. From John and Susan Edeen. *Portraits, Women Mathematicians.* Dale Seymour Publications, 1990.

Space Program [Level 1–3]

What kind of mathematics has been and is being

applied in the space program?

References: 261 (1–192) [L 2–3]; 262 (1–65) [L 1–2]; 280 (1–58) [L 2–3]; 466 (76–92) [L 2–3]; 809 (563–5) [L 3]; 979 (549–53) [L 2–3].

Speed

See **Velocity and Speed.**

Sphere Packing   [Level 2–3]

Sphere packing involves maximum utilization of space, filling bins with the greatest number of spheres possible.

References: 102 (11–8) [L 2]; 109 (96–103, 125) [L 2]; 217 (108–35) [L 3]; 1146 (18–26) [L 2]; 1186 (116–25) [L 3].

Spirals   [Level 1–3]

A spiral is a curve that begins at a point and traces a line that rotates around and away from the point according to some ratio or function. Well-defined spirals include the logarithmic spiral and the Archimedian spiral.

See also **Curves.**

References: 186 (170–98) [L 1–2]; 259 (107–43) [L 2–3]; 265 (40–5) [L 1–2]; 296 (89–92) [L 2–3]; 427 (206–16) [L 2–3]; 428 (1–464) [L 2–3]; 429 (99–109) [L 3]; 493 (44–55) [L 2]; 978 (321–7) [L 2–3]; 1205 (240–3) [L 2–3].

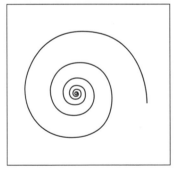

Spiral

Spirographs®

See **Instruments in Geometry.**

Spirolaterals and Worm Paths   [Level 1–2]

These designs are generated by a moving point in a plane whose path is determined by a rule. For example, "go 1 unit, turn 90°; go 2 units, turn 90°; go 3 units, turn 90°, and so on." Which rules return to their starting point? Which create closed curves?

References: 240 (144–66) [L 1–2]; 343 (205–21) [L 1–2]; 961 (279–82) [L 1]; 1043 (166–9) [L 2]; 1230 (121–4) [L 1–2].

Sports   [Level 1–3]

Statistical data on sports teams and participants is used by coaches and fans. Mathematical concepts also apply to maximizing performance in a sport. How is mathematics applied in your favorite sport?

References: 69 (23–42) [L 1–2]; 811 (450–1) [L 1–2]; 817 (327–30) [L 2–3]; 837 (528–31) [L 2]; 840 (35–52) [L 1–2]; 869 (136–41) [L 1–2]; 871 (565–9) [L 1–2]; 897 (332–5) [L 2–3]; 907 (60–4) [L 1–2]; 915 (336–42) [L 1–2]; 935 (532–5) [L 1–2]; 940 (624–7) [L 2–3]; 951 (194–5) [L 2–3]; 968 (429–30) [L 2]; 969 (346–50) [L 2–3]; 974 (658–63) [L 1–2]; 988 (366–71) [L 2–3]; 1004 (456–60) [L 2–3]; 1007 (559–63) [L 1–3]; 1014 (636–41) [L 1–2].

Square Root Algorithms   [Level 1–2]

Square roots and other roots can easily be found today using a calculator. How were square roots determined before calculators? How did these algorithms originate? Why do they work?

References: 15 (144–51) [L 1–2]; 305 (145–60) [L 1–2]; 340 (165) [L 1–2]; 813 (144–9) [L 1–2]; 962 (344–5) [L 1–2]; 1049 (218–21) [L 3]; 1222 (317–9) [L 1–2]; 1236 (175–6) [L 1–2].

Squaring the Circle   [Level 2–3]

This classic problem requires one to construct (using only a straightedge and a compass) a square with exactly the same area as a given circle.

References: 15 (302–8) [L 2–3]; 16 (96–7) [L 2–3]; 132 (90–105) [L 3]; 391 (168–72) [L 2–3]; 410 (73–80) [L 2–3]; 675 (201–4) [L 2–3].

Star Polygons   [Level 1–3]

Star polygons are concave with four or more points (acute angles), where each of the acute angles are congruent and equidistant from a centroid and each of the reflex angles are congruent and equidistant from the centroid.

References: 181 (157–79) [L 1–2]; 185 (82–91) [L 2–3]; 231 (1–154) [L 1–3]; 232 (1–192) [L 1–3]; 1071 (46–51, 54) [L 1–2].

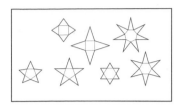

Star Polygons

Statistical Inference [Level 2–3]

Nearly every business collects data, analyzes that data, and then makes decisions based on that analysis. When using random data or a limited set of data, there is always some chance that the data will lead to a false conclusion. Statistical inference involves ways of determining the confidence level of a set of data.

References: 36 (185–92) [L 2]; 53 (210–35) [L 2–3]; 54 (127–36) [L 2–3]; 318 [L 2–3]; 319 [L 2–3]; 937 (744–6) [L 2–3].

Statistics [Level 1–3]

Statistics involves collecting, analyzing, interpreting, and presenting of numerical information.

References: 5 (594–606) [L 3]; 11 (1399–1505) [L 2]; 317 (1–196) [L 1–2]; 318 (1–174) [L 2–3]; 319 (1–190) [L 2–3]; 323 (1–120) [L 1–3]; 324 (1–110) [L 1–2]; 325 (1–429) [L 2–3]; 326 (1–142) [L 1–2]; 327 (1–210) [L 1–2]; 329 (1–145) [L 2–3]; 330 (1–166) [L 2–3]; 331 (1–150) [L 2]; 332 (1–136) [L 1–2]; 335 (1–32) [L 2–3]; 336 (1–120) [L 2–3]; 499 (159–97) [L 2]; 535 (1–246) [L 2–3]; 634 [L 3]; 635 [L 3]; 801 (623–30) [L 1–2]; 869 (136–41) [L 1–2]; 881 (139–43) [L 1–2]; 917 (132–6) [L 2–3]; 931 (283–91) [L 2–3]; 937 (744–6) [L 2–3]; 1001 (90–3) [L 1–2].

Strip Groups

See **Frieze Patterns.**

Sun Dials [Level 1–2]

How do sun dials show the time? When and where were they first used?

References: 15 (670–1) [L 1–2]; 1110 (104–6) [L 1–2]; 1167 (231–8) [L 2].

Sun Dial

Surveying

See **Earth Measurement.**

Symbolic Logic [Level 2–3]

In symbolic logic, the properties of formal logic are expressed in terms of seven basic symbols.

References: 11 (1825–1901) [L 3]; 33 (207–12) [L 2–3]; 417 (1–463) [L 1–2]; 418 (1–197) [L 3]; 419 (1–284) [L 2–3]; 500 (48–58) [L 2–3]; 527 (5–21) [L 2–3]; 541 (1–496) [L 2–3].

Symmetry [Level 1–3]

Symmetry with respect to a line is called mirror (axial or reflective) symmetry. Symmetry with respect to a point is called rotational (central) symmetry. In three dimensions, there is symmetry with respect to a plane.

References: 11 (659–711) [L 1–2]; 53 (482–505) [L 1–2]; 68 (1–11) [L 1–2]; 144 (1–160) [L 1–2]; 174 (1–168) [L 2–3]; 175 (1–125) [L 1–2]; 176 (1–40) [L 1–2]; 177 (1–125) [L 1–2]; 181 (63–85) [L 1–2]; 183 (21–36) [L 1–2]; 185 (335–400) [L 2–3]; 187 (26–77) [L 1–2]; 192 (1–124) [L 1–3]; 244 (1–48 & sftwr) [L 1–2]; 274 (1–36) [L 2–3]; 391 (115–29) [L 2–3]; 423 (405–52) [L 2–3]; 493 (405–46) [L 2–3]; 1120 (52–75) [L 2–3].

Symmetry Groups (17)

See **Crystallography Patterns.**

Symmetry in Design [Level 1–2]

Designs often use mirror symmetry, rotational symmetry, or the repeated pattern of translation symmetry.

References: 117 (1–60) [L 1–2]; 118 (1–40) [L 1–2]; 162 (1–123) [L 1–2]; 177 (1–122) [L 1–2]; 188 (1–110) [L 1–2]; 220 [L 1–2]; 223 (1–390) [L 1–2];

224 (1–281) [L 1–2]; 234 (1–160) [L 1–2]; 235 (1–542) [L 1–2]; 236 (1–153) [L 1–2]; 237 (1–100) [L 1–2]; 238 (1–467) [L 1–2]; 239 (1–93) [L 1–2]; 651 [L 2].

Symmetry in Design

Symmetry in Logos

See Logos

Symmetry in Nature   [Level 1–2]

Flowers, leaves, trees, shells, animals, and microscopic creatures are often symmetric.

References: 178 (1–100) [L 1–2]; 186 [L 1–2]; 187 [L 1–2]; 220 [L 1–2]; 223 [L 1–2].

Tangrams   [Level 1–2]

Tangrams are seven-piece geometric puzzles of triangles and quadrilaterals, which fit together to form a square and many other interesting shapes.

References: 141 (1–120) [L 1–2]; 142 (1–334) [L 1–2]; 143 (1–51) [L 1–2]; 347 (27–54) [L 1–2].

Tangram Pieces

Tensegrity   [Level 2–3]

Buckminster Fuller coined the word *tensegrity,* a contraction of tensional integrity, to describe the study of structural systems and the forces that are

transmitted from one part to another.

References: 214 (1–121) [L 2–3]; 215 (1–172) [L 3]; 216 (1–234) [L 2]; 217 (372–420) [L 2–3].

Tessellations and Tiling   [Level 1–3]

To tessellate a plane is to cover it with repeated shapes with no overlaps and no gaps between the shapes. Design patterns such as Islamic art and some of the work of M. C. Escher are tessellations.

References: 53 (494–505) [L 1–2]; 121 (147–87) [L 1–2]; 181 (1–250) [L 1–2]; 182 (1–127) [L 1–2]; 183 (1–195) [L 1–2]; 184 (1–90) [L 1–2]; 185 (1–694) [L 2–3]; 187 (130–69) [L 1–2]; 193 (1–354) [L 2–3]; 195 (1–276) [L 1–2]; 219 (1–52) [L 3]; 220 (28–31) [L 2]; 232 (117–49) [L 2–3]; 241 (95–117) [L 1–2]; 347 (161–87) [L 2–3]; 423 (167–207) [L 2]; 493 (167–208) [L 1–2]; 898 (307–10) [L 1–2]; 910 (299–306) [L 1–2].

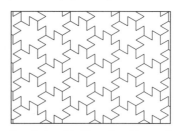

Tessellation of the Plane. From Britton and Seymour. *Introduction to Tessellations.* Dale Seymour Publications, 1989.

Tessellations, Space   [Level 1–3]

Space tessellations completely fill space with a pattern of solid shapes.

References: 201 (86–115) [L 1–3]; 202 (154–74) [L 1–2]; 208 (143–68) [L 1–2]; 219 (164–99) [L 3]; 220 (38–239) [L 3]; 423 (347–81) [L 2–3]; 493 (347–55) [L 2–3].

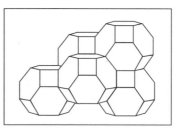

Tessellation of Space

Thales (640–550 B.C.)   [Level 1–2]

Thales founded the earliest Greek school of

mathematics and philosophy. He may have been the first to use deductive geometry.

References: 13 (14–8) [L 1–2]; 14 (64–9) [L 1–2]; 16 (43–8) [L 2]; 20 (4–6) [L 1–2]; 21 (82–3) [L 1–2]; 23 [L 1]; 52 (36) [L 1–2].

Thales. From John and Susan Edeen. *Portraits, Mathematicians Book 1.* Dale Seymour Publications, 1988.

Time and Calendars   [Level 1–3]

Every ancient culture discovered the length of the year and of the day and explored convenient ways to subdivide the day into smaller units of time.

References: 15 (651–74) [L 1–2]; 16 (374–8) [L 3]; 31 (189–202) [L 3]; 278 (1–21) [L 2]; 331 (83–90) [L 1–3]; 414 (133–51) [L 3]; 458 (191–201) [L 1–2]; 471 (19–21) [L 1–2]; 477 (1–128) [L 1]; 478 (104–11) [L 1–2]; 533 (104–11) [L 1–2]; 583 (139–52) [L 2]; 904 (304–5) [L 2–3]; 1118 (14–23) [L 3]; 1189 (21–30) [L 2].

Topology   [Level 1–3]

Topology, a branch of geometry, studies the properties of figures that do not change when stretched or bent. It is often described as "rubber-sheet geometry."

References: 5 (680–5) [L 3]; 9 (47–56) [L 2–3]; 11 (573–90) [L 1–2]; 30 (235–71) [L 2–3]; 48 (1158–81) [L 1–2]; 211 (1–319) [L 2–3]; 241 (144–66) [L 1–2]; 307 (69–94) [L 1–2]; 340 (46–80) [L 3]; 343 (55–67) [L 2]; 353 (35–47) [L 1–2]; 391 (130–45) [L 2–3]; 423 (129–37) [L 2]; 436 (1–206) [L 1–2]; 437 (1–158) [L 3]; 461 (111–26) [L 1–2]; 552 (252–81) [L 2]; 675 (185–7) [L 2]; 1202 (108–21) [L 3].

Transfinite Numbers   [Level 2–3]

A transfinite number is an infinite number, either cardinal or ordinal. These numbers have some interesting properties, such as $m = m + 1$ and $m = m \cdot m$.

References: 9 (30–8) [L 2]; 48 (979–1004) [L 2–3]; 52 (156–7) [L 1–2]; 296 (38–58) [L 2–3]; 517 [L 2–3]; 599 (41–54) [L 3]; 675 (85–6) [L 2]; 1183 [L 3].

Transformations

See **Geometric Transformations.**

Triangular Numbers

See **Figurate Numbers.**

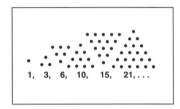

Triangular Numbers

Trigonometry   [Level 1–3]

Trigonometry is the study of functions, established from ratios of triangle measurements, and the applications of these functions.

References: 5 (220–337) [L 3]; 15 (600–32) [L 2]; 16 (158–75) [L 3]; 33 (176–200) [L 2–3]; 330 (208–20) [L 1–2]; 464 (1–32) [L 2–3]; 572 [L 2–3]; 675 (101–4, 333–75) [L 2–3]; 807 (496–8) [L 2–3].

Trisection of an Angle

See **Angle-Trisection Problem.**

Unsolved Problems   [Level 2–3]

There have always been problems that no one could solve or prove impossible to solve. These classic problems have provided an intellectual challenge to many mathematicians.

See also **Squaring the Circle, Angle-Trisection Problem, Fermat's Last Theorem.**

References: 30 (134–9) [L 3]; 53 (536–7) [L 2–3]; 120 [L 2–3]; 132 (1–350) [L 2–3]; 563 (46–72) [L 3]; 564 [L 3]; 565 [L 3]; 566 [L 3].

Vectors   [Level 1–3]

Vector quantities have both size and direction. Velocity is a vector because it is a speed in a given direction. Velocity vectors are important in navigation.

References: 5 (363–9) [L 3]; 100 (21–2) [L 2]; 121 (189–206) [L 2]; 140 (17–29) [L 3]; 431 (1–124) [L 2–3]; 432 (1–142) [L 2–3]; 433 (1–107) [L 3]; 434 [L 1–2]; 464 (33–61) [L 2–3]; 595 (136–40) [L 2]; 1132 [L 2–3].

Velocity and Speed   [Level 1–3]

Velocity, a vector quantity, is the measure of the speed and direction of an object.

See also Motion.

References: 11 (715–57) [L 2]; 396 (1–680) [L 2–3]; 407 (11–32) [L 2–3]; 431 (1–124) [L 2–3]; 432 [L 2–3]; 433 [L 3]; 434 [L 1–2]; 839 (282–7) [L 2–3]; 874 (104–7) [L 2]; 878 (601–4) [L 2–3]; 979 (549–53) [L 2–3].

Volume Problems   [Level 1–3]

Volumes of many regular geometric shapes can be calculated using formulas. Irregular volumes may require other creative problem-solving strategies.

References: 54 (14–22, 26) [L 1–2]; 827 (58–60) [L 1–2]; 864 (392–5) [L 2–3]; 984 (294–6) [L 2–3]; 1070 (356–7) [L 1–2]; 1092 (384–5) [L 2]; 1094 (642–4) [L 1–2].

Wallpaper Patterns

See Crystallography Patterns, Frieze Patterns.

Weights and Measures

See Measurement.

Western European Mathematics   [Level 1–3]

As the mathematical knowledge of ancient Greece and Asia was compared and combined, Western Europe began exploring new areas of mathematics and extending existing ones. Which countries and which mathematicians led these developments?

References: 11 [L 1–2]; 12 (77–92) [L 1–2]; 13 (131–43) [L 1–2]; 14 (292–530) [L 1–2]; 16 (246–532) [L 2–3]; 596 [L 1–2]; 469 (168–229) [L 1–2].

Women   [Level 1–3]

Despite the lack of opportunity for women in mathematics, several women have made significant contributions to the development of mathematics. Progress has been made recently in recognizing and encouraging women in mathematics.

***See also* Germain, Hypatia, Kovalevsky, Lovelace, Noether, Modern Mathematicians.**

References: 11 [L 1–2]; 21 [L 1–2]; 22 (1–138) [L 1]; 25 (1–36) [L 1]; 26 (1–250) [L 1–2]; 42 (1–12) [L 1–2]; 43 (1–249) [L 1–2]; 44 (1–123) [L 1–2]; 45 (1–187) [L 1–2]; 46 (1–200) [L 1–2]; 442 [L 1–2]; 443 [L 2]; 444 [L 1–2]; 466 (20, 30–2) [L 2]; 519 (1–305) [L 1–2]; 522 (1–28) [L 1–2]; 588 [L 2]; 589 [L 1–2]; 590 [L 2]; 591 [L 2–3]; 592 [L 1–2]; 593 [L 1–2]; 663 [L 1–2]; 1008 (150–4) [L 1–2]; 1034 (354–8) [L 1–2].

Karen Uhlenbeck. From John and Susan Edeen. *Portraits, Women Mathematicians.* Dale Seymour Publications, 1990.

Zero   [Level 1–2]

The symbol *0* stands for the absence of quantity. It is an essential symbol for a place-value numeration system.

References: 15 (69–72) [L 1–2]; 16 [L 2]; 33 (1–49) [L 1–2]; 76 (23–6) [L 1–2]; 415 (1–14) [L 1–2]; 675 (27–30, 49–50) [L 1–2].

References
for Math
Projects

Books Listed by Number

Abbreviations used: NCTM—The National Council of Teachers of Mathematics. MAA—The Mathematical Association of America. COMAP—Consortium for Mathematics and Its Applications.

1   James, Glenn, and Robert James. *Mathematics Dictionary.* 5th ed. New York: Van Nostrand Reinhold Co., 1992.

2   Karush, William. *Webster's New World Dictionary of Mathematics.* New York: Simon & Schuster, 1989.

3   Karush, William. *The Crescent Dictionary of Mathematics.* Palo Alto, CA: Dale Seymour Publications, 1962.

4   Abdelnoon, R. E. Jason. *The Silver Burdett Mathematical Dictionary.* Morristown, NJ: Silver Burdett & Ginn, 1979.

5   Gellert, W., M. Hellwich, H. Kastner, and H. Kustner, eds. *The VNR Concise Encyclopedia of Mathematics.* 2d ed. New York: Van Nostrand Reinhold Co., 1989.

6   Newman, James R. *The Universal Encyclopedia of Mathematics.* New York: Simon & Schuster, 1964.

7   Dolan, Dan, ed. *Mathematics Teacher Resource Handbook.* Millwood, NY: Kraus International Publications, 1993.

8   Nichols, Eugene D., and Sharon L. Schwartz. *Mathematics Dictionary and Handbook.* Hondale, PA: Nichols Schwartz Publishing Co., 1993.

9   Dalton, LeRoy, and Henry Snyder. *Topics for Mathematics Clubs.* Reston, VA: NCTM, 1988.

10   Bergamini, David. *Mathematics.* Alexandria, VA: Time-Life Books, 1980.

11   Newman, James R. *The World of Mathematics.* 4 vols. Redmond, WA: Tempus Books, 1988.

12   Struik, Dirk J. *A Concise History of Mathematics.* 4th ed. New York: Dover Publications, 1987.

13   Ball, W. W. Rouse. *A Short Account of the History of Mathematics.* New York: Dover Publications, 1980.

14   Smith, D. E. *History of Mathematics.* Vol. 1. New York: Dover Publications, 1951.

15   Smith, D. E. *History of Mathematics.* Vol. 2. New York: Dover Publications, 1951.

16   Boyer, Carl B. *A History of Mathematics.* 2d ed. New York: John Wiley & Sons, 1991.

17   Bell, E. T. *Men of Mathematics.* New York: Simon & Schuster, 1965.

18   Albers, Donald J., and G. L. Alexanderson. *Mathematical People.* Chicago: Contemporary Books, 1985.

19   Reimer, Luetta, and Wilbert Reimer. *Mathematicians Are People, Too.* Vol. 1. Palo Alto, CA: Dale Seymour Publications, 1990.

20   Turnbull, Herbert Westren. *The Great Mathematicians.* New York: Simon & Schuster, 1962.

21   Johnson, Art. *Classic Math: History Topics for the Classroom.* Palo Alto, CA: Dale Seymour Publications, 1994.

22   Reimer, Luetta, and Wilbert Reimer. *Mathematicians Are People, Too.* Vol. 2. Palo Alto, CA: Dale Seymour Publications, 1994.

23   Edeen, Susan, and John Edeen. *Portraits for Classroom Bulletin Boards Mathematicians.* Book 1. Palo Alto, CA: Dale Seymour Publications, 1988.

24   Edeen, Susan, and John Edeen. *Portraits for Classroom Bulletin Boards Mathematicians.* Book 2. Palo Alto, CA: Dale Seymour Publications, 1988.

25   Edeen, Susan, and John Edeen. *Portraits for Classroom Bulletin Boards Women Mathematicians.* Palo Alto, CA: Dale Seymour Publications, 1990.

26   Perl, Teri. *Math Equals: Biographies of Women Mathematicians.* Menlo Park, CA: Addison-Wesley Publishing Co., 1978.

27   Peace, Nigel R. *Discovering Mathematics.* Books 1 and 2. London: Macmillan Education, 1987.

28   Sawyer, W. W. *Prelude to Mathematics.* New York: Dover Publications, 1982.

29   Bendick, Jeanne, and Marcia Levin. *Mathematics Illustrated Dictionary.* New York: McGraw-Hill, 1965.

30   Courant, Richard, and Herbert Robbins. *What Is Mathematics?* London: Oxford Univ. Press, 1941.

31   Halmos, Paul R. *I Want to Be a Mathematician.* Washington, D.C.: MAA, 1985.

32 Kline, Morris. *Mathematics and the Search for Knowledge.* Oxford, England: Oxford Univ. Press, 1985.

33 Rucker, Rudy. *Mind Tools.* Boston: Houghton Mifflin Co., 1987.

34 Sawyer, W. W. *Mathematician's Delight.* Baltimore, MD: Penguin Books, 1943.

35 Sawyer, W. W. *The Search for Pattern.* Baltimore, MD: Penguin Books, 1970.

36 Sharron, Sidney, Bob Reyes, et al. *Applications in Mathematics.* Reston, VA: NCTM, 1979.

37 Kastner, Bernice. *Applications of Secondary School Mathematics.* Reston, VA: NCTM, 1978.

38 Saunders, Hal. *When Are We Ever Gonna Have to Use This?* 3d ed. Palo Alto, CA: Dale Seymour Publications, 1988.

39 Alexanderson, G. L. *Pólya Picture Album: Encounters of a Mathematician.* Cambridge, MA: Birkhäuser, 1987.

40 Taylor, Harold, and Loretta Taylor. *George Pólya: Master of Discovery.* Palo Alto, CA: Dale Seymour Publications, 1993.

41 Pólya, George. *How to Solve It.* Princeton, NJ: Princeton Univ. Press, 1973.

42 Greenes, Carole. *Sonya Kovalevsky.* Providence, RI: Janson Publications, 1989.

43 Keith, Sandra, and Philip Keith, eds. *National Conference on Women in Math and the Sciences.* St. Cloud, MN: St. Cloud University, 1990.

44 Perl, Teri. *Women and Numbers.* San Carlos, CA: Wide World Publishing/Tetra, 1993.

45 Perl, Teri, and Joan Manning. *Women, Numbers, and Dreams.* Santa Rosa, CA: National Women's History Project, 1982.

46 Alcoze, Thom, et al. *Multiculturism in Mathematics, Science, and Technology.* Menlo Park, CA: Addison-Wesley Publishing Co., 1993.

47 Zaslavsky, Claudia. *Africa Counts.* Brooklyn, NY: Lawrence Hill Books, 1973.

48 Kline, Morris. *Mathematical Thought from Ancient to Modern Times.* 3 Vols. New York: Oxford Univ. Press, 1972.

49 Motz, Lloyd, and Jefferson Weaver. *Story of Mathematics.* New York: Plenum Press, 1993.

50 Aaboe, Asger. *Episodes from the Early History of Mathematics.* Washington, D.C.: MAA, 1964.

51 Khurgin, Y. *Did You Say Mathematics?* Moscow: Mir Publishers, 1974.

52 Pappas, Theoni. *The Joy of Mathematics.* San Carlos, CA: Wide World Publishing/Tetra, 1986.

53 Garfunkel, Solomon, Lynn Steen, and Joseph Malkevich, et al. *For All Practical Purposes.* New York: W. H. Freeman, 1991.

54 Steen, Lynn A. *On the Shoulders of Giants.* Washington, D.C.: National Academy Press, 1990.

55 Dunham, William. *Journey Through Genius: The Great Theorems of Mathematics.* New York: John Wiley & Sons, 1990.

56 Madison, Bernard L., and Therese A. Hart. *A Challenge of Numbers: People in the Mathematical Sciences.* Washington, D.C.: National Academy Press, 1989.

57 Isaacs, Daintith, and Martin Isaacs, eds. *Concise Science Dictionary.* New York: Oxford Univ. Press, 1991.

58 Walker, Peter, ed. *Chambers Science and Technology Dictionary.* Edinburgh, England: W & R Chambers, 1988.

59 Abbott, Edwin. *Flatland.* New York: Dover Publications, 1952.

60 Burger, Dionys. *Sphereland.* New York: Harper & Row, 1965.

61 Bezuszka, Stanley, Lou D'Angelo, and Margaret Kenney. *The Wonder Square* (Boston College Math Inst. Booklet 2). Chestnut Hill, MA: Boston College Press, 1976.

62 Bezuszka, Stanley, et al. *Perfect Numbers* (Boston College Math Inst. Booklet 3). Chestnut Hill, MA: Boston College Press, 1980.

63 Bezuszka, Stanley, Lou D'Angelo, and Margaret Kenney. *Applications of Series* (Boston College Math Inst. Booklet 4). Chestnut Hill, MA: Boston College Press, 1976.

64 Bezuszka, Stanley, Lou D'Angelo, and Margaret Kenney. *Applications of Finite Differences* (Boston College Math Inst. Booklet 9). Chestnut Hill, MA: Boston College Press, 1976.

65 Kenney, Margaret. *The Super Sum* (Boston College Math Inst. Booklet 10). Chestnut Hill, MA: Boston College Press, 1976.

66 Kenney, Margaret. *The Incredible Pascal Triangle* (Boston College Math Inst. Booklet 11). Chestnut Hill, MA: Boston College Press, 1976.

67 Kenney, Margaret. *A Lesson in Mathematical Doodling* (Boston College Math Inst. Booklet. 12) Chestnut Hill, MA: Boston College Press, 1976.

68 Souviney, Randall, et al. *Mathematical Investigations.* Book 1. Palo Alto, CA: Dale Seymour Publications, 1990.

69 Souviney, Randall, et al. *Mathematical Investigations.* Book 2. Palo Alto, CA: Dale Seymour Publications, 1992.

70 Souviney, Randall, et al. *Mathematical Investigations.* Book 3. Palo Alto, CA: Dale Seymour Publications, 1992.

71 Hess, Adrien T. *Four-Dimensional Geometry.* Reston, VA: NCTM, 1977.

72 Henderson, Linda D. *The Fourth-Dimension and Non-Euclidean Geometry in Modern Art.* Princeton, NJ: Princeton Univ. Press, 1983.

73 Hess, Adrien, Glenn Allinger, and Lyle Andersen. *Mathematics Projects Handbook.* Reston, VA: NCTM, 1989.

74 Urdang, Lawrence. *The Facts on File Dictionary of Numerical Allusions.* New York: Facts on File, 1986.

75 Gibson, Carl, et al. *The Facts on File Dictionary of Mathematics.* New York: Facts on File, 1988.

76 Wells, David. *The Penguin Dictionary of Curious and Interesting Numbers.* New York: Penguin Books, 1986.

77 Smeltzer, Donald. *Man and Number.* Buchanan, NY: Emerson Books, 1958.

78 Henry, Boyd. *Every Number Is Special.* Palo Alto, CA: Dale Seymour Publications, 1985.

79 Wisner, Robert J. *A Panorama of Numbers.* Glenview, IL: Scott, Foresman, & Co., 1970.

80 Morrison, Philip, and Phylis Morrison. *Powers of Ten.* New York: W. H. Freeman, 1982.

81 Bezuszka, Stanley, and Margaret Kenney. *Number Treasury.* Palo Alto, CA: Dale Seymour Publications, 1982.

82 Veltman, John. *Binary Power.* Palo Alto, CA: Dale Seymour Publications, 1992.

83 Henry, Boyd. *Those Amazing Reciprocals.* Palo Alto, CA: Dale Seymour Publications, 1992.

84 Brown, Stephen I. *Some Prime Comparisons.* Reston, VA: NCTM, 1978.

85 Ribenboim, Paulo. *The Little Book of Big Primes.* New York: Springer-Verlag, 1991.

86 Shoemaker, Richard W. *Perfect Numbers.* Reston, VA: NCTM, 1973.

87 McLeish, John. *Number: The History of Numbers and How They Shape Our Lives.* New York: Ballantine, 1991.

88 Shapiro, Max S., ed. *Mathematics Encyclopedia.* Garden City, NY: Doubleday & Co., 1977.

89 Eves, Howard. *An Introduction to the History of Mathematics.* New York: Holt, Reinhart and Winston, 1964.

90 Steen, Lynn Arthur, ed. *Mathematics Today.* New York: Springer-Verlag, 1978.

91 Garland, Trudi. *Fascinating Fibonaccis.* Palo Alto, CA: Dale Seymour Publications, 1987.

92 Brother Alfred Brousseau. *Introduction to Fibonacci Discovery.* Santa Clara, CA: Fibonacci Assoc., 1965.

93 Bicknell, Marjorie, and Verner E. Hoggatt. *A Primer for the Fibonacci Numbers.* Santa Clara, CA: Fibonacci Assoc., 1972.

94 Seymour, Dale. *Visual Patterns in Pascal's Triangle.* Palo Alto, CA: Dale Seymour Publications, 1986.

95 Green, Thomas M., and Charles L. Hamberg. *Pascal's Triangle.* Palo Alto, CA: Dale Seymour Publications, 1986.

96 Niven, Ivan. *Numbers: Rational and Irrational.* Washington, D.C.: MAA, 1961.

97 Davis, Philip. *The Lore of Large Numbers.* Washington, D.C.: MAA, 1961.

98 Dolan, Stan, et al. *Functions.* New York: Cambridge Univ. Press, 1991.

99 Lund, Charles, and Edwin Andersen. *Graphing Calculator Activities.* Menlo Park, CA: Addison-Wesley Innovative Learning Publications, 1992.

100 Hallenberg, Arthur E., et al. *Historical Topics in Algebra.* Reston, VA: NCTM, 1971.

101 Posamentier, Alfred S., and Charles T. Salkind. *Challenging Problems in Algebra.* Palo Alto, CA: Dale Seymour Publications, 1988.

102 Dalton, LeRoy C. *Algebra in the Real World.* Palo Alto, CA: Dale Seymour Publications, 1983.

103 Carlson, Ronald, and Mary Jean Winter. *Algebra Experiments II: Exploring Nonlinear Functions.* Menlo Park, CA: Addison-Wesley Innovative Learning Publications, 1993.

104 Olds, C. D. *Continued Fractions.* Washington, D.C.: MAA, 1963.

105 Beckmann, Petr. *History of Pi.* New York: St. Martin's Press, 1971.

106 Pethoud, Robert. *Pi in the Sky.* Tucson, AZ: Zephr Press, 1993.

107 Apostol, Tom. *Story of Pi.* Pasadena, CA: California Institute of Technology, 1989. Video.

108 Dolan, Stan, et al. *Foundations.* New York: Cambridge Univ. Press, 1991.

109 Peterson, Ivars. *Islands of Truth: A Mathematical Mystery Cruise.* New York: W. H. Freeman, 1990.

110 Room, Adrian. *The Guinness Book of Numbers.* London: Guinness Publishing, 1989.

111 Seymour, Dale, and Peg Shedd. *Techniques in Finite Differences.* Palo Alto, CA: Dale Seymour Publications, 1973.

112 Bochinski, Julianne. *The Complete Handbook of Science Fair Projects.* New York: John Wiley & Sons, 1991.

113 Center for Statistical Education, ASA. *Student Poster Projects: Winners of the 1991–92 ASA Competition.* Palo Alto, CA: Dale Seymour Publications, 1994.

114 Paulos, John. *Innumeracy.* New York: Hill & Wang, 1988.

115 Kogelman, Stanley, and Joseph Warren. *Mind over Math.* New York: McGraw-Hill, 1978.

116 Kremer, Ron. *Exploring with Squares and Cubes.* Palo Alto, CA: Dale Seymour Publications, 1989.

117 Quintin, Jonathan. *Star Mosaics.* Palo Alto, CA: Dale Seymour Publications, 1993.

118 Shaw, Sheilah. *Kaleidometrics.* Norfolk, England: Tarquin Publications, 1981.

119 Apostal, Tom. *Similarity.* Pasadena, CA: California Institute of Technology, 1990. Video and Guide.

120 Yates, Robert. *The Trisection Problem.* Reston, VA: NCTM, 1971.

121 Elliott, H. A., James R. MacLean, and Janet M. Jorden. *Geometry in the Classroom: New Concepts and Methods.* Toronto: Holt, Rinehart and Winston of Canada, 1968.

122 Kenney, Margaret J., Stanley J. Bezuszka, and Joan D. Mastin. *Informal Geometry Explorations.* Palo Alto, CA: Dale Seymour Publications, 1992.

123 Pottage, John. *Geometrical Investigations.* Reading, MA: Addison-Wesley Publishing Co., 1983.

124 Sommer, Robert. *The Mind's Eye: Imagery in Everyday Life.* Palo Alto, CA: Dale Seymour Publications, 1978.

125 Pedoe, Dan. *Geometry and the Visual Arts.* New York: Dover Publications, 1976.

126 Ivins Jr., William M. *Art and Geometry: A Study in Space Intuitions.* New York: Dover Publications, 1946.

127 Stepelman, Jay. *Milestones in Geometry.* New York: Macmillan, 1970.

128 Genise, L. Roland, Ronald Genise, and Michael E. Burke. *René's Place: Exploring Euclidean Geometry.* Menlo Park, CA: Addison-Wesley Innovative Learning Publications, 1993.

129 Posamentier, Alfred. *Excursions in Advanced Euclidean Geometry.* Menlo Park, CA: Addison-Wesley Innovative Learning Publications, 1984.

130 Sykes, Mabel. *Source Book of Problems for Geometry,* 1912. Reprint, Palo Alto, CA: Dale Seymour Publications, 1994.

131 Posamentier, Alfred S., and Charles T. Salkind. *Challenging Problems in Geometry.* Palo Alto, CA: Dale Seymour Publications, 1988.

132 Tietze, Heinrich. *Famous Problems of Mathematics.* New York: Graylock Press, 1965.

133 Lindgren, Harry. *Recreational Problems in Geometric Dissections and How to Solve Them.* New York: Dover Publications, 1972.

134 Runion, Garth E. *The Golden Section.* Palo Alto, CA: Dale Seymour Publications, 1990.

135 Huntley, H. E. *The Divine Proportion.* New York: Dover Publications, 1970.

136 Kolpas, Sidney J. *The Pythagorean Theorem: Eight Classic Proofs.* Palo Alto, CA: Dale Seymour Publications, 1992.

137 Loomis, Elisha Scott. *The Pythagorean Proposition.* Reston, VA: NCTM, 1968.

138 Swetz, Frank J., and T. I. Kao. *Was Pythagoras Chinese?* Reston, VA: NCTM, 1977.

139 Apostol, Tom. *Theorem of Pythagoras.* Pasadena, CA: California Institute of Technology, 1988. Video.

140 Friedricks, K. O. *From Pythagoras to Einstein.* Washington, D.C.: MAA, 1965.

141 Seymour, Dale. *Tangramath.* Oak Lawn, IL: Creative Publications, 1971.

142 Read, Ronald. *Tangrams: 330 Puzzles.* New York: Dover Publications, 1965.

143 Loyd, Sam. *The Eighth Book of Tan: 700 Tangrams by Sam Loyd.* New York: Dover Publications, 1968.

144 Kennedy, Joe, and Diane Thomas. *Kaleidoscope Math.* Oak Lawn, IL: Creative Publications, 1978.

145 Boys, C. V. *Soap Bubbles: Their Colors and the Forces That Mold Them.* New York: Dover Publications, 1959.

146 Bentley, W. A., and W. J. Humphreys. *Snow Crystals: 2453 Illustrations.* New York: Dover Publications, 1931.

147 Reed, Brenda Lee. *Decorative Paper Snowflakes.* New York: Dover Publications, 1987.

148 Murray, William D., and Francis J. Rigney. *Paper Folding for Beginners.* New York: Dover Publications, 1960.

149 Olson, Alton T. *Mathematics Through Paper Folding.* Reston, VA: NCTM, 1975.

150 Row, T. Sundara. *Geometric Exercises in Paper Folding.* New York: Dover Publications, 1966.

151 Silvey, Linda, and Loretta Taylor. *Paper and Scissors Polygons and More.* Palo Alto, CA: Dale Seymour Publications, 1995.

152 Botermans, Jack. *Paper Capers.* New York: Henry Holt & Co., 1986.

153 Kenneway, Eric. *Complete Origami.* New York: St. Martin's Press, 1987.

154 Weiss, Stephen. *Wings and Things: Origami That Flies.* New York: St. Martin's Press, 1984.

155 Collins, John M. *The Gliding Flight.* Berkeley, CA: Ten Speed Press, 1989.

156 Kline, Richard. *The Ultimate Paper Airplane.* New York: Fireside Books, 1985.

157 Chatani, Masahiro. *Paper Magic: Pop-Up Paper Craft.* Tokyo: Ondorisha Publishing, 1988.

158 Hiner, Mark. *Paper Engineering for Pop-Up Books and Cards.* Norfolk, England: Tarquin Publications, 1985.

159 Chatani, Masahiro. *American Houses: Origami Architecture.* New York: Kodansha International, 1988.

160 Kempe, A. B. *How to Draw a Straight Line.* Reston, VA: NCTM, 1877

161 Seymour, Dale, and Reuben Schadler. *Creative Constructions.* Oak Lawn, IL: Creative Publications, 1974.

162 Seymour, Dale. *Geometric Design.* Palo Alto, CA: Dale Seymour Publications, 1988.

163 Posamentier, Alfred S., and William Wernick. *Advanced Geometric Constructions.* Palo Alto, CA: Dale Seymour Publications, 1988.

164 Gillespie, Norm. *Mira Activities for High School.* Toronto, CA: Mira Math Co., 1973.

165 Dayoub, Iris Mack, and Johnny W. Lott. *Geometry: Constructions and Transformations.* Palo Alto, CA: Dale Seymour Publications, 1977.

166 Brown, Richard G. *Transformational Geometry.* Palo Alto, CA: Dale Seymour Publications, 1973.

167 Seymour, Dale, Joyce Snider, and Linda Silvey. *Line Designs*. Oak Lawn, IL: Creative Publications, 1974.

168 Seymour, Dale. *Introduction to Line Designs*. Palo Alto, CA: Dale Seymour Publications, 1992.

169 Somerveil, Edith L. *A Rhythmic Approach to Mathematics*. Reston, VA: NCTM, 1906.

170 Millington, Jon. *Curve Stitching*. Norfolk, England: Tarquin Publications, 1989.

171 Pohl, Victoria. *How to Enrich Geometry Using String Designs*. Reston, VA: NCTM, 1986.

172 Winter, John. *String Sculpture*. Oak Lawn, IL: Creative Publications, 1972.

173 Sarff, Laura, and Jan Harem. *Symmography: Linear Thread Design*. Worcester, MA: Davis Publications, 1979.

174 Weyl, Hermann. *Symmetry*. Princeton, NJ: Princeton Univ. Press, 1980.

175 Tarasov, L. *This Amazingly Symmetrical World*. Moscow: Mir Publishers, 1986.

176 Wiltshire, Alan. *Symmetry Patterns*. Norfolk, England: Tarquin Publications, 1989.

177 Kim, Scott. *Inversions*. New York: W. H. Freeman, 1989.

178 Haeckel, Ernst. *Art Forms in Nature*. New York: Dover Publications, 1974.

179 Hornung, Clarence P. *Hornung's Handbook of Designs and Devices*. New York: Dover Publications, 1946.

180 Capitman, Barbara Baer. *American Trademark Designs*. New York: Dover Publications, 1976.

181 Seymour, Dale, and Jill Britton. *Introduction to Tessellations*. Palo Alto, CA: Dale Seymour Publications, 1989.

182 Bezuszka, Stanley, Margaret Kenney, and Linda Silvey. *Tessellations: The Geometry of Patterns*. Oak Lawn, IL: Creative Publications, 1977.

183 Ranucci, E. R., and J. L. Teeters. *Creating Escher-Type Drawings*. Oak Lawn, IL: Creative Publications, 1977.

184 Kenney, Margaret J., and Stanley Bezuszka. *Tessellations Using Logo*. Palo Alto, CA: Dale Seymour Publications, 1987.

185 Grunbaum, Branko, and G. C. Shephard. *Tilings and Patterns*. New York: W. H. Freeman, 1987.

186 Boles, Martha, and Rochelle Newman. *Universal Patterns*. Bradford, MA: Pythagorean Press, 1980.

187 Boles, Martha, and Rochelle Newman. *The Surface Plane*. Bradford, MA: Pythagorean Press, 1992.

188 Albarn, Keith, et al. *The Language of Pattern*. New York: Harper & Row, 1974.

189 Ernst, Bruno, *The Magic Mirror of M. C. Escher*. Norfolk, England: Tarquin Publications, 1985.

190 Escher, M. C. *The Graphic Work of M. C. Escher*. New York: Ballantine Books, 1960.

191 Locker, J. L. *The World of M. C. Escher*. New York: Harry N. Abrams, 1971.

192 Coxeter, H. S. M., M. Emmer, R. Penrose, and M. L. Teuber, eds. *M. C. Escher: Art and Science*. New York: North-Holland, 1986.

193 Schattschneider, Doris. *Visions of Symmetry: Notebooks, Periodic Drawings, and Related Works of M. C. Escher*. New York: W. H. Freeman, 1990.

194 Escher, M. C. *Escher on Escher: Exploring the Infinite*. New York: Harry N. Abrams, 1986.

195 Britton, Jill, and Walter Britton. *Teaching Tessellating Art*. Palo Alto, CA: Dale Seymour Publications, 1992.

196 Seymour, Dale. *Polyhedra Blocks*. Palo Alto, CA: Dale Seymour Publications, 1994.

197 Seymour, Dale. *Advanced Polyhedra Blocks*. Palo Alto, CA: Dale Seymour Publications, 1995.

198 Pedersen, Jean, and Peter Hilton. *Build Your Own Polyhedra*. Menlo Park, CA: Addison-Wesley Innovative Learning Publications, 1988.

199 Beard, Robert S. *Patterns in Space*. Palo Alto, CA: Creative Publications, 1973.

200 Pugh, Anthony. *Polyhedra: A Visual Approach*. Palo Alto, CA: Dale Seymour Publications, 1990.

201 Pearce, Peter. *Polyhedra Primer*. Palo Alto, CA: Dale Seymour Publications, 1978.

202 Holden, Alan. *Shapes, Space, and Symmetry*. New York: Columbia Univ. Press, 1971.

203 Fetter, Schmalzried, Eckert, Schattschneider, and Klotz. *The Platonic Solids Activity Book.* Berkeley, CA: Key Curriculum Press, 1991.

204 Brest, Hilary, et al. *Stella Octangula Activity Book.* Berkeley, CA: Key Curriculum Press, 1991.

205 Smart, Margaret, and Mary Laycock. *Create a Cube.* Hayward, CA: Activity Resources Co., 1985.

206 Jenkins, Gerald, and Anne Wild. *Make Shapes.* Books 1–3. Norfolk, England: Tarquin Publications, 1990.

207 Jenkins, Gerald, and Anne Wild. *Mathematical Curiosities.* Books 1–3. Norfolk, England: Tarquin Publications, 1989.

208 Coffin, Stewart T. *The Puzzling World of Polyhedral Dissections.* New York: Oxford Univ. Press, 1991.

209 Wenninger, Magnus J. *Polyhedron Models.* New York: Cambridge Univ. Press, 1970.

210 Cundy, H. Martyn, and A. P. Rollett. *Mathematical Models.* New York: Oxford Univ. Press, 1961.

211 Weeks, Jeffrey R. *The Shape of Space.* New York: Marcel Dekker, 1985.

212 Wenninger, Magnus J. *Spherical Models.* New York: Cambridge Univ. Press, 1979.

213 Coxeter, H. S. M. *Regular Polytopes.* London: Methuen & Co., 1947.

214 Pugh, Anthony. *An Introduction to Tensegrity.* Berkeley, CA: Univ. of California Press, 1976.

215 Kenner, Hugh. *Geodesic Math.* Berkeley, CA: Univ. of California Press, 1976.

216 Fuller, R. Buckminster, and Robert Marks. *The Dymaxion World of Buckminister Fuller.* New York: Anchor Press/Doubleday, 1973.

217 Fuller, R. Buckminster. *Synergetics: Explorations in the Geometry of Thinking.* New York: Macmillan, 1975.

218 Kahn, Lloyd, ed. *Dome.* Books 1 and 2. Bolinas, CA: Pacific Domes, 1971.

219 Williams, Robert. *The Geometrical Foundation of Natural Structure.* New York: Dover Publications, 1979.

220 Pearce, Peter. *Structure in Nature Is a Source for Design.* Cambridge, MA: MIT Press, 1978.

221 Field, Robert. *Geometric Patterns from Roman Mosaics and How to Draw Them.* Norfolk, England: Tarquin Publications, 1988.

222 Troutman, Andria, and Sonia Forseth. *Math Art Posters.* Palo Alto, CA: Creative Publications, 1973.

223 Stevens, Peter S. *Handbook of Regular Patterns.* Cambridge, MA: MIT Press, 1984.

224 Washburn, Dorothy K., and Donald W. Crowe. *Symmetries of Culture: Theory and Practice of Plane Pattern Analysis.* Seattle, WA: Univ. of Washington Press, 1988.

225 Yamaguchi, Makato. *Kusudama: Ball Origami.* New York: Japan Publications, 1990.

226 Fusé, Tomoko. *Origami Boxes.* New York: Japan Publications, 1989.

227 Fusé, Tomoko. *Unit Origami: Multidimensional Transformations.* New York: Japan Publications, 1990.

228 Chatani, Masahiro. *Pop-Up Greeting Cards.* New York: Ondorisha Publishing, 1986.

229 Biddle, Steve, and Megumi Biddle. *The New Origami.* New York: St. Martin's Press, 1993.

230 Bourgoin, J. *Arabic Geometrical Pattern and Design.* New York: Dover Publications, 1973.

231 El-Said, Issam, and Ayse Parman. *Geometric Concepts in Islamic Art.* Palo Alto, CA: Dale Seymour Publications, 1976.

232 Critchlow, Keith. *Islamic Patterns: An Analytical and Cosmological Approach.* New York: Shocken Books, 1976.

233 Meehan, Aidan. *Celtic Design: Knotwork—The Secret Method of the Scribes.* New York: Thames & Hudson, 1991.

234 Meehan, Aidan. *Celtic Design: A Beginner's Manual.* New York: Thames & Hudson, 1991.

235 Meyer, Franz Sales. *Handbook of Ornament.* New York: Dover Publications, 1957.

236 Enciso, Jorge. *Design Motifs of Ancient Mexico.* New York: Dover Publications, 1953.

237 Sides, Dorothy Smith. *Decorative Art of the Southwestern Indians.* New York: Dover Publications, 1961.

238 Dye, Daniel Sheets. *Chinese Lattice Designs.* New York: Dover Publications, 1974.

239 Vinciolo, Federico. *Renaissance Patterns for Lace, Embroidery, and Needlepoint.* New York: Dover Publications, 1971.

240 Silvey, Linda, Stanley Bezuszka, and Margaret Kenney. *Designs From Mathematical Patterns.* Palo Alto, CA: Dale Seymour Publications, 1990.

241 Mottershead, Lorraine. *Metamorphosis.* Palo Alto, CA: Dale Seymour Publications, 1977.

242 Henry, Boyd. *Experiments with Patterns in Mathematics.* Palo Alto, CA: Dale Seymour Publications, 1987.

243 Foster, Lorraine L. *The Alhambra Past and Present: A Geometer's Odyssey.* Northridge, CA: California State Univ. Northridge, 1992.

244 Kim, Scott. *Letterforms and Illusion.* New York: W. H. Freeman, 1989.

245 Shepard, Roger. *Mind Sights.* New York: W. H. Freeman, 1990.

246 Ernst, Bruno. *Adventures with Impossible Figures.* Norfolk, England: Tarquin Publications, 1986.

247 Block, J. R., and Harold E. Yuker. *Can You Believe Your Eyes?* New York: Gardner Press, 1989.

248 Luckiesh, M. *Visual Illusions: Their Causes, Characteristics, and Applications.* New York: Dover Publications, 1965.

249 Turner, Harry. *Triad Optical Illusions and How to Design Them.* New York: Dover Publications, 1978.

250 Pappas, Theoni. *What Do You See? An Optical Illusion Slide Show.* San Carlos, CA: Wide World Publishing/Tetra, 1989.

251 Barrett, Cyril. *An Introduction to Optical Art.* New York: E. P. Dutton & Co., 1971.

252 Marks, Mickey Klar, and Edith Alberts. *Op-Tricks: Creating Kinetic Art.* Philadelphia, PA: J. B. Lippincott Co., 1972.

253 McLoughlin Brothers staff. *The Magic Mirror: An Antique Optical Toy.* New York: Dover Publications, 1979.

254 Moscovich, Ivan. *The Magic Cylinder Book.* Norfolk, England: Tarquin Publications, 1988.

255 Armstrong, Tim. *Make Moving Patterns.* Norfolk, England: Tarquin Publications, 1982.

256 Kremer, John. *Turntable Illusions: Kinetic Optical Illusions for Your Turntable.* Fairfield IA: Open Horizons Publishing, 1992.

257 Grafton, Carol Belanger. *Optical Designs in Motion with Moiré Overlays.* New York: Dover Publications, 1976.

258 Oster, Gerald. *The Science of Moiré Patterns.* Barrington, NJ: Edmund Scientific Co., 1969.

259 Dixon, Robert. *Mathographics.* New York: Dover Publications, 1987.

260 Gill, Robert W. *Basic Perspective.* London: Thames & Hudson, 1974.

261 Kastner, Bernice. *Space Mathematics: NASA.* Palo Alto, CA: Dale Seymour Publications, 1987.

262 Merseth, Katherine, dir. *Math Space Mission.* Palo Alto, CA: Dale Seymour Publications, 1987.

263 Baynes, John. *How Maps Are Made.* New York: Facts On File, 1987.

264 Blackwell, William. *Geometry in Architecture.* Berkeley, CA: Key Curriculum Press, 1984.

265 Grillo, Paul Jacques. *Form, Function, and Design.* New York: Dover Publications, 1960.

266 Garland, Trudi, and Charity Kahn. *Math and Music: Harmonius Connections.* Palo Alto, CA: Dale Seymour Publications, 1994.

267 Fey, James T., et al. *Computing and Mathematics.* Reston, VA: NCTM, 1984.

268 Schultz, Harris, and William Leonard. *Mathematical Topics for Computer Instruction.* Palo Alto, CA: Dale Seymour Publications, 1990.

269 Thornburg, David. *Discovering Apple Logo.* Menlo Park, CA: Addison Wesley Innovative Learning Publications, 1983.

270 Burke, Michael, and Roland Genise. *Logo and Models of Computation.* Reading, MA: Addison-Wesley Publishing Co., 1987.

271 Malkevitch, Joseph, and Gary Froelich. *The Mathematical Theory of Elections.* Arlington, MA: COMAP, 1989.

272 Cozzens, Margaret, and Richard Porter. *Recurrence Relations: "Counting Backwards."* Arlington, MA: COMAP, 1989.

273 Zagare, Frank C. *The Mathematics of Conflict.* Arlington, MA: COMAP, 1989.

274 Crowe, Donald. *Symmetry, Rigid Motions, and Patterns.* Arlington, MA: COMAP, 1986.

275 Cozzens, Margaret B., and Richard D. Porter. *Problem Solving Using Graphs.* Arlington, MA: COMAP, 1987.

276 Bennett, Sandi, et al. *The Apportionment Problem: The Search for the Perfect Democracy.* Arlington, MA: COMAP, 1986.

277 Bennett, Sandi, et al. *Fair Divisions: Getting Your Fair Share.* Arlington, MA: COMAP, 1986.

278 Francis, Richard L. *A Mathematical Look at the Calendar.* Arlington, MA: COMAP, 1988.

279 Djang, Fred D. *Applications of Geometrical Probability.* Arlington, MA: COMAP, 1988.

280 Martin, William B. *Spheres and Satellites.* Arlington, MA: COMAP, 1988.

281 Francis, Richard. *Mathematician's Coloring Book.* Arlington, MA: COMAP, 1989.

282 Kumar, G. Surya. *Decision Making and Math Models.* Arlington, MA: COMAP, 1989.

283 Rogers, James R. *A Uniform Approach to Rate and Ratio Problems.* Arlington, MA: COMAP, 1989.

284 Laycock, Mary. *Bucky for Beginners.* Hayward, CA: Activity Resources, 1984.

285 Oliver, June. *Polysymetrics.* Norfolk, England: Tarquin Publications, 1979.

286 Pedersen, Jean, and Kent Pedersen. *Geometric Playthings.* Palo Alto, CA: Dale Seymour Publications, 1973.

287 Joseph, George Gheverghese. *The Crest of the Peacock: Non-European Roots of Mathematics.* London: J. B. Tauris & Co., 1991.

288 Hoggatt, Verner E. *Fibonacci and Lucas Numbers.* Santa Clara, CA: Fibonacci Association, 1969.

289 Meyer, Rochele Wilson. *Explore Sorts.* Arlington, MA: COMAP, 1990.

290 Metallo, Frances Rosebell. *The Abacus: Its History and Applications.* Arlington, MA: COMAP, 1990.

291 Malkevitch, Joseph. *Codes Galore.* Arlington, MA: COMAP, 1990.

292 Pólya, George. *Mathematical Discovery: On Understanding, Learning, and Teaching Problem Solving.* New York: John Wiley & Sons, 1981.

293 Shasha, Dennis. *Codes, Puzzles, and Conspiracy.* New York: W. H. Freeman, 1992.

294 Slocum, Jerry, and Jack Boterman. *Puzzles Old and New.* Seattle, WA: Univ. of Washington Press, 1987.

295 Gardiner, A. *Mathematical Puzzling.* New York: Oxford Univ. Press, 1987.

296 Zippin, Leo. *Uses of Infinity.* Washington, D.C.: MAA, 1962.

297 Isenberg, Cyril. *Science of Soap Films and Soap Bubbles.* New York: Dover Publications, 1978.

298 Clift, R., and J. R. Grace. *Bubbles, Drops, and Particles.* San Diego, CA: Academic Press, 1978.

299 Barber, Jacqueline, and Carolyn Willard. *Bubble Festival.* Berkeley, CA: Lawrence Hall of Science, 1992.

300 Diamond, Anna. *A Book of Baubles.* Kuala Lumpur, Malaysia: Anna Diamond, 1988.

301 Newman, Claire M., Thomas E. Obremski, and Richard Scheaffer. *Exploring Probability.* Palo Alto, CA: Dale Seymour Publications, 1987.

302 Rowntree, Derek. *Probability Without Tears: A Primer for Non-Mathematicians.* New York: Charles Scribner & Sons, 1984.

303 McGervey, John D. *Probabilities in Everyday Life.* New York: Ivy Books, 1986.

304 Benjamin, Arthur, and Michael Shermer. *Mathemagics.* Los Angeles: Lowell House, 1993.

305 Flansburg, Scott. *Math Magic.* New York: William Morrow & Co., 1993.

306 Emekwulu, Paul. *Magic of Numbers.* Norman, OK: Novelty Books, 1993.

307 Gardner, Martin. *Mathematics, Magic, and Mystery.* New York: Dover Publications, 1956.

308 Schimmel, Annemarie. *Mystery of Numbers.* New York: Oxford Univ. Press, 1992.

309 Kelly, Gerard W. *Short-Cut.* New York: Dover Publications, 1984.

310 Orkin, Mike. *Can You Win?* New York: W. H. Freeman, 1991.

311 Thorp, Edward O. *The Mathematics of Gambling.* Secaucus, NJ: Lyle Stuart, 1984.

312 Packel, Edward. *Mathematics of Games and Gambling.* Washington, D.C.: MAA, 1981.

313 Thorp, Edward O. *Beat the Dealer.* New York: Blaisdell Publishing, 1962.

314 Guy, Richard. *Fair Game.* Arlington, MA: COMAP, 1989.

315 Williams, David, and Thomas Scott. *Investigating Mathematics with the TI-81.* Sunnyvale, CA: Stokes Publishing, 1993.

316 Rowntree, Derek. *Statistics Without Tears: A Primer for Non-Mathematicians.* New York: Charles Scribner & Sons, 1982.

317 Kennedy, Gavin. *Invitation to Statistics.* New York: Basil Blackwell, 1983.

318 Phillips Jr., John L. *Statistical Thinking.* 2d ed. New York: W. H. Freeman, 1982.

319 Phillips, John L. *How to Think About Statistics.* New York: W. H. Freeman, 1988.

320 Landwehr, James M., and Ann E. Watkins. *Exploring Data.* Palo Alto, CA: Dale Seymour Publications, 1986.

321 Landwehr, James M., Jim Swift, and Ann E. Watkins. *Exploring Surveys and Information from Samples.* Palo Alto, CA: Dale Seymour Publications, 1987.

322 Gnanadesikan, Mrudulla, Richard L. Scheaffer, and Jim Swift. *Art and Techniques of Simulation.* Palo Alto, CA: Dale Seymour Publications, 1987.

323 Barbella, Peter, James Kepner, and Richard Scheaffer. *Exploring Measurements.* Palo Alto, CA: Dale Seymour Publications, 1994.

324 Burrill, Gail, ed. *From Home Runs to Housing Costs: Data Resource.* Palo Alto, CA: Dale Seymour Publications, 1994.

325 Moore, David S. *Statistics: Concepts and Controversies.* New York: W. H. Freeman, 1991.

326 Huff, Darrell. *How to Lie with Statistics.* New York: W. W. Norton, 1982.

327 Runyon, Richard. *Winning with Statistics.* Reading, MA: Addison-Wesley Publishing Co., 1977.

328 Tanur, Judith, et al. *Statistics: A Guide to the Unknown.* Pacific Grove, CA: Wadsworth & Brooks/Cole, 1989.

329 Mosteller, Frederick, et al. *Statistics by Example: Weighing Chances.* Menlo Park, CA: Addison-Wesley Innovative Learning Publications, 1973.

330 Benice, Daniel D. *Mathematics: Ideas and Applications.* New York: Academic Press, 1978.

331 Abell, George O., David Morrison, and Sidney C. Wolff. *Exploration of the Universe.* Philadelphia, PA: Saunders College Publishing, 1991.

332 Dolan, Stan, et al. *Living with Uncertainty.* New York: Cambridge Univ. Press, 1991.

333 King, Glen, et al. *Statistical Abstract of the United States.* Washington, D.C.: U.S. Government Printing Office, 1993.

334 Dolan, Stan, et al. *The Normal Distribution.* New York: Cambridge Univ. Press, 1992.

335 Kelly, Brendan. *Using the TI-81 Graphing Calculator to Explore Statistics.* Burlington, Ontario: Brendan Kelly Publishing, 1992.

336 Burrill, Gail, and Patrick Hopfensperger. *Exploring Statistics with the TI-81.* Menlo Park, CA: Addison-Wesley Innovative Learning Publications, 1993.

337 Kelly, Brendan. *Using the TI-81 Graphing Calculator to Explore Functions.* Burlington, Ontario: Brendan Kelly Publishing, 1991.

338 Kelly, Brendan. *Programming the TI-81 & TI-85 Graphing Calculator to Explore Mathematics.* Burlington, Ontario: Brendan Kelly Publishing, 1992.

339 Hammersly, J. M., and D. C. Handscomb. *Monte Carlo Methods.* New York: John Wiley & Sons, 1964.

340 Peterson, Ivars. *The Mathematical Tourist.* New York: W. H. Freeman, 1988.

341 Stewart, Ian. *The Problems of Mathematics.* New York: Oxford Univ. Press, 1992.

342 Gardner, Martin. *Aha! Gotcha: Paradoxes to Puzzle and Delight.* New York: W. H. Freeman, 1982.

343 Gardner, Martin. *Knotted Doughnuts and Other Mathematical Entertainments.* New York: W. H. Freeman, 1986.

344 Gardner, Martin. *Mathematical Carnival.* Washington, D C.: MAA, 1989.

345 Gardner, Martin. *Wheels, Life, and Other Mathematical Amusements.* New York: W. H. Freeman, 1983.

346 Stewart, Ian. *Another Fine Math You've Got Me Into. . . .* New York: W. H. Freeman, 1992.

347 Gardner, Martin. *Time Travel and Other Mathematical Bewilderness.* New York: W. H. Freeman, 1988.

348 Gardner, Martin. *The New Ambidextrous Universe.* New York: W. H. Freeman, 1990.

349 Gardner, Martin. *Mathematical Magic Show.* Washington, D.C.: MAA, 1990.

350 Gardner, Martin. *Penrose Tiles to Trapdoor Ciphers.* New York: W. H. Freeman, 1989.

351 Ball, W. W. Rouse, and H. S. M. Coxeter. *Mathematical Recreations and Essays.* Toronto, Canada: Univ. of Toronto Press, 1974.

352 Gardner, Martin. *Riddles of the Sphinx and Other Mathematical Puzzle Tales.* Washington, D.C.: MAA, 1988.

353 Hunter, J. A. H., and Joseph S. Madachy. *Mathematical Diversions.* New York: Dover Publications, 1975.

354 Graham, L. A. *The Surprise Attack in Mathematical Problems.* New York: Dover Publications, 1968.

355 Gardner, Martin. *Perplexing Puzzles and Tantalizing Teasers.* New York: Dover Publications, 1969.

356 Andrews, W. S. *Magic Squares and Cubes.* New York: Dover Publications, 1960.

357 Benson, William H., and Oswald Jacoby. *New Recreations with Magic Squares.* New York: Dover Publications, 1976.

358 Moran, Jim. *The Wonders of Magic Squares.* New York: Vintage Books, 1981.

359 Martin, George E. *Polyominoes: A Guide to Puzzles and Problems in Tiling.* Washington, D.C.: MAA, 1991.

360 Golomb, Solomon W. *Polyominoes.* New York: Charles Scribner & Sons, 1965.

361 Paige, Donald D. *Problem Solving with Ominoes.* Palo Alto, CA: Dale Seymour Publications, 1987.

362 Brooke, Maxey. *150 Puzzles in Crypt-Arithmetic.* New York: Dover Publications, 1969.

363 Jayne, Caroline Furness. *String Figures and How to Make Them.* New York: Dover Publications, 1962.

364 Bell, R. C. *Board and Table Games from Many Civilizations.* New York: Dover Publications, 1979.

365 Moscovich, Ivan. *Mind Benders: Games of Shape.* New York: Penguin Books, 1986.

366 Agostini, Franco, and Nicola Alberto De Carlo. *Intelligence Games.* New York: Fireside Books, 1985.

367 Ewing, John, and Czes Kosinowski. *Puzzle It Out: Cubes, Groups, and Puzzles.* Cambridge, England: Univ. of Cambridge Press, 1982.

368 Ideal Toy staff. *Alexander's Star Puzzle: The Ideal Solution.* Newark, NJ: Ideal Toy Corporation, 1982.

369 Filipiak, Anthony S. *Mathematical Puzzles and Other Brain Twisters.* New York: Bell Publishing Co., 1942.

370 Coffin, Stewart T. *Puzzle Craft.* Lincoln, MA: Stewart T. Coffin, 1985.

371 Slocum, Jerry, and Jack Botermans. *New Books of Puzzles: 101 Classic and Modern Puzzles to Make and Solve.* New York: W. H. Freeman, 1992.

372 Hordern, L. E. *Sliding Piece Puzzles: Recreations in Mathematics.* New York: Oxford Univ. Press, 1986.

373 Ideal Toy staff. *Rubik's Cube: The Ideal Solution.* Hollis, NY: Ideal Toy Corporation, 1980.

374 Saaty, Thomas L., and Paul C. Kainen. *The Four-Color Problem.* New York: Dover Publications, 1986.

375 Bunch, Bryan H. *Mathematical Fallacies and Paradoxes.* New York: Van Nostrand Reinhold, 1982.

376 Cutler, Ann. *The Trachenberg Speed System of Mathematics.* Westport, CT: Greenwood Press, 1960.

377 Howard, W. J. *Doing Simple Math in Your Head.* Coos Bay, OR: Coast Publishing, 1992.

378 Sticker, Henry. *How to Calculate Quickly.* New York: Dover Publications, 1955.

379 Lieberthal, Edwin M. *The Complete Book of Fingermath.* New York: McGraw-Hill, 1979.

380 Julius, Edward H. *Rapid Math Tricks and Tips.* New York: John Wiley & Sons, 1992.

381 Kenney, Margaret, and Christian Hirsch, eds. *Discrete Mathematics Across the Curriculum K–12.* Reston, VA: NCTM, 1991.

382 Sacco, William, Wayne Copes, Clifford Sloyer, and Robert Stark. *Glyphs: Getting the Picture.* Providence, RI: Janson Publications, 1987.

383 Sacco, William, Wayne Copes, Clifford Sloyer, and Robert Stark. *Queues: Will This Wait Never End!* Providence, RI: Janson Publications, 1987.

384 Sacco, William, Wayne Copes, Clifford Sloyer, and Robert Stark. *Graph Theory: Euler's Rich Legacy.* Providence, RI: Janson Publications, 1987.

385 Sacco, William, et al. *Mathematics and Medicine: How Serious Is the Injury?* Providence, RI: Janson Publications, 1987.

386 Sacco, William, Wayne Copes, Clifford Sloyer, and Robert Stark. *Dynamic Programming: An Elegant Problem Solver.* Providence, RI: Janson Publications, 1987.

387 Sacco, William, Wayne Copes, Clifford Sloyer, and Robert Stark. *Information Theory: Saving Bits.* Providence, RI: Janson Publications, 1987.

388 Perham, Bernadette, and Arnold Perham. *Matrix Theory.* Menlo Park, CA: Addison-Wesley Innovative Learning Publications, 1993.

389 Perham, Bernadette, and Arnold Perham. *Game Theory.* Menlo Park, CA: Addison-Wesley Innovative Learning Publications, 1993.

390 Perham, Bernadette, and Arnold Perham. *Linear Programming.* Menlo Park, CA: Addison-Wesley Innovative Learning Publications, 1993.

391 Perham, Bernadette, and Arnold Perham. *Markov Chain Theory.* Menlo Park, CA: Addison-Wesley Innovative Learning Publications, 1993.

392 Perham, Bernadette, and Arnold Perham. *Graph Theory.* Menlo Park, CA: Addison-Wesley Innovative Learning Publications, 1993.

393 Barnette, David. *Map-Coloring, Polyhedra, and the Four-Color Problem.* Washington, D.C.: MAA, 1983.

394 Grossman, Israel, and Magnus Wilhelm. *Groups and Their Graphs.* Washington, D.C.: MAA, 1964.

395 Whitmer, John. *Spreadsheets in Math and Science Technology.* Bowling Green, OH: School Science & Math Assoc., 1992.

396 Newton, Issac. *Mathematical Principles.* Berkeley, CA: Univ. of California Press, 1934. Translation.

397 Beckman, Charlene, and Theodore Sundstrom. *Exploring Calculus with a Graphing Calculator.* Menlo Park, CA: Addison-Wesley Publishing Co., 1992.

398 DeTemple, Duane, and Jack Robertson. *The Calc Handbook: Conceptual Activites for Learning Calculus.* Palo Alto, CA: Dale Seymour Publications, 1991.

399 Dolan, Stan, et al. *Calculus Methods.* New York: Cambridge Univ. Press, 1992.

400 Dolan, Stan, et al. *Introductory Calculus.* New York: Cambridge Univ. Press, 1990.

401 Wilson, Robin J. *Graphs and Their Uses.* Washington, D.C.: MAA, 1990.

402 Department of Mathematics and Computer Science. North Carolina School of Science and Mathematics. *Matrices.* Reston, VA: NCTM, 1988.

403 Sinkov, Abraham. *Elementary Cryptanalysis: A Mathematical Approach.* Washington, D.C.: MAA, 1966.

404 Boltyanski, V., and A. Soifer. *Geometric Etudes in Combinatorial Mathematics.* Colorado Springs, CO: Center for Excellence in Mathematics Education, 1991.

405 Soifer, Alexander. *How Does One Cut a Triangle?* Colorado Springs, CO: Center for Excellence in Mathematics Education, 1990.

406 Péter, Rózsa. *Playing with Infinity: Mathematical Explorations and Excursions.* New York: Dover Publications, 1961.

407 Sawyer, W. W. *What Is Calculus About?* Washington, D.C.: MAA, 1961.

408 Steen, Lynn Arthur. *Calculus for a New Century: A Pump, Not a Filter.* Washington, D.C.: MAA, 1988.

409 Coxeter, H. S. M., and S. L. Greitzer. *Geometry Revisited.* Washington, D.C.: MAA, 1967.

410 Banchoff, Thomas F. *Beyond the Third Dimension.* New York: Scientific American Library, 1990.

411 Manning, Henry P. *The Fourth Dimension Simply Explained.* New York: Dover Publications, 1960.

412 Gardner, Martin. *The Magic Numbers of Dr. Matrix.* Buffalo, NY: Prometheus Books, 1985.

413 Oystein, Ore. *Invitation to Number Theory.* Washington, D.C.: MAA, 1967.

414 Schiffer, M. M., and L. Bowden. *Role of Mathematics in Science.* Washington, D.C.: MAA, 1984.

415 Lytel, Allan. *ABCs of Boolean Algebra.* Indianapolis, IN: Howard W. Sams Co., 1966.

416 Adler, Irving. *Logic for Beginners.* New York: John Day Co., 1964.

417 Carney, James D., and Richard K. Scheer. *Fundamentals of Logic.* New York: Macmillan, 1964.

418 Stolyar, Abram Aronovich. *Introduction to Elementary Mathematical Logic.* New York: Dover Publications, 1970.

419 Copi, Irving M., and Keith Emerson Ballard. *Introduction to Logic.* 5th ed. New York: Macmillan, 1978.

420 Fadiman, Clifton. *Fantasia Mathematica.* New York: Fireside Books, 1958.

421 Lieber, Lillian. *Education of T. C. MITS.* New York: W. W. Norton, 1972.

422 Bühler, W. K. *Gauss: A Biographical Study.* New York: Springer-Verlag, 1981.

423 Kappraff, Jay. *Connections: The Geometric Bridge Between Art and Science.* New York: McGraw-Hill, 1991.

424 Kahn, David. *Code Breakers.* New York: Macmillan, 1967.

425 Halberstam, H., and K. F. Roth. *Sequences.* New York: Springer-Verlag, 1983.

426 Downs, J. W. *Practical Conic Sections.* Palo Alto, CA: Dale Seymour Publications, 1993.

427 Yates, Robert C. *Curves and Their Properties.* Reston, VA: NCTM, 1952.

428 Cook, Theodore Andrea. *The Curves of Life.* New York: Dover Publications, 1979.

429 Lockwood, E. H. *A Book of Curves.* New York: Cambridge Univ. Press, 1961.

430 Wahl, Mark. *A Mathematical Mystery Tour.* Tucson, AZ: Zephyr Press, 1988.

431 Dolan, Stan, et al. *Newton's Laws of Motion.* New York: Cambridge Univ. Press, 1992.

432 Dolan, Stan, et al. *Modeling with Force and Motion.* New York: Cambridge Univ. Press, 1992.

433 Dolan, Stan, et al. *Modeling with Circular Motion.* New York: Cambridge Univ. Press, 1992.

434 Epstein, Lewis Carol. *Thinking Physics.* San Francisco: Insight Press, 1992.

435 Fendel, D., and D. Resek. *Foundations of Higher Mathematics: Exploration and Proof.* Reading, MA: Addison-Wesley Publishing Co., 1990.

436 Barr, Stephen. *Experiments in Topology.* New York: Thomas Y. Crowell Co., 1964.

437 Chinn, W. G., and N. E. Steenrod. *First Concepts in Topology.* Washington, D.C.: MAA, 1966.

438 Hildebrandt, Stefan, and Anthony Tromba. *Mathematics and Optimal Form.* New York: W. H. Freeman, 1985.

439 Solow, Daniel. *Reading, Writing, and Doing Math Proofs: Proof Techniques for Geometry.* Palo Alto, CA: Dale Seymour Publications, 1984.

440 Solow, Daniel. *Reading, Writing, and Doing Math Proofs: Advanced Math.* Palo Alto, CA: Dale Seymour Publications, 1984.

441 Hofstadter, Douglas R. *Gödel, Escher, Bach: An Eternal Golden Braid.* New York: Vintage Books, 1979.

442 Toole, Betty A. *Ada, The Enchantress of Numbers.* Mill Valley, CA: Strawberry Press, 1992.

443 Stein, Dorothy. *Ada: A Life and a Legacy.* Cambridge, MA: MIT Press, 1985.

444 Baum, Joan. *The Calculating Passion of Ada Byron.* Hamden, CT: Archon Books, The Shoestring Press, 1987.

445 Malacy, Don. *Charles Babbage, Father of the Computer*. New York: Crowell-Collier Press, 1970.

446 Morrison, Phillip, and Emily Morrison, eds. *Charles Babbage and His Calculating Engines*. New York: Dover Publications, 1961.

447 Moseley, Mabeth. *Irascible Genius; the Life of Charles Babbage*. Chicago: Henry Regnery Co., 1964.

448 Coolidge, Julian Lowell. *The Mathematics of Great Amateurs*. New York: Dover Publications, 1963.

449 Smith, David E., and Macia L. Latham, trans. *The Geometry of René Descartes*. New York: Dover Publications, 1954.

450 Heath, Thomas L., trans. *The 13 Books of Euclid's Elements*. New York: Dover Publications, 1956.

451 Devaney, Robert L. *Chaos, Fractals and Dynamics: Computer Experiments in Mathematics*. Menlo Park, CA: Addison-Wesley Innovative Learning Publications, 1990.

452 Gleick, James. *Chaos: Making a New Science*. New York: Penguin Books, 1987.

453 Schroeder, Manfried. *Fractals, Chaos, Power Laws*. New York: W. H. Freeman, 1991.

454 Field, Michael, and Martin Golubitsky. *Symmetry in Chaos*. New York: Oxford Univ. Press, 1992.

455 Peitgen, Heinz-Otto, et al. *Fractals for the Classroom*. Vol. 1. New York: Springer-Verlag/NCTM, 1992.

456 Peitgen, Heinz-Otto, et al. *Fractals for the Classroom*. Vol. 2. New York: Springer-Verlag/NCTM, 1992.

457 Mandelbrot, Benoit B. *The Fractal Geometry of Nature*. New York: W. H. Freeman, 1983.

458 Gardner, Martin. *Fractal Music, Hypercards, and More*. New York: W. H. Freeman, 1992.

459 Briggs, John. *Fractals: The Patterns of Chaos*. New York: Touchstone Books, 1992.

460 Briggs, John, and David Peat. *Turbulent Mirror*. New York: Harper & Row, 1989.

461 Pappas, Theoni. *Mathematics Appreciation*. San Carlos, CA: Wide World Publishing/Tetra, 1986.

462 Flato, Moshe. *Power of Mathematics*. New York: McGraw-Hill, 1990.

463 Hogben, Lancelot. *Mathematics for the Millions*. New York: W. W. Norton, 1967.

464 Dolan, Stan, et al. *Mathematical Methods*. New York: Cambridge Univ. Press, 1992.

465 Stanfield, Anthony, Karl Smith, and Andrew Bleloch. *How to Model It*. New York: McGraw-Hill, 1990.

466 Egsgard, John, et al. *Making Connections with Mathematics*. Providence, RI: Janson Publications, 1988.

467 Cadwell, J. H. *Topics in Recreational Mathematics*. New York: Cambridge Univ. Press, 1966.

468 Meadows, Jack. *The Great Scientists*. New York: Oxford Univ. Press, 1987.

469 Hogben, Lancelot. *Mathematics in the Making*. New York: Doubleday & Co., 1960.

470 Bezuszka, Stanley, Mary Farrey, and Margaret Kenney. *Contemporary Motivated Mathematics*. Book 1. Chestnut Hill, MA: Boston College Press, 1972.

471 Bezuszka, Stanley, Mary Farrey, and Margaret Kenney. *Contemporary Motivated Mathematics*. Book 2. Chestnut Hill, MA: Boston College Press, 1986.

472 Bezuszka, Stanley, Mary Farrey, and Margaret Kenney. *Contemporary Motivated Mathematics*. Book 3. Chestnut Hill, MA: Boston College Press, 1980.

473 Bezuszka, Stanley, Lou D'Angelo, and Margaret Kenney. *Contemporary Motivated Mathematics*. Book 4. Chestnut Hill, MA: Boston College Press, 1976.

474 Bezuszka, Stanley, Lou D'Angelo, and Margaret Kenney. *Contemporary Motivated Mathematics*. Book 9. Chestnut Hill, MA: Boston College Press, 1976.

475 Kenney, Margaret. *Contemporary Motivated Mathematics*. Book 12. Chestnut Hill, MA: Boston College Press, 1976.

476 Bezuszka, Stanley, Jeanne Cavanaugh, and Margaret Kenney. *Contemporary Motivated Mathematics*. Book 13. Chestnut Hill, MA: Boston College Press, 1984.

477 Burns, Marilyn. *This Book Is About Time*. Boston, MA: Little, Brown & Co., 1978.

478 Bendick, Jeanne. *How Much and How Many?* New York: Franklin Watts, 1989.

479 Diagram Group. *Comparisons*. New York: St. Martin's Press, 1980.

480 Sneider, Cary, and Alan Gould. *Height-O-Meters*. Berkeley, CA: Lawrence Hall of Science, 1988.

481 Pedde, Lawrence, et al. *Metric Manual.* Washington, D.C.: U.S. Government Printing Office, 1978.

482 Shoemaker, Robert. *Metric for Me.* South Beloit, IL: Blackhawk Publishing, 1993.

483 Swart, William. *Navigation.* Mt. Pleasant, MI: Tricon Mathematics, 1992.

484 Moeschl, Richard. *Exploring the Sky.* Chicago: Independent Publishers Group, 1989.

485 Ross, Kathryn. *NCEER Interim Bibliography of Earthquake Education Materials.* Washington, D.C.: NSTA & FEMA, 1989.

486 Cook, Nancy. *Measuring Earthquakes.* Menlo Park, CA: Addison-Wesley Innovative Learning Publications, 1994.

487 Pollard, Jeanne. *Building Toothpick Bridges.* Palo Alto, CA: Dale Seymour Publications, 1985.

488 Salvadori, Mario. *Why Buildings Stand Up.* New York: McGraw-Hill, 1980.

489 Salvadori, Mario. *Art of Construction.* Chicago: Chicago Review Press, 1990.

490 Abhau, Marcy, Rolaine Copeland, and Greta Greenberger. *Architecture in Education.* Philadelphia, PA: Foundation for Architecture, 1986.

491 Zevi, Bruno. *Architecture as Space.* New York: DeCapo Press, 1993.

492 Norwich, John, et al. *Great Architecture of the World.* New York: Bonanza Books, 1975.

493 Hoffman, Paul. *Archimedes Revenge: The Challenge of the Unknown.* New York: W. W. Norton, 1988.

494 Richardson, Terry. *A Guide to Metrics.* Ann Arbor, MI: Prakken Publications, 1978.

495 Henkin, Leon. *Mathematical Induction.* Washington, D.C.: MAA. Film.

496 Thomas, David A. *The Math-Computer Connection.* New York: Franklin Watts, 1986.

497 Cohen, Marcus, et al. *Student Research Projects in Calculus.* Washington, D.C.: MAA, 1991.

498 Nelson, David, George Joseph, and Julian Williams. *Multicultural Mathematics.* New York: Oxford Univ. Press, 1993.

499 Berlinghoff, William, and Kerry Grant. *Mathematics Sampler: Topics for the Liberal Arts.* New York: Ardsley House, 1992.

500 Stwertk, Albert. *Recent Revolutions in Mathematics.* New York: Franklin Watts, 1987.

501 Pullan, J. M. *The History of the Abacus.* New York: Praeger Publishers, 1969.

502 Hunter, J. A. H. *Challenging Mathematical Teasers.* New York: Dover Publications, 1980.

504 Elffers, Joost, Fred Leeman, and Michael Schuyt. *Anamorphoses: Games of Perception and Illusion in Art.* New York: Abrams, 1976.

505 Albers, D., G. Alexanderson, and C. Reid. *More Mathematical People.* San Diego, CA: Harcourt Brace Javanovich, 1990.

506 Dudley, Underwood. *A Budget of Trisection.* New York: Springer-Verlag, 1987.

507 Klein, Felix. *Famous Problems from Elementary Geometry.* New York: Dover Publications, 1956.

508 Reid, Constance. *A Long Way from Euclid.* New York: T. Y. Crowell, 1963.

509 Boole, George. *Collected Logical Works.* Peru, IL: Open Court, 1952.

510 Newell, Virginia K., and Joella Gipson. *Black Mathematicians and Their Works.* Ardmore, PA: Dorrance and Co., 1980.

511 Glaser, Anton. *History of Binary and Other Nondecimal Numeration.* Los Angeles: Tomash Publishing, 1981.

512 Ouchi, Hajime. *Japanese Optical and Geometric Art.* New York: Dover Publications, 1977.

513 Sommerville, D. M. Y. *Elements of Non-Euclidean Geometry.* New York: Dover Publications, 1958.

514 Johnson, D. A., and W. H. Glenn. *Calculating Devices.* Portsmouth, NH: John Murray, 1964.

515 Wood, Mary. *Tamari Balls.* Tunbridge Wells, England: Search Press, 1991.

516 Fulves, Karl. *Self-Working Number Magic.* New York: Dover Publications, 1983.

517 Jourdain, Philip E. B., trans. *Contributions to the Founding of the Theory of Transfinite Numbers.* New York: Dover Publications, 1955.

518 Dauben, Joseph. *Georg Cantor: His Mathematics and Philosophy of the Infinite.* Cambridge, MA: Harvard Univ. Press, 1979

519 Koblitz, Ann Hibner. *Convergence of Lives: Sofia Kovalerskaia: Scientist, Writer, Revolutionary.* New Brunswick, NJ: Rutgers Univ. Press, 1993.

520 Hallerberg, Arthur E. *Mathematical Proof: An Elementary Approach.* New York: Hafner Press, 1974.

521 Edwards, Ronald. *Alge Cadabra! Algebra Magic Tricks.* Pacific Grove, CA: Critical Thinking Press, 1992.

522 National Women's History Project. *Outstanding Women in Mathematics and Science.* Windsor, CA: National Women's History Project, 1991.

523 Dilson, Jesse. *The Abacus: A Pocket Computer.* New York: St. Martin's Press, 1968.

524 Robbin, Tony. *Fourfield: Computers, Art, and the Fourth Dimension.* Boston: Bulfinch Press, 1992.

525 Chatani, Masahiro, and Keiko Nakazawa. *Great American Buildings: Origami Cutouts.* New York: Kodansha International, 1991.

526 Fulves, Karl. *More Self-Working Card Tricks.* New York: Dover Publications, 1984.

527 Iglewicz, Boris, and Judith Stoyle. *An Introduction to Mathematical Reasoning.* New York: Macmillan, 1973.

528 Rucker, Rudyr. *The Fourth Dimension.* Boston: Houghton Mifflin Co., 1994.

529 Sanders, Cathi. *Perspective Drawing with the Geometer's Sketchpad.* Berkeley, CA: Key Curriculum Press, 1995.

530 Serra, Michael. *Patty Paper Geometry.* Berkeley, CA: Key Curriculum Press, 1994.

531 Frank, Phillip. *Einstein: His Life and Times.* New York: Alfred A. Knopf, 1963.

532 Dilke, O. A. W. *Mathematics and Measurement.* Berkeley, CA: Univ. of California Press, 1987.

533 Richards, Joan L. *Mathematical Visions.* Boston: Academic Press, 1988.

534 Srivastava, Jane Jones. *Averages.* New York: Crowell, 1975.

535 Williams, Bill. *A Sampler on Sampling.* New York: John Wiley & Sons, 1978.

536 Yoshino, Yozo. *The Japanese Abacus Explained.* New York: Dover Publications, 1963.

537 Cotter, Joan A. *Activities for the Abacus.* Hutchinson, MN: Activities for Learning, 1988.

538 Kojima, Takashi. *Advanced Abacus.* Tokyo: Charles E. Tuttle Co., 1991.

539 Lassiter, Luther. *Billiards for Everyone.* New York: Grosset & Dunlap, 1965.

540 Hoppe, Willie. *Billiards as It Should Be Played.* Chicago: Henry Regnery Co., 1941.

541 Carroll, Lewis. *Symbolic Logic.* New York: Clarkson N. Potter Publishers, 1977.

542 Levitz, Kathleen, and Hilbert Levitz. *Logic and Boolean Algebra.* Woodbury, NY: Barron's Educational Series, 1979.

543 Smullyan, Raymond. *Forever Undecided.* New York: Alfred A. Knopf, 1987.

544 Fraga, Robert, ed. *Calculus Problems for a New Century.* Washington, D.C.: MAA, 1993.

545 Straffin, Philip, ed. *Applications of Calculus.* Washington, D.C.: MAA, 1993.

546 Jackson, Michael B., and John R. Ramsay, eds. *Calculus Problems for Student Investigation.* Washington, D.C.: MAA, 1993.

547 Solow, Anita, ed. *Learning by Discovery: A Lab Manual for Calculus.* Washington, D.C.: MAA, 1993.

548 Dudley, Underwood, ed. *Readings for Calculus.* Washington, D.C.: MAA, 1993.

549 Constance Reid. *From Zero to Infinity.* 4th ed. Washington, D.C.: MAA, 1992.

550 Kasner, Edward, and James R. Newman. *Mathematics and the Imagination.* Redmond, WA: Tempus Books, 1989.

551 Devlin, Keith. *Mathematics: The New Golden Age.* London: Penguin Books, 1988.

552 Steinhaus, M. *Mathematical Snapshots.* New York: Oxford Univ. Press, 1969.

553 Dewdney, A. K. *The Tinkertoy Computer.* New York: W. H. Freeman, 1993.

554 Moritz, Robert O. *Memorabilia Mathematica: The Philomaths Quotation Book.* Washington, D.C.: MAA, 1942.

555 Schmalz, Rosemary. *Out of the Mouths of Mathematicians: A Quotation Book for Philomaths.* Washington, D.C.: MAA, 1993.

556 Heath, Thomas L. *A Manual of Greek Mathematics.* New York: Dover Publications, 1931.

557 Gillings, Richard J. *Mathematics in the Time of the Pharaohs.* Cambridge, MA: MIT Press, 1972.

558 Woods, Geraldine. *Science in Ancient Egypt.* New York: Franklin Watts, 1988.

559 Moss, Carol. *Science in Ancient Mesopotamia.* New York: Franklin Watts, 1988.

560 Beshore, George. *Science in Ancient China.* New York: Franklin Watts, 1988.

561 Temple, Robert. *The Genius of China.* New York: Simon & Schuster, 1986.

562 Roberts, Joe. *Lure of the Integers.* Washington, D.C.: MAA, 1992.

563 Vos Savant, Marilyn. *World's Most Famous Math Problem, Is It Solved?* New York: St. Martin's Press, 1993.

564 Edwards, Harold. *Fermat's Last Theorem.* New York: Springer-Verlag, 1977.

565 Ribenboim, Paulo. *Thirteen Lectures on Fermat's Last Theorem.* New York: Springer-Verlag, 1979.

566 Weil, André. *Number Theory.* Cambridge, MA: Birkhäuser, 1984.

567 Kanigel, Robert. *A Man Who Knew Infinity: Ramanujan.* New York: Charles Scribner & Sons, 1991.

568 Neale, Robert, and Thomas Hull. *Origami, Plain and Simple.* New York: St. Martin's Press, 1994.

569 Wölfflin, Heinrich. *The Art of Albrecht Dürer.* New York: Phaidon Publishers, 1971.

570 Cole, Alison. *Perspective.* New York: Dorling Kindersley, 1992.

571 Devaney, Robert L. *Transition to Chaos.* New York: Science Television, 1990.

572 Apostol, Tom. *Sines and Cosines.* Parts I and II. Reston, VA: NCTM. Video.

573 Lyng, Merwin J. *Dancing Curves: A Dynamic Demonstration of Geometric Principles.* Reston, VA: NCTM, 1978.

574 Lockwood, James R., and Garth E. Runion. *Deductive Systems: Finite and Non-Euclidean Geometries.* Reston, VA: NCTM, 1978.

575 MAA staff. *Mathematical Scientists at Work.* 1st & 2d eds. Washington, D.C.: MAA, 1992.

576 Steen, Lynn Arthur, ed. *Mathematics Books: Recommendations for High School and Public Libraries.* Washington, D.C.: MAA, 1992.

577 Sachs, Leroy, ed. *Projects to Enrich School Mathematics: Level 2 and Level 3.* Reston, VA: NCTM, 1988.

578 Chace, A. B., ed. *The Rhind Mathematical Papyrus.* Reston, VA: NCTM, 1979.

579 Hardy, G. H. *Ramanujan.* New York: Chelsea Publishing Company, 1978.

580 Movshovitz-Hadar, and Webb. *Mathematical Paradoxes.* Dedham, MA: Janson Publications, 1994.

581 Flegg, Graham. *Numbers: Their History and Meaning.* New York: Schocken Books, 1983.

582 Devi, Shakuntala. *Figuring—The Joy of Numbers.* New York: Harper & Row, 1977.

583 Asimov, Isaac. *Asimov on Numbers.* Garden City, NY: Doubleday & Co., 1977.

584 Asimov, Isaac. *How Did We Find Out About Numbers?* New York: Walker & Co., 1973.

585 Wyler, Rose, and Gerald Ames. *It's All Done with Numbers.* Garden City, NY: Doubleday & Co., 1979.

586 Friedberg, Richard. *An Adventurer's Guide to Number Theory.* New York: McGraw-Hill, 1968.

587 Asimov, Isaac. *Realm of Numbers.* Boston: Houghton Mifflin, 1959.

588 Grinstein, Louise S., and Paul J. Campbell, eds. *Women of Mathematics.* Westport, CT: Greenwood Press, 1987.

589 Osen, Lynn M. *Women in Mathematics.* Cambridge, MA: MIT Press, 1974.

590 Kenchaft, Patricia Clark, ed. *Winning Women into Mathematics.* Washington, D.C.: MAA, 1991.

591 Jacobs, Judith E., ed. *Perspectives on Women and Mathematics.* Columbus, OH: Ohio State Univ., 1978.

592 Genshaft, Judy, and Jack Naglieri. *A Mindset for Math.* Newton, MA: Education Development Center, 1987.

593 Afflack, Ruth. *Beyond Equals.* Oakland, CA: Mills College, 1982.

594 Van Der Waerden, B. L. *A History of Algebra.* Berlin: Springer-Verlag, 1985.

595 Paullos, John Allen. *Beyond Numeracy.* New York: Alfred A. Knopf, 1991.

596 Kline, Morris. *Mathematics in Western Culture.* Oxford, England: Oxford Univ. Press, 1978.

597 Davis, Philip J., and Reuben Hirsh. *The Mathematical Experience.* Cambridge, MA: Birkhäuser, 1981.

598 Gowar, Norman. *An Invitation to Mathematics.* Oxford, England: Oxford Univ. Press, 1979.

599 Guillen, Michael. *Bridges to Infinity.* Los Angeles: Jeremy P. Tarcher, 1983.

600 Honsberger, Ross. *Mathematical Gems II.* Washington, D.C.: MAA, 1976.

601 Foster, Lorraine L. *Archimedean and Archimedian Dual Polyhedra.* Northridge, CA: California State Univ. Northridge, 1991.

602 Critchlow, Keith. *Order in Space.* New York: Viking Press, 1969.

603 Tufse, Edward R. *The Visual Display of Quantitative Information.* Cheshire, CT: Graphics Press, 1983.

604 Menninger, Karl. *Number Words and Number Symbols: A Cultural History of Numbers.* Cambridge, MA: MIT Press, 1977.

605 Ifrah, Georges. *From One to Zero: A Universal History of Numbers.* New York: Viking Press, 1985.

606 Hardy, G. H. and E. M. Wright. *Introduction to the Theory of Numbers.* Oxford: Oxford Univ. Press, 1980.

607 Dudley, U. *Elementary Number Theory.* San Francisco: W. H. Freeman, 1978.

608 Sloane, N. J. A. *A Handbook of Integer Sequences.* New York: Academic Press, 1973.

609 Knopp, K. *Infinite Sequences and Series.* New York: Dover Publications, 1956.

610 Seebach, J. Arthur, and Lynn Arthur Steen, eds. *Mathematics Magazine: 50 Year Index.* Washington, D.C.: MAA, 1978.

611 NCTM. *The Mathematics Teacher: Cumulative Indices.* Reston, VA: NCTM, 1984.

612 May, Kenneth O. *Index of the American Mathematical Monthly.* Washington, D.C.: MAA, 1977.

613 Tyanaga, Shôkichi, and Yukiuosi Kawada, eds. *Encyclopedic Dictionary of Mathematics.* Cambridge, MA: MIT Press, 1986.

614 Borwein, Johnathan M., and Peter B. Borwein. *A Dictionary of Real Numbers.* Belmont, CA: Wadsworth, 1990.

615 Bestgen, Barbara J., and Robert E. Reys. *Films in the Mathematics Classroom.* Reston, VA: NCTM, 1982.

616 Thomas, David A. *Math Projects for Young Scientists.* New York: Franklin Watts, 1988.

617 Yan, Li, and Du Shiran. *Chinese Mathematics: A Concise History.* Oxford: Clarendon Press, 1987.

618 Gardner, Martin. *Hexaflexagons and Other Mathematical Diversions.* Chicago: Univ. of Chicago Press, 1988.

619 Chartrand, Gary, and Linda Lesniak. *Graphs and Digraphs.* Boston: Prindle, Weber and Schmidt, 1979.

620 Rosenfeld, B. A. *A History of Non-Euclidean Geometry: Evolution of the Concept of a Geometric Space.* New York: Springer-Verlag, 1988.

621 Dijksterhuis, E. J. *Archimedes.* Princeton, NJ: Princeton Univ. Press, 1987.

622 Westfall, Richard S. *Never at Rest: A Biography of Isaac Newton.* New York: Cambridge Univ. Press, 1983.

623 Mahoney, Michael S. *The Mathematical Career of Pierre de Fermat, 1601–1665.* Princeton, NJ: Princeton Univ. Press, 1973.

624 MacHale, Desmond. *George Boole: His Life and Work.* Dublin: Boole Press, 1985.

625 Hoffmann, Banesh. *Albert Einstein: Creator and Rebel.* New York: Viking Press, 1972.

626 Dick, Auguste. *Emmy Noether, 1882–1935.* Cambridge, MA: Birkhäuser, 1981.

627 Bedini, Silvio. *The Life of Benjamin Banneker.* New York: Charles Scribner & Sons, 1972.

628 Collins, A. Frederick. *Rapid Math Without a Calculator.* Secaucus, NJ: Citadel Press, 1987.

629 Bicknell, Marjorie, and Vernon Hoggatt, eds. *Fibonacci's Problem Book.* San Jose, CA: San Jose Univ. Fibonacci Assoc., 1974.

630 Weaver, Warren. *Lady Luck: The Theory of Probability.* New York: Dover Publications, 1982.

631 Niven, Ivan M. *Mathematics of Choice or How to Count Without Counting.* Washington, D.C.: MAA, 1975.

632 Hacking, Ian. *The Emergence of Probability.* New York: Cambridge Univ. Press, 1975.

633 Rucker, Rudolf. *Geometry, Relativity, and the Fourth Dimension.* New York: Dover Publications, 1977.

634 Stigler, Stephen M. *The History of Statistics: The Measurement of Uncertainty Before 1900.* Cambridge, MA: Harvard Univ. Press, 1986.

635 Gani, J. *The Making of Statisticians.* New York: Springer-Verlag, 1982.

636 Moclenov, P. S., and A. S. Parkhomenko. *Geometric Transformations.* New York: Academic Press, 1965.

637 Yaglom, I. M. *Geometric Transformations.* Washington, D.C.: MAA, 1979.

638 Halmos, Paul R. *Naive Set Theory.* New York: Springer-Verlag, 1974.

639 Pólya, George. *Induction and Analogy in Mathematics.* Princeton, NJ: Princeton Univ. Press, 1954.

640 Williams, John D. *The Complete Strategist: Being a Primer on the Theory of Games of Strategy.* New York: Dover Publications, 1986.

641 Bowen, Earl K., Gordon D. Prichett, and John C. Saber. *Mathematics with Applications in Management and Economics.* Homewood, IL: Richard D. Irwin, 1987.

642 Hillier, Frederick S. and Gerald J. Lieberman. *Introduction to Operations Research.* New York: McGraw-Hill, 1980.

643 French, Simon. *Readings in Decision Analysis.* New York: Chapman and Hall, 1989.

644 Budden, F. J. *The Fascination of Groups.* New York: Cambridge Univ. Press, 1972.

645 Goldberg, Samuel I. *Introduction to Difference Equations.* New York: John Wiley & Sons, 1958.

646 Kemeny, John G. *Man and the Computer.* New York: Charles Scribner & Sons, 1972.

647 Dewdney, A. K. *The Armchair Universe: An Exploration of Computer Worlds.* New York: W. H. Freeman, 1988.

648 Goldstine, Herman H. *The Computer from Pascal to von Neumann.* Princeton, NJ: Princeton Univ. Press, 1972.

649 Sharkley, John. *Celtic Mysteries: The Ancient Religion.* New York: Crossroad, 1975.

650 Bain, G. *Celtic Art: The Methods of Construction.* New York: Dover Publications, 1973.

651 Shubnikov, A. V., et al. *Symmetry in Science and Art.* New York: Plenum, 1974.

652 Rademacher, Hans. *The Enjoyment of Mathematics.* New York: Dover Publications, 1990.

653 Davis, Morton D. *Game Theory: A Nontechnical Introduction.* New York: Basic Books, 1970.

654 Fauvel, John, Raymond Flood, and Robin Wilson. *Möbius and His Band: Mathematics and Astronomy in Nineteenth-Century Germany.* New York: Oxford Univ. Press, 1993.

655 Williams, Michael R. *A History of Computing Technology.* Englewood Cliffs, NJ: Prentice Hall, 1993.

656 French, Simon. *Sequencing and Scheduling.* New York: John Wiley & Sons, 1982.

657 Piers, Anthony. *Ox.* New York: Avon, 1976.

658 Elffers, Joost, and Michael Schuyt. *Tangrams.* New York: Abrams, 1979.

659 Closs, M. F. *Native American Mathematics.* Austin, TX: Univ. of Texas Press, 1986.

660 Heath, T. L. *History of Greek Mathematics.* New York: Dover Publications, 1981.

661 Mikami, Y. *The Development of Mathematics in China and Japan.* New York: Chelsea, 1974.

662 Cantor, G. *The Mathematics of Sonya Kovalevskaya.* New York: Springer-Verlag, 1984.

663 Clark, Ronald W. *Einstein: The Life and Times.* New York: World Publishing Co., 1971.

664 Bondi, H. *Relativity and Common Sense.* Garden City, NY: Doubleday & Co., 1964.

665 Stevens, Peter S. *Patterns in Nature.* Boston: Little, Brown & Co., 1974.

666 Feininger, Andreas. *The Anatomy of Nature.* New York: Dover Publications, 1956.

667 Finkel, Leslie. *Kaleidoscopic Designs and How to Create Them.* New York: Dover Publications, 1980.

668 Churchill, E. Richard. *Instant Paper Airplanes.* New York: Sterling Publishing Co., 1988.

669 Wienen, Norbert. *I Am a Mathematician.* Garden City, NY: Doubleday & Co., 1956.

670 Belsky, Nancy Ann. *Building Kites: Flying High with Math.* Palo Alto, CA: Dale Seymour Publications, 1995.

671 Kremer, Ron. *From Crystals to Kites: Exploring Three Dimensions.* Palo Alto, CA: Dale Seymour Publications, 1995.

672 Greger, Margaret. *Kites for Everyone.* Richmond, WA: M. Gregor, 1984.

673 Alic, Margaret. *Hypatia Heritage.* Boston: Beacon Press, 1986.

674 Allman, G. J. *Greek Geometry from Thales to Euclid.* New York: Arno Press, 1976.

675 Baumgart, J., et al. *Historical Topics for the Mathematics Classroom.* Reston, VA: NCTM, 1989.

800 Schatzman, Gary. "252/7: A Divisibility Pattern." *Mathematics Teacher* (October 1986): 542–6.

801 Lightner, James E. "A Brief Look at the History of Probability and Statistics." *Mathematics Teacher* (November 1991): 623–30.

802 Jamski, William D. "A Different Look at πr^2." *Mathematics Teacher* (April 1978): 273–4.

803 DeTemple, Duane. "A Direct Derivation of the Equations of the Conic Sections." *Mathematics Teacher* (March 1990): 190–3.

804 Camp, Dane R. "A Fractal Excursion." *Mathematics Teacher* (April 1991): 265–75.

805 Davis, Edward J., and Ed Middlebrooks. "Algebra and a Super Card Trick." *Mathematics Teacher* (May 1983): 326–8.

806 Szetela, Walter. "General Divisibility Test for Whole Numbers." *Mathematics Teacher* (March 1980): 223–5.

807 Bonsangue, Martin V. "A Geometrical Approach to the Six Trigonometric Ratios." *Mathematics Teacher* (September 1993): 496–8.

808 Keeports, David. "A Map-Coloring Algorithm." *Mathematics Teacher* (December 1991): 759–63.

809 Thoemke, Sharon, and Pam Shriver. "A Mathematical Model for the Height of a Satellite." *Mathematics Teacher* (October 1993): 563–5.

810 Lefton, Phylis. "Matrix Method for Generating Pythagorean Triples." *Mathematics Teacher* (February 1987): 103–8.

811 Watson, James O. "American's Pastime" *Mathematics Teacher* (September 1993): 450–1.

812 Gaughan, Edward D. "An 'Almost' Diophantine Equation." *Mathematics Teacher* (May 1980).

813 Carmony, Lowell. "Analysis of a Truck Driver's Square Root Algorithm." *Mathematics Teacher* (February 1981): 144–9.

814 Dunham, William. "An 'Ancient/Modern' Proof of Heron's Formula." *Mathematics Teacher* (April 1985): 258–9.

815 Flusser, Peter. "An Ancient Problem." *Mathematics Teacher* (May 1981): 389–90.

816 Snow, Joanne R. "An Application of Number Theory to Cryptology." *Mathematics Teacher* (January 1989): 18–26.

817 Eisner, Milton P. "An Application of Quadratic Equations to Baseball." *Mathematics Teacher* (May 1986): 327–30.

818 Posamentier, Alfred S., and Naom Gordan. "An Astounding Revelation on the History of Pi." *Mathematics Teacher* (January 1984): 52, 47.

819 Wahl, M. Stoessel. "An Easy-to-Paste Model of the Rhombic Dodecahedron." *Mathematics Teacher* (November 1978): 689–93.

820 Benson, John, and Debra Borkovitz. "A New Angle for Constructing Pentagons." *Mathematics Teacher* (April 1982): 288–90.

821 Thornton, Carol A. "A New Look, Pythagoras!" *Mathematics Teacher* (February 1981): 98–100.

822 Smith, Arthur. "Angles of Elevation of the Pyramids of Egypt." *Mathematics Teacher* (February 1982): 124–7.

823 Iles, Kim, and Lester S. Wilson. "An Improvement of a Historic Construction." *Mathematics Teacher* (January 1980): 32–4.

824 Tisdale III, Joseph C. "An Interest in Interest." *Mathematics Teacher* (February 1989): 126–7.

825 Autrey, Malanie Ann, and Joe Dan Austin. "A Novel Way to Factor Quadratic Polynomials." *Mathematics Teacher* (February 1979): 127–8.

826 Escultura, Eddie. "Number Tricks Explained with Algebra." *Mathematics Teacher* (January 1983): 20–1.

827 Stannard, W. A. "Applying the Technique of Archimedes to the 'Birdcage' Problem." *Mathematics Teacher* (January 1979): 58–60.

828 Litwiller, Bonnie, and David Duncan. "Apportionment Examples: An Application of Decimal Ordering." *Mathematics Teacher* (February 1983): 89–91.

829 Sconyers, James M. "Approximation of Area Under a Curve." *Mathematics Teacher* (February 1984): 92–3.

830 Hilsenrath, Joseph, and Bruce Field "Program to Simulate the Galton Quincunx." *Mathematics Teacher* (November 1983): 571–3.

831 Marche, M. M. "A Pythagorean Curiosity." *Mathematics Teacher* (November 1984): 611–3.

832 Dence, Joseph B., and Thomas P. Dence "A Rapidly Converging Recursive Approach to Pi." *Mathematics Teacher* (February 1993): 121–4.

833 Shilgalis, Thomas W. "Archimedes and Pi." *Mathematics Teacher* (March 1989): 204–6.

834 Cotspeich, Richard "'Archimedes' Pi—An Introduction to Iteration." *Mathematics Teacher* (March 1988): 208–10.

835 Merkowitz, Lee "Area = Perimeter." *Mathematics Teacher* (March 1981): 222–3.

836 McGowan, William E. "A Recursive Approach to the Construction of the Deltahedra." *Mathematics Teacher* (March 1978): 204–10.

837 May, E. Lee. "Are Seven-Game Baseball Playoffs Fairer?" *Mathematics Teacher* (October 1992): 528–31.

838 Brown, Susan A. "A Surprising Fact About Pythagorean Triples." *Mathematics Teacher* (October 1985): 540–1.

839 Borlaug, Victoria A. "A Tonka® Toy Truck Does the Trick." *Mathematics Teacher* (April 1993): 282–7.

840 Bickenbach, Edwin F. "Baseball Statistics." *Mathematics Teacher* (May 1979): 35–52.

841 McMillan, Robert D. "Babylonian Quadratics." *Mathematics Teacher* (January 1984): 63–5.

842 Crouse, Richard. "Binomial Coefficients and the Partitioning of N-Dimensional Space." *Mathematics Teacher* (November 1978): 698–701.

843 Mullenex, James. "Box Plots: Basic and Advanced." *Mathematics Teacher* (February 1990): 108–12.

844 Carlson, Ronald. "Buffon's Needle Problem on a Computer." *Mathematics Teacher* (November 1981): 638–40.

845 Donahue, Richard. "Calculating Palindromic Sums by Computer." *Mathematics Teacher* (April 1984): 269–71.

846 Lauber, Murray. "Casting Out Nines: An Explanation and Extensions." *Mathematics Teacher* (November 1990): 661–5.

847 Noone Jr., E. T. "Chuck-a-Luck: Learning Probability Concepts with Games of Chance." *Mathematics Teacher* (February 1988): 121–3.

848 Dieffenbach, Robert M. "Combinatorial Scheduling." *Mathematics Teacher* (April 1990): 269–73.

849 Kimberling, Clark. "Complex Roots: The Bairstow-Hitchcock Method." *Mathematics Teacher* (April 1986): 278–82.

850 Pizarro, Antonio. "Computer-Generated Magic Squares." *Mathematics Teacher* (September 1986): 471–6.

851 Kimberling, Clark. "Conics." *Mathematics Teacher* (May 1984): 363–8.

852 Austin, Joe Dan. "Construction with an Unmarked Protractor." *Mathematics Teacher* (April 1982): 291–5.

853 Wright, Marie A. "Conventional Cryptography." *Mathematics Teacher* (March 1993): 249–51.

854 Landauer, Edwin. "Counting Using License Plates and Phone Numbers." *Mathematics Teacher* (March 1984): 183–7.

855 Reesink, Carole J. "Crystals: Through the Looking Glass with Planes, Points, and Rotational Symmetries." *Mathematics Teacher* (May 1987): 377–88.

856 Catranides, Peter. "Curve-Stitching the Cardioid and Related Curves." *Mathematics Teacher* (December 1978): 726–32.

857 Kolpas, Sidney J. "David Copperfield's Orient Express Card Trick." *Mathematics Teacher* (October 1992): 568–70.

858 Meeks, Kay I. "Decimals, Rounding, and Apportionment." *Mathematics Teacher* (October 1992): 523–5.

859 Lamon, Richard A. "Dense, Denser, Densest." *Mathematics Teacher* (November 1976): 547–8.

860 Francis, Richard L. "Did Gauss Discover That, Too?" *Mathematics Teacher* (April 1986): 288–93.

861 Brown, Joseph. "Digits Count: Significant Digits and Calculators." *Mathematics Teacher* (May 1991): 344–6.

862 Wilcock, Douglas. "Discover Pick's Theorem." *Mathematics Teacher* (September 1992): 424–5.

863 Kimberling, Clark. "Emmy Noether, Greatest Woman Mathematician." *Mathematics Teacher* (March 1982): 246–9.

864 Cohen, Donald. "Estimating the Volumes of Solid Figures with Curved Surfaces." *Mathematics Teacher* (May 1991): 392–5.

865 Wasclovich, Dorothy. "Euclid and Descartes: A Partnership." *Mathematics Teacher* (December 1991): 706–9.

866 Dunham, William. "Euclid and the Infinitude of Primes." *Mathematics Teacher* (January 1987): 16–7.

867 Taylor, Jerry. "Euler, the Master Calculator." *Mathematics Teacher* (September 1983): 424–8.

868 DiDomenico, Angelo. "Eureka! Pythagorean Triples from the Multiplication Table." *Mathematics Teacher* (January 1983): 48–51.

869 Hinders, Duane C. "Examples of the Use of Statistics in Society." *Mathematics Teacher* (February 1990): 136–41.

870 Nagase, Goro. "Existence of Real Roots of a Radical Equation." *Mathematics Teacher* (May 1987): 369–70.

871 Olson, Alton T. "Exploring Baseball Data." *Mathematics Teacher* (October 1987): 565–9.

872 Kern, Jane F., and Cherry C. Mauk. "Exploring Fractals . . . A Problem-Solving Adventure Using Mathematics and Logo." *Mathematics Teacher* (March 1990): 179–85; 244.

873 Messer, Robert. "Factorial!" *Mathematics Teacher* (January 1984): 50–1.

874 Daniels, David S. "Fast Brakes." *Mathematics Teacher* (February 1989): 104–7; 111.

875 Eynden, Charles Vanden. "Fermat's Last Theorem." *Mathematics Teacher* (November 1989): 637–40.

876 Kost, Franklin. "Finance Charges on Credit Card Accounts." *Mathematics Teacher* (November 1987): 624–30.

877 Esty, Warren W. "Finding Points of Intersection of Polar Coordinate Graphs." *Mathematics Teacher* (September 1991): 472–8.

878 Malone, Jim. "Four Labs to Introduce Quadratic Functions." *Mathematics Teacher* (November 1989): 601–4.

879 Bannon, Thomas J. "Fractals and Transformations." *Mathematics Teacher* (March 1991): 178–85.

880 Wagner, Sue S. "Fun with Repeating Decimals." *Mathematics Teacher* (March 1979): 209–12.

881 Heiny, Robert L. "Gambling, Casinos, and Game Simulation." *Mathematics Teacher* (February 1981): 139–43.

882 Rector, Robert E. "Game Theory: An Application of Probability." *Mathematics Teacher* (February 1987): 138–42.

883 Cohen, Martin, and William A. Juraschek. "GCD, LCM, and Boolean Algebra." *Mathematics Teacher* (November 1976): 602–5.

884 Gerber, Daniel T. "Gears, Ratios, and the Bicycle." *Mathematics Teacher* (September 1989): 466–8.

885 Pizarro, Antonio. "Generating Magic Squares Whose Orders Are Multiples of Four." *Mathematics Teacher* (March 1989): 216–21.

886 Wenninger, Magnus J. "Geodesic Domes by Euclidean Construction." *Mathematics Teacher* (October 1978): 582.

887 Reesink, Carole J. "Geomegy or Geolotry: What Happens When Geology Visits Geometry Class?" *Mathematics Teacher* (September 1982): 454–61.

888 Robertson, Jack M. "Geometric Constructions Using Hinged Mirrors." *Mathematics Teacher* (May 1986): 380–6.

889 Van Beynen, John, and Robert L. McGinty. "Geometric Interpretation of Series." *Mathematics Teacher* (March 1981): 218–21.

890 Carr, M. Jane. "Get Away from the Table! Make Interest More Interesting." *Mathematics Teacher* (December 1986): 703–5.

891 Reagan, James. "Get the Message? Cryptographs, Mathematics, and Computers." *Mathematics Teacher* (October 1986): 547–53.

892 Aieta, Joseph F. "Getting to the Roots of the Problem." *Mathematics Teacher* (May 1978): 414–7.

893 Gibb, Allan. "Giving Geometry Students an Added Edge." *Mathematics Teacher* (April 1982): 296–301.

894 Alexander, Robert D., et al. "Graphical Properties of Sequences and Equations." *Mathematics Teacher* (November 1977): 665–72.

895 Embse, Charles Vonder. "Graphing Powers and Roots of Complex Numbers." *Mathematics Teacher* (October 1993): 589–97.

896 Hughes, Barnabas. "Hawaiian Number Systems." *Mathematics Teacher* (March 1982): 253–6.

897 Woodward, Ernest. "How Many Games in a Tournament?" *Mathematics Teacher* (May 1989): 332–5.

898 Teeters, Joseph L. "How to Draw Tessellations of the Escher Type." *Mathematics Teacher* (April 1974): 307–10.

899 Rubillo, James M. "Illustrating the Euler Line." *Mathematics Teacher* (May 1987): 389–93.

900 Gonzales, Michael G., and William J. Carr. "Impact of the Black Death (1348–1405): on World Population: Then and Now." *Mathematics Teacher* (February 1986): 92–4.

901 Goldberg, Dorothy. "In Celebration: Newton's Principia, 1687–1987." *Mathematics Teacher* (December 1987): 711–4.

902 Love, William P. "Infinity: The Twilight Zone of Mathematics." *Mathematics Teacher* (April 1989): 284–92.

903 Mulligan, Catherine Herr. "Interest in Mathematics—It's in the Cards." *Mathematics Teacher* (February 1989): 100–3.

904 Stensholt, Boonchai Kuekiatngam, and Eivind Stensholt. "Invertable Points of Time." *Mathematics Teacher* (April 1988): 304–5.

905 Beamer, James E. "Lessons Learned While Approximating Pi." *Mathematics Teacher* (February 1987): 154–9.

906 Maxfield, Margaret W. "Linear Measurement U.S. Square Measurement; or, Why the Queen Used Two Pi R." *Mathematics Teacher* (January 1988): 51–3.

907 Musser, Gary L. "Line Reflections in the Complex Plane—A Billiards Player's Delight." *Mathematics Teacher* (January 1978): 60–4.

908 Aviv and Rachlin. "Magic Cubes: A Total Experience." *Mathematics Teacher* (September 1981): 464–72.

909 McCranie, Judson. "Magic Squares of All Orders." *Mathematics Teacher* (November 1988): 674–8.

910 Ranucci, Ernest R. "Master of Tessellations: M. C. Escher, 1898–1972." *Mathematics Teacher* (April 1974): 299–306.

911 Flores, Alfino. "Mathematical Connections with a Spirograph®." *Mathematics Teacher* (February 1992): 129–38.

912 Witkowski, Joseph C. "Mathematical Modeling and the Presidential Election." *Mathematics Teacher* (October 1992): 520–1.

913 Wood, Eric F. "Mathematics and Meteorology." *Mathematics Teacher* (November 1986): 602–3.

914 Woodward and Tolleson. "Mathematics Expressed in Trademarks." *Mathematics Teacher* (September 1981): 437–9.

915 Battista, Michael T. "Mathematics in Baseball." *Mathematics Teacher* (April 1993): 336–42.

916 Jeffrey, Neil J. "Mathematics in Photography." *Mathematics Teacher* (December 1980): 657–62.

917 Haigh, William E. "Microcomputer Unit: Generating Random Numbers." *Mathematics Teacher* (February 1986): 132–6.

918 Vest, Floyd. "Modeling the Cost of Homeownership." *Mathematics Teacher* (November 1986): 610–3.

919 Hinders, Duane C. "Monte Carlo, Probability, Algebra, and Pi." *Mathematics Teacher* (May 1981): 335–9.

920 Swetz, Frank. "Mysticism and Magic in Number Squares of Old China." *Mathematics Teacher* (January 1978): 50–6.

921 Hering, Hermann. "Nearly Isosceles Pythagorean Triples—Once More." *Mathematics Teacher* (December 1986): 724–5.

922 Lefton, Phyllis. "Number Theory and Public-Key Cryptography." *Mathematics Teacher* (January 1991): 34–62.

923 Pagni, David L. "Number Theory for Secondary Schools?" *Mathematics Teacher* (January 1979): 20–2.

924 Boag, Tom, Charles Boberg, and Lyn Hughes. "On Archimedean Solids." *Mathematics Teacher* (May 1979): 371–6.

925 Schwartzman, Steven. "On Population and Resources." *Mathematics Teacher* (November 1983): 605–8.

926 Staib, John, and Larry Staib. "Pascal Pyramid." *Mathematics Teacher* (September 1978): 505–10.

927 Varnadore, James. "Pascal's Triangle and Fibonacci Numbers." *Mathematics Teacher* (April 1991): 314–6.

928 Grinstein, Louise S. "Pascal's Triangle: Some Recent References." *Mathematics Teacher* (September 1981): 449–50.

929 Parker, Andy. "Pattern Discovery with Binary Trees." *Mathematics Teacher* (May 1979): 337.

930 Shoemaker, Richard W. "Patterns in Powers of Digits." *Mathematics Teacher* (April 1988): 294–8.

931 Dunn, Samuel L., et al. "People, People, People." *Mathematics Teacher* (April 1978): 283–91.

932 Nowak, Ray S. "Periodic Pictures." *Mathematics Teacher* (February 1987): 126–33.

933 Hollingsworth, Caroline. "Perplexed by Hexed® (Pentominoes)." *Mathematics Teacher* (October 1984): 560–2.

934 Polis, Christopher. "Pick's Theorem Extended and Generalized." *Mathematics Teacher* (May 1991): 399.

935 Litwiller, Bonnie H., and David R. Duncan. "Playoff Series and Pascal's Triangle." *Mathematics Teacher* (October 1992): 532–5.

936 Miller, William A. "Polygonal Numbers and Recursion." *Mathematics Teacher* (October 1990): 555–62.

937 Mogall, Robert G. "Popular Measures of Central Tendency." *Mathematics Teacher* (December 1990): 744–6.

938 Sconyers, James M. "Prime Numbers—A Locust's View." *Mathematics Teacher* (February 1981): 105–8.

939 Kimberling, Clark. "Primes." *Mathematics Teacher* (September 1983): 434–7.

940 Serba, Don. "Probability and Basketball." *Mathematics Teacher* (November 1981): 624–7.

941 Lappan, Glenda, and M. J. Winter. "Probability Simulation in Middle School." *Mathematics Teacher* (September 1980): 446–9.

942 Miller, William A., and Linda Wagner. "Pythagorean Dissection Puzzles." *Mathematics Teacher* (April 1993): 302–8.

943 Tirman, Alvin. "Pythagorean Triples." *Mathematics Teacher* (November 1986): 652–5.

944 DiDomencio, Angelo S. "Pythagorean Triples from the Addition Table." *Mathematics Teacher* (May 1985): 346–8.

945 Nievergelt, Yves. "Quadratic Formulas." *Mathematics Teacher* (September 1992): 461–5.

946 Esty, Warren W. "Rates and Taxes." *Mathematics Teacher* (May 1992): 376–9.

947 Perham, Betty. "Recognizing Quadratic Equations with No Real Roots." *Mathematics Teacher* (March 1979): 195–6.

948 DeTemple, Duane. "Reflection Borders for Patchwork Quilts." *Mathematics Teacher* (February 1986): 138–43.

949 McGinty, Robert, and William Mutch. "Repeating Decimals: Geometric Patterns and Open-Ended Questions." *Mathematics Teacher* (October 1982): 600–2.

950 Galanor, Stewart. "Riemann's Rearrangement Theorem." *Mathematics Teacher* (November 1987): 675–81.

951 Tannone, Michael A. "Round Robin Schedules." *Mathematics Teacher* (March 1983): 194–5.

952 Camp, Dane R. "Secret Codes with Matrices." *Mathematics Teacher* (December 1985): 676–80.

953 Wood, Eric F. "Self-Checking Codes—An Application of Modular Arithmetic." *Mathematics Teacher* (April 1987): 312–6.

954 DeTemple, Duane W. "Simple Constructions for the Regular Pentagon and Heptadecagon." *Mathematics Teacher* (May 1989): 361–5.

955 Hoffman, Dale T. "Smart Soap Bubbles Can Do Calculus." *Mathematics Teacher* (May 1979): 377–85.

956 Dolan, Daniel T. "Some Irrational Results with Irrational Numbers." *Mathematics Teacher* (April 1981): 258–61.

957 Schwartzman, Steven. "Some Little-Known Rules and Why They Work." *Mathematics Teacher* (October 1985): 554–8.

958 Soler, Frank P. "Some Mathematical Applications of Pari-Mutual Wagering." *Mathematics Teacher* (May 1987): 394–9.

959 Markowitz, Lee. "Some Variations on a Mathematical Card Trick." *Mathematics Teacher* (November 1983): 618–9.

960 Janski, William D. "Spherical Geodesics." *Mathematics Teacher* (March 1981): 227–8; 236.

961 Brannan, Richard, and Scott McFadden. "Spirolaterals." *Mathematics Teacher* (April 1981): 279–82.

962 Goodman, Terry A., and John Bernard. "Square Roots from Anywhere." *Mathematics Teacher* (May 1979): 344–5.

963 Meyer, Ruth Ann, and James E. Riley. "Studying Decimal Fractions with Microcomputers." *Mathematics Teacher* (February 1987): 144–8.

964 Graham, Ronald. "The Combinatorial Mathematics of Scheduling." *Scientific American* (March 1978): 124–32.

965 Stover, Donald W. "Teaching Quadratic Problem Solving." *Mathematics Teacher* (January 1978): 13–6.

966 Sandefur, James T. "Technology, Linear Equations, and Buying a Car." *Mathematics Teacher* (October 1992): 562–7.

967 Millman, Richard, and Romona Speranza. "The Artist's View of Points and Lines." *Mathematics Teacher* (February 1991): 133.

968 Byrne, Dan. "The Bank Shot." *Mathematics Teacher* (September 1986): 429–30.

969 Kurtzke, John F. "The Baseball Schedule: A Modest Proposal." *Mathematics Teacher* (May 1990): 346–50.

970 Crowley, Mary L. "The 'Difference' in Babbage's Difference Equation." *Mathematics Teacher* (May 1985): 366–72.

971 Sullivan, John J. "The Election of a President." *Mathematics Teacher* (October 1972): 493–501.

972 Schielack Jr., Vincent P. "The Fibonacci Sequence and the Golden Ratio." *Mathematics Teacher* (May 1987): 357–8.

973 Parzynski, William. "The Geometry of Microwave Antennas." *Mathematics Teacher* (April 1984): 294–6.

974 Graening, Jay. "The Geometry of Tennis." *Mathematics Teacher* (November 1982): 658–63.

975 Dickey, Edwin M. "The Golden Ratio: A Golden Opportunity to Investigate Multiple Representations of a Problem." *Mathematics Teacher* (October 1993): 554–7.

976 Verno, Ralph. "The Golden Section and Conic Sections." *Mathematics Teacher* (April 1974): 361–3.

977 Ercolano, Joseph. "The Harmonic Mean as a Factor in Currency Conversion." *Mathematics Teacher* (February 1979): 146–8.

978 Maor, Eli. "The Logorithmic Spiral." *Mathematics Teacher* (April 1974): 321–7.

979 Anderson, Bill, and John Lamb. "The Mathematical Aspects of a Lunar Shuttle Landing." *Mathematics Teacher* (October 1981): 549–53.

980 Austin, Joe Dan. "The Mathematics of Genetics." *Mathematics Teacher* (November 1977): 685–90.

981 Pinker, Aron. "The Method of Centroids in Plane Geometry." *Mathematics Teacher* (May 1980): 378–85.

982 Guilotte, Henry P. "The Method of Finite Differences: Some Applications." *Mathematics Teacher* (September 1986): 466–70.

983 Travers, Kenneth J., and Kenneth G. Gray. "The Monte Carlo Method: A Fresh Approach to Teaching Probabilistic Concepts." *Mathematics Teacher* (May 1981): 327–34.

984 McKim, James. "The Problem of Galaxa: Infinite Area Versus Finite Volume." *Mathematics Teacher* (April 1981): 294–6.

985 Hirstein, James J., and Sidney L. Rachlin. "The Pythagorean Theorem on an Isometric Geoboard." *Mathematics Teacher* (February 1980): 141–4.

986 Sastry, K. R. S. "The Quadratic Formula: A Historic Approach." *Mathematics Teacher* (November 1988): 670.

987 Johnson, Alonza F. "The Rule of 78: A Rule That Outlived Its Useful Life." *Mathematics Teacher* (September 1988): 450–3; 480.

988 Eisner, Milton P. "The Shape of a Baseball Field." *Mathematics Teacher* (May 1993): 366–71.

989 Cibes, Margaret. "The Sierpinski Triangle: Deterministic Versus Random Models." *Mathematics Teacher* (November 1990): 617–21.

990 Ballew, David W. "The Wheel of Aristotle." *Mathematics Teacher* (October 1972): 507.

991 Kleiner, Israel. "Thinking the Unthinkable: The Story of Complex Numbers." *Mathematics Teacher* (October 1988): 583–92.

992 Kilmer, Jeane E. "Triangles of Equal Area and Perimeter and Inscribed Circles." *Mathematics Teacher* (January 1988): 65–70.

993 Lamb, John F. "Trisecting an Angle—Almost." *Mathematics Teacher* (March 1988): 220–2.

994 Duncan, David R., and Bonnie H. Litwiller. "Turning Landslides into Cliffhangers: An Analysis of Presidential Election Returns." *Mathematics Teacher* (November 1986): 605–8.

995 Maurer, Stephen B. "Two Meanings of Algorithmic Mathematics." *Mathematics Teacher* (September 1984): 430–5.

996 Waits, Bert K. "Using a Calculator to Find Rational Roots." *Mathematics Teacher* (May 1978): 418–9.

997 Ginther, John, and William Ewbank. "Using a Microcomputer to Simulate the Birthday Coincidence Problems." *Mathematics Teacher* (December 1982): 769–75.

998 Beamer, James E. "Using Puzzles to Teach the Pythagorean Theorem." *Mathematics Teacher* (May 1989): 336–41.

999 Haak, Sheila. "Using the Monochord: The Mathematics of Musical Scales." *Mathematics Teacher* (March 1982): 238–44.

1000 Nowlin, Donald. "What Are My Car Payments Going to Be?" *Mathematics Teacher* (April 1993): 299–300.

1001 Scheaffer, Richard. "What Is Data Analysis?" *Mathematics Teacher* (February 1990): 90–3.

1002 Kluepfel, Charles. "When Are Logarithms Used?" *Mathematics Teacher* (April 1981): 250–3.

1003 Saunders, Hal. "When Are We Ever Gonna Have to Use This?" *Mathematics Teacher* (January 1980): 7–16.

1004 Ott, Jack A., and Anthony Contento. "Where Is the Ball Going?" *Mathematics Teacher* (September 1986): 456–60.

1005 Lubecke, André Michelle. "Which Mean Do You Mean?" *Mathematics Teacher* (January 1991): 24.

1006 Corbet, James J., and J. Susan Milton. "Who Killed the Cook?" *Mathematics Teacher* (April 1978): 263–6.

1007 Ott, Jack A. "Who's Going to Win the Playoff?" *Mathematics Teacher* (October 1985): 559–63.

1008 Fabricant, M., S. Svitak, and C. Kenschaft. "Why Women Succeed in Mathematics." *Mathematics Teacher* (February 1990): 150–4.

1009 Barnes, Sue. "Now and Then: From Cashier to Scan Coordinator." *Mathematics Teaching in the Middle School* (April 1994): 59–64.

1010 Ehrmann, Rita M. "Minimal Surfaces Revisited." *Mathematics Teacher* (February 1976): 146–52.

1011 Mercer, Joseph O. "Some Surprising Probabilities from Bingo." *Mathematics Teacher* (December 1993): 726–31.

1012 Reinford, Daniel J. "The Generality of a Simple Area Formula." *Mathematics Teacher* (December 1993): 738–40.

1013 Crouse, Richard J., and Clifford W. Sloyer. "Mathematics and Medical Indexes: A Life-Saving Connection." *Mathematics Teacher* (November 1993): 624–6.

1014 Plummer, Robert, Maita Levine, and Raymond H. Rolwing. "Using the TI-81 to Analyze Sports Data." *Mathematics Teacher* (November 1993): 636–41.

1015 Glidden, Peter L., and Erin K. Fry. "Two Proofs that Only Five Regular Polyhedra Exist." *Mathematics Teacher* (November 1993): 657–61.

1016 Woodward, Ernest, and Marilyn Woodward. "Expected Value and the Wheel of Fortune Game." *Mathematics Teacher* (January 1994): 13–7.

1017 Morgan, John L., and John L. Ginther. "The Magic of Mathematics." *Mathematics Teacher* (March 1994): 150–3.

1018 Lambert, J. B., et. al. "Maya Arithmetic." *American Scientist* (1980): 249–55.

1019 Rahn, James R., and Barry A. Berndes. "Using Logarithms to Explore Power and Exponential Functions." *Mathematics Teacher* (March 1994): 161–8.

1020 Mulcrone, T. F. "Benjamin Banneker, Pioneer Negro Mathematician." *Mathematics Teacher* (February 1976): 155–60.

1021 Malestsky, Evan M. "Ancient Babylonian Mathematics." *Mathematics Teacher* (April 1976): 295–8.

1022 Bolduc Jr., Elroy J. "A Discovery Approach to the Cube Root Algorithm." *Mathematics Teacher* (May 1976): 402–3.

1023 Pasquali, Giorgio. "Discovering a Formula that Generates Even Perfect Numbers." *Mathematics Teacher* (October 1976): 469–70.

1024 McCaffrey, Kenneth J. "Digital Sum Divisibility Tests." *Mathematics Teacher* (December 1976): 670–4.

1025 Yazbak, Najib. "Some Unusual Tests of Divisibility." *Mathematics Teacher* (December 1976): 667–8.

1026 Maor, Eli. "A Mathematician's Repertoire of Means." *Mathematics Teacher* (January 1977): 20–5.

1027 Skidell, Akiva. "The Harmonic Mean: A Nomograph and Some Problems." *Mathematics Teacher* (January 1977): 30–4.

1028 Troccolo, Joseph A. "A Strip of Wallpaper." *Mathematics Teacher* (January 1977): 55–8.

1029 Swetz, Frank. "The 'Piling up of Squares' in Ancient China." *Mathematics Teacher* (January 1977): 72–9.

1030 Blaisdell, Fred, and Art Indelicato. "Finding Chord Factors of Geodesic Domes." *Mathematics Teacher* (February 1977): 117–24.

1031 Harnel, Thomas R., and Ernest Woodward. "Developing Mathematics on a Pool Table." *Mathematics Teacher* (February 1977): 154–63.

1032 Slawsky, Norman. "The Artist as a Mathematician." *Mathematics Teacher* (April 1977): 298–308.

1033 Spencer, Neville. "Celebrating the Birthday Problem." *Mathematics Teacher* (April 1977): 348–53.

1034 Perl, Teri. "The Ladies' Diary . . . Cira 1700." *Mathematics Teacher* (April 1977): 354–8.

1035 Reyerson, Hardy C. "Anyone Can Trisect an Angle." *Mathematics Teacher* (April 1977): 319–21.

1036 Lott, Johnny, and Iris Mack Dayoub. "What Can Be Done with a Mira?" *Mathematics Teacher* (May 1977): 394–9.

1037 Shilgalis, Thomas W. "Maps: Geometry in Geography." *Mathematics Teacher* (May 1977): 400–4.

1038 Litwiller, Bonnie H., and David R. Duncan. "Poker Probabilities: A New Setting." *Mathematics Teacher* (December 1977): 766–71.

1039 Troccolo, Joseph A. "Randomness in Physics and Mathematics." *Mathematics Teacher* (December 1977): 772–4.

1040 Maor, Eli. "What Is There So Mathematical About Music?" *Mathematics Teacher* (September 1979): 414–22.

1041 Litwiller, Bonnie H., and David R. Duncan. "The Probability of Winning Dice Games." *Mathematics Teacher* (September 1979): 458–61.

1042 Wagner, Clifford H. "Determining Fuel Consumption—An Exercise in Applied Mathematics." *Mathematics Teacher* (February 1979): 134–6.

1043 Schwandt, Alice Kaseberg. "Spirolaterals: An Advanced Investigation from an Elementary Standpoint." *Mathematics Teacher* (March 1979): 166–9.

1044 Martin, George E. "Duplicating the Cube with a Mira." *Mathematics Teacher* (March 1979): 204–8.

1045 Austin, Joe Dan, and Kathleen Ann Austin. "Constructing and Trisecting Angles with Integer Angle Measures." *Mathematics Teacher* (April 1979): 290–3.

1046 Peterson, Gregory K. "Cube Roots on a Calculator—Some More Thoughts." *Mathematics Teacher* (September 1979): 448–9.

1047 Waits, Bert K., and James E. Schultz. "An Iterative for Computing Solutions to Equations Using a Calculator." *Mathematics Teacher* (December 1979): 685–9.

1048 Spieler, Robert. "Roman Numeral Puzzle." *Mathematics Teacher* (February 1980): 108, 156.

1049 Dorn, Carl, and Samuel Councilman. "Some Properties of the Calculator Square Root Function." *Mathematics Teacher* (March 1980): 218–21.

1050 Olson, Melfried. "Beyond the Usual Constructions." *Mathematics Teacher* (May 1980): 361–4.

1051 Sterrett, Andrew. "Electing a President in a Three-Candidate Race." *Mathematics Teacher* (November 1980): 635.

1052 Fawcett, George. "Camera Calculations." *Mathematics Teacher* (May 1981): 366–7, 398.

1053 Doebling, Mary Jo. "Mathematics of Buying a Car: A Basic Skills Unit." *Mathematics Teacher* (March 1981): 184–6, 238.

1054 Houser, Larry H. "Baseball Monte Carlo Style." *Mathematics Teacher* (May 1981): 340–1.

1055 Knorr, W. "Techniques of Fractions in Ancient Egypt and Greece." *Historia Mathematica* (1982): 133–71.

1056 Dewdney, A. K. "Yin and Yang: Recursion and Iteration, the Tower of Hanoi, and the Chinese Rings." *Scientific American* (November 1984): 19–28.

1057 Knill, George, and George Fawcett. "The Mathematics of Sight." *Mathematics Teacher* (November 1981): 636–7.

1058 Sullivan, John J. "Apportionment—A Decennial Problem." *Mathematics Teacher* (January 1982): 20–5.

1059 Obermeyer, Dean D. "Another Look at the Quadratic Formula." *Mathematics Teacher* (February 1982): 146–52.

1060 Johnson, Alonzo F. "The t in $i = prt$." *Mathematics Teacher* (October 1982): 595–7.

1061 Blake, Rick N., and Charles Verhille. "Semiregular Polyhedra." *Mathematics Teacher* (October 1982): 577–81.

1062 Bland, Paul, and Betty Givan. "Analysis of Two Car-Buying Strategies." *Mathematics Teacher* (February 1983): 124–7.

1063 Palmaccio, Richard J. "Shipboard Weather Observation." *Mathematics Teacher* (March 1983): 165–8.

1064 Beimler, Gerald. "Harmonic Series Revisited." *Mathematics Teacher* (March 1983): 178–9.

1065 Lyon, Betty Clayton. "How Is Area Related to Perimeter?" *Mathematics Teacher* (May 1983): 360–3.

1066 Olson, Melfried, Gerald K. Goff, and Murray Blose. "Triangular Numbers: The Building Blocks of Figurate Numbers." *Mathematics Teacher* (November 1983): 624–5.

1067 Lee, Kil S., and Wayne Marx. "Demonstrating the Efficiency of Linear Programming." *Mathematics Teacher* (December 1983): 664–6.

1068 Richbart, Lynn A. "Exotic Horse-Race Wagering and Combinations." *Mathematics Teacher* (January 1984): 35–6.

1069 Kimberling, Clark. "Generate Your Own Random Numbers." *Mathematics Teacher* (February 1984): 118–23.

1070 Eid, Frederick. "A Discovery Involving Volume." *Mathematics Teacher* (May 1984): 356–7.

1071 Kimberling, Clark. "Circles and Star Polygons." *Mathematics Teacher* (January 1985): 46–51, 54.

1072 Addicks, Tom. "Logo in the Mathematics Curriculum." *Mathematics Teacher* (September 1986): 424–8.

1073 Seo, Kenzo. "An Alternative Perspective on the Optical Property of Ellipses." *Mathematics Teacher* (November 1986).

1074 Brazier, Pearl W., and Joseph E. Chance. "Two Problems That Illustrate the Technique of Computer Simulation." *Mathematics Teacher* (December 1986): 726–31.

1075 Harvey, H. R., and B. J. Williams. "Aztec Arithmetic: Positional Notation and Area Calculation." *Science* (October 1980): 499–505.

1076 Mitchen, John. "Paradoxes in Averages." *Mathematics Teacher* (April 1989): 250–3.

1077 Irby, Ken. "Figuring Out a Jigsaw Puzzle." *Mathematics Teacher* (April 1989): 260–3.

1078 Stimpson, Virginia C. "What Do We Mean by Area and Perimeter?" *Mathematics Teacher* (May 1989): 342–4.

1079 Ranucci, Ernest R. "The World of Buckminister Fuller." *Mathematics Teacher* (October 1978): 568–77.

1080 Adele, Gail H. "When Did Euclid Live? An Answer Plus a Short History of Geometry." *Mathematics Teacher* (September 1989): 460–3.

1081 Olson, Alton T. "Recursion Mathematics." *Mathematics Teacher* (October 1989): 571–2, 576.

1082 Daniels, David S. "Mathematical Modeling: Lemonade from Lemons." *Mathematics Teacher* (October 1989): 516–9.

1083 Jones, Graham. "Mathematical Modeling in a Feast of Rabbits." *Mathematics Teacher* (December 1989): 770–3.

1084 Channell, Dwayne E. "Problem Solving with Simulation." *Mathematics Teacher* (December 1989): 713.

1085 Swetz, Frank. "When and How Can We Use Modeling?" *Mathematics Teacher* (December 1989): 722–6.

1086 Cohen, Donald. "Can a Purchaser Save Money by Financing?" *Mathematics Teacher* (January 1993): 62–3.

1087 Pritchard, Mary Kim. "Mathematical Iteration Through Computer Programming." *Mathematics Teacher* (February 1993): 150–6.

1088 Lamb, John F. "Two Egyptian Construction Tools." *Mathematics Teacher* (February 1993): 166–7.

1089 Nowlin, Donald. "Practical Geometry Problems: The Case of the Ritzville Pyramids." *Mathematics Teacher* (March 1993): 198–200.

1090 Kennedy, Jane B. "Area and Perimeter Connections." *Mathematics Teacher* (March 1993): 218–21, 231–2.

1091 Cannon, Lawrence O., and Joe Elich. "Pleasures and Perils of Iteration." *Mathematics Teacher* (March 1993): 233–9.

1092 Lavric, Boris. "The Volume of a Cone." *Mathematics Teacher* (May 1993): 384–5.

1093 Jones, Kevin S. "The Birthday Problem Again." *Mathematics Teacher* (May 1993): 373–7.

1094 Swetz, Frank J. "The Incredible Shrinking Can: Mathematics of Diminishing Returns Revealed." *Mathematics Teacher* (November 1993): 642–4.

1095 Bezuszka, Stanley J., and Margaret Kenney. "Implementing the Discrete Mathematics Standards: Focusing on Recursion." *Mathematics Teacher* (November 1993): 676–80.

1096 Fishman, Joseph. "Analyzing Energy and Resource Problems." *Mathematics Teacher* (November 1993): 628–33.

1097 Wallace, Edward C. "Exploring Regression with a Graphing Calculator." *Mathematics Teacher* (December 1993).

1098 Risoen, John, and Jane Stanzel. "A Truck Driver Looks at Square Roots." *Arithmetic Teacher* (November 1978).

1099 Eels, W. C. "Number Systems of the North American Indian." *American Mathematical Monthly* (1913): 263–72, 293–9.

1100 Wood, Denis. "The Power of Maps." *Scientific American* (May 1993): 85–93.

1101 Stewart, Ian. "Rise and Fall of the Lunar M-Pire." *Scientific American* (April 1993): 120–1.

1102 Dunker, Kenneth F., and Basile G. Rabbat. "Why American's Bridges Are Crumbling." *Scientific American* (March 1993): 66–73.

1103 Stephens, Peter W., and Alan I. Goldman. "Structure of Quasicrystals." *Scientific American* (April 1991): 44–53.

1104 Kotlick, Edward C., Thomas J. Hendrickson, and Kenneth D. Marshall. "The Acoustics of Harpsichord." *Scientific American* (February 1991): 110–15.

1105 Greenberg, Donald P. "Computers and Architecture." *Scientific American* (February 1991): 104–9.

1106 Scaglia, Gustina. "Building the Cathedral in Florence." *Scientific American* (January 1991): 66–76.

1107 Ross, Phillip E. "Buckytubes." *Scientific American* (December 1991): 24.

1108 Stewart, Ian. "Concentration: A Winning Strategy." *Scientific American* (October 1991): 126–8.

1109 Cerf, Vinton G. "Networks." *Scientific American* (September 1991): 72–85.

1110 Stewart, Ian. "What in Heaven Is a Digital Sundial?" *Scientific American* (August 1991): 104–6.

1111 Stewart, Ian. "Short Trek to Infinity." *Scientific American* (December 1991): 144–7.

1112 Freeman, Wendy L. "The Expansion Rate and Size of the Universe." *Scientific American* (November 1992): 54–61.

1113 Stewart, Ian. "Murder at Ghastleigh Grange (Networks)." *Scientific American* (October 1992): 118–20.

1114 Bennett, Charles H., Gilles Blassard, and Arthur K. Ekert. "Quantum Cryptography." *Scientific American* (October 1993): 50–7.

1115 Fagan, Paul J., and Michael D. Ward. "Building Molecular Crystals." *Scientific American* (July 1993): 48–55.

1116 Jescauage-Bernard, Karen, and Anders Crofoot. "Mapping to Preserve a Watershed." *Scientific American* (May 1993): 134.

1117 Sen, Amartya. "The Economics of Life and Death." *Scientific American* (May 1993): 40–7.

1118 Dewey, A. K. "A Program for Rotating Hypercubes Includes Four-Dimensional Dementia." *Scientific American* (April 1986): 14–23.

1119 Walker, Jearl. "Methods and Optics of Perceiving Color in Black-and-White Grating." *Scientific American* (March 1986): 112–8.

1120 Haber, Howard E., and Gordon L. Kane. "Is Nature Supersymmetric?" *Scientific American* (June 1986): 52–75.

1121 Mathews, Max V., and John R. Pierce. "Computer as a Musical Instrument." *Scientific American* (February 1987): 126–33.

1122 Walker, Jearl. "Music and Ammonia Vapor Excite the Color Pattern of Soap Film." *Scientific American* (August 1987): 104–7.

1123 Dewdney, A. K. "Imagination Meets Geometry in the Crystalline Realm of Latticeworms." *Scientific American* (June 1988): 120–3.

1124 Boulez, Piene, and Andrew Gerzso. "Computers in Music." *Scientific American* (April 1988): 44–51.

1125 Archer, J. Clark, et al. "Geography of U.S. Presidential Elections." *Scientific American* (July 1988): 44–53.

1126 Dewdney, A. K. "How to Pan for Primes in Numerical Gravel." *Scientific American* (July 1988): 120–3.

1127 Krantz, William B., Kevin J. Gleason, and Nelson Caine. "Patterned Ground." *Scientific American* (December 1988): 68–77.

1128 Borein, Jonathan M., and Peter B. Borwein. "Rasmanujan and Pi." *Scientific American* (February 1988): 112–7.

1129 Keyfitz, Nathan. "The Growing Human Population." *Scientific American* (September 1989): 118–27.

1130 Goldberger, Ary L., David R. Rigney, and Bruce J. West. "Chaos and Fractals in Human Physiology." *Scientific American* (February 1990): 42–9.

1131 Jürgens, Hartmut, Dietmar Saupe, and Heinz-Otto Peitgen. "The Language of Fractals." *Scientific American* (August 1990): 60–7.

1132 Nahin, Paul J. "Oliver Heaviside." *Scientific American* (June 1990).

1133 Berry, R. Stephen. "When Melting and Freezing Points Are Not the Same." *Scientific American* (August 1990): 68–74.

1134 Anderson, Roy M., and Robert M. Mey. "Understanding the AIDS Pandemic." *Scientific American* (May 1992): 58–69.

1135 Hauck, George F. W. "The Roman Aqueduct of Nines." *Scientific American* (March 1989): 98–105.

1136 Reid-Green, Keith S. "The History of Census Tabulation." *Scientific American* (February 1989): 98–103.

1137 Dewdney, A. K. "Tinkertoy Computer That Plays Tic-Tac-Toe." *Scientific American* (October 1989): 120–3.

1138 Gwinner, Eberhard. "Internal Rhythms in Bird Migration." *Scientific American* (April 1986).

1139 Rouvray, Dennis H. "Predicting Chemistry from Topology." *Scientific American* (September 1986): 40–7.

1140 Walker, Jearl. "Calculating the Distance to the Sun by Observing the Trail of a Meteor." *Scientific American* (March 1987): 122–6.

1141 Walker, Jearl. "Making a Barometer That Works with Water in Place of Mercury." *Scientific American* (April 1987): 122–7.

1142 Hiatt, Arthur A. "Finding Areas Under Curves with Hand-Held Calculators." *Scientific American* (May 1978): 420–3.

1143 Prielipp, Robert W. "Perfect Numbers, Abundant Numbers, and Deficient Numbers." *Mathematics Teacher* (December 1970): 692–6.

1144 Almgren, Frederick J., and Jean E. Taylor. "The Geometry of Soap Films and Soap Bubbles." *Scientific American* (July 1976): 82–93.

1145 Drake, S., and J. MacLachlan. "Galileo's Discovery of the Parabolic Trajectory." *Scientific American* (March 1975): 102–10.

1146 Gardner, Martin. "Some Packing Problems That Cannot Be Solved by Sitting on the Suitcase." *Scientific American* (October 1979): 18–26.

1147 Hellman, Martin E. "The Mathematics of Public-Key Cryptography." *Scientific American* (August 1979): 146–57.

1148 Gardner, Martin. "The Random Number Omega Bids Fair to Hold the Mysteries of the Universe." *Scientific American* (November 1979): 20–34.

1149 Gardner, Martin. "The Imaginableness of the Imaginary Numbers." *Scientific American* (August 1979): 18–24.

1150 Walker, Jearl. "How to Measure the Size of the Earth with Only a Foot Rule or a Stopwatch." *Scientific American* (May 1979): 172–82.

1151 Walker, Jearl. "Boomerang! How to Make Them and Also How They Fly." *Scientific American* (March 1979): 162–72.

1152 Walker, Jearl. "How to Build a Simple Seismograph to Record Earthquake Waves at Home." *Scientific American* (July 1979): 152–9.

1153 Gwatkin, Davidson R., and Sarah K. Brandel. "Life-Expectancy and Population Growth in the Third World." *Scientific American* (May 1982): 57–65.

1154 Gardner, Martin. "The Coloring of Unusual Maps Leads to Uncharted Territory." *Scientific American* (February 1980): 14–19.

1155 Hofstadter, Douglas R. "Beyond Rubik's Cube: Spheres, Pyramids, Dodecahedrons, and God Knows What Else." *Scientific American* (July 1982): 16–31.

1156 Pomerance, Carl. "The Search for Prime Numbers." *Scientific American* (December 1982): 136–47.

1157 Blair, Douglas H., and Robert A. Pollack. "Rational Collective Choice." *Scientific American* (August 1983): 88–95.

1158 Walker, Jearl. "The Physics of the Follow, the Draw, and the Massé." *Scientific American* (July 1983): 124–35.

1159 Gardner, Martin. "The Mathematics of Elections." *Scientific American* (October 1980): 16–26.

1160 Hofstradter, Douglas R. "The Magic Cube's Cubies are Twiddled by Cubes and Solved by Cubemeisters." *Scientific American* (March 1981): 20–39.

1161 Cohen, I. Bernard. "Newton's Discovery of Gravity." *Scientific American* (March 1981): 166–81.

1162 Gardner, Martin. "Gauss' Congruence Theory Was Mod as Early as 1801." *Scientific American* (February 1981): 17–20.

1163 Glahn, Else. "Chinese Building Standards in the 12th Century." *Scientific American* (May 1981): 162–73.

1164 Gardner, Martin. "The Abstract Parabola Fits the Concrete World." *Scientific American* (August 1981): 16–27.

1165 Bland, Robert G. "The Allocation of Resources by Linear Programming." *Scientific American* (June 1981): 126–45.

1166 Hutchins, Carleen Maley. "The Acoustics of Violin Plates." *Scientific American* (September 1981): 171–86.

1167 Walker, Jearl. "The Physics of the Patterns of Frost on a Window, Plus an Easy-to-Read Sundial." *Scientific American* (December 1980): 231–8.

1168 Lewis, Harry R., and Chistos H. Papodimitrion. "The Efficiency of Algorithms." *Scientific American* (January 1978): 96–110.

1169 Gardner, Martin. "In Which a Mathematical Aesthetic Is Applied to Modern Minimal Art." *Scientific American* (November 1978): 22.

1170 Gardner, Martin. "A Möbius Band." *Scientific American* (August 1978): 18–25.

1171 Walker, Jearl. "Introducing the Musha." *Scientific American* (February 1978): 156–61.

1172 Walker, Jearl. "Moiré Effects, the Kaleidoscope, and Other Victorian Diversions." *Scientific American* (December 1978): 182–8.

1173 Kihlstedt, Folke T. "The Crystal Palace." *Scientific American* (October 1984): 132–45.

1174 Mark, Robert, and William W. Clark. "Gothic Structural Experimentation." *Scientific American* (November 1984): 176–85.

1175 Wirth, Niklaus. "Data Structure and Algorithms." *Scientific American* (September 1984): 60–9.

1176 Wolfran, Stephen. "Computer Software in Science and Mathematics." *Scientific American* (September 1984): 188–99.

1177 Cliff, Andrew, and Peter Haggett. "Island Epidemics." *Scientific American* (May 1984): 138–47.

1178 Hayes, Brian. "Turning Turtle Gives One a View of Geometry from the Inside Out." *Scientific American* (February 1984): 14–20.

1179 Friberg, Jöran. "Numbers and Measures in the Earliest Written Records." *Scientific American* (February 1984): 110–9.

1180 Edwards, Harold M. "Fermat's Last Theorem." *Scientific American* (October 1978): 104–22.

1181 Walker, Jearl. "Thinking About Physics While Scared to Death." *Scientific American* (October 1983): 163.

1182 Gardner, Martin. "The Topology of Knots." *Scientific American* (September 1983): 18–28.

1183 Dauben, Joseph W. "Georg Cantor and the Origins of Transfinite Set Theory." *Scientific American* (June 1983): 122.

1184 Gardner, Martin. "One Checker Jumping, the Amazon Game, Weird Dice, Card Tricks, and Other Playful Pastimes." *Scientific American* (February 1978): 19–33.

1185 Finder, Nicholas V. "Computer Poker." *Scientific American* (July 1978): 144–51.

1186 Sloane, N. J. A. "The Packing of Spheres." *Scientific American* (January 1984): 116–25.

1187 Gardner, Martin. "In Which Players of Ticktacktoe are Taught to Hunt Bigger Game." *Scientific American* (April 1979): 18–28.

1188 Tormey, Alan, and Judith Farr Tormey. "Renaissance Intarsia: The Art of Geometry." *Scientific American* (July 1982): 136.

1189 Gardner, Martin. "On Altering the Past, Delaying the Future, and Other Ways of Tampering with Time." *Scientific American* (March 1979): 21–30.

1190 Rothman, Tony. "The Short Life of Évariste Galois." *Scientific American* (April 1982): 136–49.

1191 Gardner, Martin. "Graphs That Can Help Cannibals, Missionaries, Wolves, Goats, and Cabbages Get There from Here." *Scientific American* (March 1980): 24–38.

1192 Gingerich, Owen. "The Galileo Affair." *Scientific American* (August 1982): 133–43.

1193 Drake, Stillman. "Newton's Apple and Galileo's Dialogue." *Scientific American* (August 1980): 150–7.

1194 Gardner, Martin. "Dr. Matrix, Like Dr. Holmes, Comes to an Untimely and Mysterious End." *Scientific American* (September 1980): 20–4.

1195 Frohlich, Cliff. "The Physics of Somersaulting and Twisting." *Scientific American* (March 1980): 154–65.

1196 Orans, S. "Kaleidoscopes and Mathematics." *Arithmetic Teacher* (1973): 576–9.

1197 Thomas, David Emil. "Mirror Images." *Scientific American* (December 1980): 206–30.

1198 Dorn, Harold, and Robert Mark. "The Architecture of Christopher Wren." *Scientific American* (July 1981): 160–75.

1199 Keyfitz, Nathan. "The Population of China." *Scientific American* (February 1984): 38–47.

1200 Denning, Peter J., and Robert C. Brown. "Operating Systems." *Scientific American* (September 1984): 94–106.

1201 Lesk, Michael. "Computer Software for Information Management." *Scientific American* (September 1984): 163–74.

1202 Thorsfon, William P., and Jeffrey R. Weeks. "The Mathematics of Three-Dimensional Manifolds." *Scientific American* (July 1984): 108–21.

1203 Stanley, Steven M. "Mass Extinctions in the Ocean." *Scientific American* (June 1984): 64–83.

1204 Wheeler, Mary L. "Check-Digit Schemes." *Mathematics Teacher* (April 1994): 228–30.

1205 Moskowitz, Stuart. "Investigating Circles and Spirals with a Graphing Calculator." *Mathematics Teacher* (April 1994): 240–3.

1206 Walton, Karen Doyle. "Albert Dürer's Renaissance Connections Between Mathematics and Art." *Mathematics Teacher* (April 1994): 278–82.

1207 Hopley, Ronald B. "Nested Platonic Solids: A Class Project in Solid Geometry." *Mathematics Teacher* (May 1994): 312–8.

1208 Floyd, Jeffrey K. "A Discrete Analysis of 'Final Jeopardy.'" *Mathematics Teacher* (May 1994): 328–31.

1209 Mooshovitz-Hadar, N. "Mathematical Induction: A Focus on the Conceptual Framework." *School Science & Math Journal* (December 1993): 408–17.

1210 Walker, Jearl. "Anamorphic Pictures." *Scientific American* (July 1981): 176–87.

1211 Lee, Elvin J., and Joseph Madachy. "The History of Discovery of Amicable Numbers." *Journal of Recreational Math* Vol. 5.

1212 Dacey, Raymond. "Variations on a Theme by Pólya." *Mathematics Teacher* (November 1973): 598–9.

1213 Gridgeman, N. T. "Coprimes and Randomness." *Mathematics Teacher* (November 1973): 663–4.

1214 Westwood, Jack R. "Construction of a Slide Rule with Compass and Straightedge." *Mathematics Teacher* (February 1973): 162–4.

1215 White, Paul A. "An Application of Clock Arithmetic." *Mathematics Teacher* (November 1973): 645–7.

1216 Mosteller, Frederick. "Understanding the Birthday Problem." *Mathematics Teacher* (May 1962): 322–5.

1217 Stilwell, Kenneth. "The Quadratic Formula—An Enrichment Approach." *Mathematics Teacher* (May 1972): 472–3.

1218 Mann III, Nathaniel. "Modulo Systems: One More Step." *Mathematics Teacher* (March 1972): 207–9.

1219 Henry, Boyd. "Modulo-Seven Arithmetic—A Perfect Example of Field Properties." *Mathematics Teacher* (October 1972): 525–8.

1220 Duncan, Dewey C. "Instant Insanity: That Ubitquitous Baffler." *Mathematics Teacher* (February 1972): 131–5.

1221 Pinker, Avon. "Convergence of Some Iteration Formulas and Solutions of Recurrence Formulas." *Mathematics Teacher* (January 1972): 61–7.

1222 Tarte, Edward C. "Teaching the Square Root Algorithm by the Discovery Approach." *Mathematics Teacher* (April 1974): 317–9.

1223 Smith, Stanley A. "Rolling Curves." *Mathematics Teacher* (March 1974): 239–42.

1224 Ballew, David. "Numeration Systems with Unusual Bases." *Mathematics Teacher* (May 1974): 413–5.

1225 Firl, Donald H. "The Move to Metric: Some Considerations." *Mathematics Teacher* (November 1974): 581–5.

1226 Lichtenberg, Donovan R. "More about Triangles with the Same Area and the Same Perimeter." *Mathematics Teacher* (November 1974): 659–60.

1227 Flynn, Michael J. "The Computer's Impact on Mathematics: Numerical and Monte Carlo Methods." *Mathematics Teacher* (May 1974): 458–60.

1228 Schroeder, Lee L. "Buffon's Needle Problem: An Exciting Application of Many Mathematical Concepts." *Mathematics Teacher* (February 1974): 183–6.

1229 Prielipp, Robert. "Are Triangles That Have the Same Area and the Same Perimeter Congruent?" *Mathematics Teacher* (February 1974): 157–9.

1230 Odds, Frank C. "Spirolaterals." *Mathematics Teacher.* (February 1973): 121–4.

1231 Carson, George S. "Soma Cubes." *Mathematics Teacher* (November 1973): 583–92.

1232 Vervoort, Gerardus. "Inching Our Way Towards the Metric System." *Mathematics Teacher* (April 1973): 297–302.

1233 Struik, D. J. "On Ancient Chinese Mathematics." *Mathematics Teacher* (October 1963): 424–32.

1234 Guggenbuhl, L. "Mathematics in Ancient Egypt: A Checklist." *Mathematics Teacher* (November 1965): 630–4.

1235 Bidwell, James K. "Mayan Arithmetic." *Mathematics Teacher* (November 1967): 762–8.

1236 Hansen, Viggo P. "Square Root and Cube Root Extraction in 1788." *Mathematics Teacher* (February 1968): 175–6.

1237 Indelicato, Arthur. "Generating Random Numbers Using Modular Arithmetic." *Mathematics Teacher* (May 1969): 385–91.

1238 Piele, Donald T. "Population Explosion: An Activity Lesson." *Mathematics Teacher* (October 1974): 496–502.

1239 Jones, Robert L. "The Nine-Point Circle on a Geoboard." *Mathematics Teacher* (February 1976): 141–4.

1240 Beamer, J. E. "The Tale of a Kite." *Arithmetic Teacher* (1975): 382–6.

1241 *The Cryptogram.* Mundelein, IL: American Cryptogram Association.

Abacus: A Pocket Computer. by Jesse Dilson. New York: St. Martin's Press, 1968.

Abacus: Its History and Applications. by Frances Rosebell Metallo. Arlington, MA: COMAP, 1990.

ABCs of Boolean Algebra. by Allan Lytel. Indianapolis, IN: Howard W. Sams Co., 1966.

Activities for the Abacus. by Joan A. Cotter. Hutchinson, MN: Activities for Learning, 1988.

Ada, The Enchantress of Numbers. by Betty A. Toole. Mill Valley, CA: Strawberry Press, 1992.

Ada: A Life and a Legacy. by Dorothy Stein. Cambridge, MA: MIT Press, 1985.

Advanced Abacus. by Takashi Kojima. Tokyo: Charles E. Tuttle Co., 1991.

Advanced Geometric Constructions. by Alfred S. Posamentier, and William Wernick. Palo Alto, CA: Dale Seymour Publications, 1988.

Advanced Polyhedra Blocks. by Dale Seymour. Palo Alto, CA: Dale Seymour Publications, 1995.

Adventurer's Guide to Number Theory. by Richard Friedberg. New York: McGraw–Hill, 1968.

Adventures with Impossible Figures. by Bruno Ernst. Norfolk, England: Tarquin Publications, 1986.

Africa Counts. by Claudia Zaslavsky. Brooklyn, NY: Lawrence Hill Books, 1973.

Aha! Gotcha: Paradoxes to Puzzle and Delight. by Martin Gardner. New York: W. H. Freeman, 1982.

Albert Einstein: Creator and Rebel. by Banesh Hoffmann. New York: Viking Press, 1972.

Alexander's Star Puzzle: The Ideal Solution. by Ideal Toy staff. Newark, NJ: Ideal Toy Corporation, 1982.

Alge Cadabra! Algebra Magic Tricks. by Ronald Edwards. Pacific Grove, CA: Critical Thinking Press, 1992.

Algebra Experiments II: Exploring Nonlinear Functions. by Ronald Carlson, and Mary Jean Winter. Menlo Park, CA: Addison-Wesley Innovative Learning Publications, 1993.

Algebra in the Real World. by LeRoy C. Dalton. Palo Alto, CA: Dale Seymour Publications, 1983.

Alhambra Past and Present: A Geometer's Odyssey. by Lorraine L. Foster. Northridge, CA: California State Univ. Northridge, 1992.

American Houses: Origami Architecture. by Masahiro Chatani. New York: Kodansha International, 1988.

American Trademark Designs. by Barbara Baer Capitman. New York: Dover Publications, 1976.

Anamorphoses: Games of Perception and Illusion in Art. by Joost Elffers, Fred Leeman, and Michael Schuyt. New York: Abrams, 1976.

Anatomy of Nature. by Andreas Feininger. New York: Dover Publications, 1956.

Another Fine Math You've Got Me Into. . . . by Ian Stewart. New York: W. H. Freeman, 1992.

Applications in Mathematics. by Sidney Sharron, Bob Reyes, et al. Reston, VA: NCTM, 1979.

Applications of Calculus. by Philip Straffin, ed. Washington, D.C.: MAA, 1993.

Applications of Finite Differences (Boston College Math Inst. Booklet 9). by Stanley Bezuszka, Lou D'Angelo, and Margaret Kenney. Chestnut Hill, MA: Boston College Press, 1976.

Applications of Geometrical Probability. by Fred D. Djang. Arlington, MA: COMAP, 1988.

Applications of Secondary School Mathematics. by Bernice Kastner. Reston, VA: NCTM, 1978.

Applications of Series (Boston College Math Inst. Booklet 4). by Stanley Bezuszka, Lou D'Angelo, and Margaret Kenney. Chestnut Hill, MA: Boston College Press, 1976.

Apportionment Problem: The Search for the Perfect Democracy. by Sandi Bennett, et al. Arlington, MA: COMAP, 1986.

Arabic Geometrical Pattern and Design. by J. Bourgoin. New York: Dover Publications, 1973.

Archimedean and Archimedian Dual Polyhedra. by Lorraine L. Foster. Northridge, CA: California State Univ. Northridge, 1991.

Archimedes Revenge: The Challenge of the Unknown. by Paul Hoffman. New York: W. W. Norton, 1988.

Archimedes. by E. J. Dijksterhuis. Princeton, NJ: Princeton Univ. Press, 1987.

Architecture as Space. by Bruno Zevi. New York: DeCapo Press, 1993.

Architecture in Education. by Marcy Abhau, Rolaine Copeland, and Greta Greenberger. Philadelphia, PA: Foundation for Architecture, 1986.

Armchair Universe: An Exploration of Computer Worlds. by A. K. Dewdney. New York: W. H. Freeman, 1988.

Art and Geometry: A Study in Space Intuitions. by William M. Ivins Jr. New York: Dover Publications, 1946.

Art and Techniques of Simulation. by Mrudulla Gnanadesikan, Richard L. Scheaffer, and Jim Swift. Palo Alto, CA: Dale Seymour Publications, 1987.

Art Forms in Nature. by Ernst Haeckel. New York: Dover Publications, 1974.

Art of Albrecht Dürer. by Heinrich Wölfflin. New York: Phaidon Publishers, 1971.

Art of Construction. by Mario Salvadori. Chicago: Chicago Review Press, 1990.

Asimov on Numbers. by Isaac Asimov. Garden City, NY: Doubleday & Co., 1977.

Averages. by Jane Jones Srivastava. New York: Crowell, 1975.

Basic Perspective. by Robert W. Gill. London: Thames & Hudson, 1974.

Beat the Dealer. by Edward O. Thorp. New York: Blaisdell Publishing, 1962.

Beyond Equals. by Ruth Afflack. Oakland, CA: Mills College, 1982.

Beyond Numeracy. by John Allen Paullos. New York: Alfred A. Knopf, 1991.

Beyond the Third Dimension. by Thomas F. Banchoff. New York: Scientific American Library, 1990.

Billiards as It Should Be Played. by Willie Hoppe. Chicago: Henry Regnery Co., 1941.

Billiards for Everyone. by Luther Lassiter. New York: Grosset & Dunlap, 1965.

Binary Power. by John Veltman. Palo Alto, CA: Dale Seymour Publications, 1992.

Black Mathematicians and Their Works. by Virginia K. Newell, and Joella Gipson. Ardmore, PA: Dorrance and Co., 1980.

Board and Table Games from Many Civilizations. by R. C. Bell. New York: Dover Publications, 1979.

Book of Baubles. by Anna Diamond. Kuala Lumpur, Malaysia: Anna Diamond, 1988.

Book of Curves. by E. H. Lockwood. New York: Cambridge Univ. Press, 1961.

Bridges to Infinity. by Michael Guillen. Los Angeles: Jeremy P. Tarcher, 1983.

Bubble Festival. by Jacqueline Barber, and Carolyn Willard. Berkeley, CA: Lawrence Hall of Science, 1992.

Bubbles, Drops, and Particles. by R. Clift, and J. R. Grace. San Diego, CA: Academic Press, 1978.

Bucky for Beginners. by Mary Laycock. Hayward, CA: Activity Resources, 1984.

Budget of Trisection. by Underwood Dudley. New York: Springer-Verlag, 1987.

Build Your Own Polyhedra. by Jean Pedersen, and Peter Hilton. Menlo Park, CA: Addison-Wesley Innovative Learning Publications, 1988.

Building Kites: Flying High with Math. by Nancy Ann Belsky. Palo Alto, CA: Dale Seymour Publications, 1995.

Building Toothpick Bridges. by Jeanne Pollard. Palo Alto, CA: Dale Seymour Publications, 1985.

Calc Handbook: Conceptual Activites for Learning Calculus. by Duane DeTemple, and Jack Robertson. Palo Alto, CA: Dale Seymour Publications, 1991.

Calculating Devices. by D. A. Johnson, and W. H. Glenn. Portsmouth, NH: John Murray, 1964.

Calculating Passion of Ada Byron. by Joan Baum. Hamden, CT: Archon Books, The Shoestring Press, 1987.

Calculus for a New Century: A Pump, Not a Filter. by Lynn Arthur Steen. Washington, D.C.: MAA, 1988.

Calculus Methods. by Stan Dolan, et al. New York: Cambridge Univ. Press, 1992.

Calculus Problems for a New Century. by Robert Fraga, ed. Washington, D.C.: MAA, 1993.

Calculus Problems for Student Investigation. by Michael B. Jackson, and John R. Ramsay, eds. Washington, D.C.: MAA, 1993.

Can You Believe Your Eyes? by J. R. Block, and Harold E. Yuker. New York: Gardner Press, 1989.

Can You Win? by Mike Orkin. New York: W. H. Freeman, 1991.

Celtic Art: The Methods of Construction. by G. Bain. New York: Dover Publications, 1973.

Celtic Design: A Beginner's Manual. by Aidan Meehan. New York: Thames & Hudson, 1991.

Celtic Design: Knotwork—The Secret Method of the Scribes. by Aidan Meehan. New York: Thames & Hudson, 1991.

Celtic Mysteries: The Ancient Religion. by John Sharkley. New York: Crossroad, 1975.

Challenge of Numbers: People in the Mathematical Sciences. by Bernard L. Madison, and Therese A. Hart. Washington, D.C.: National Academy Press, 1989.

Challenging Mathematical Teasers. by J. A. H. Hunter. New York: Dover Publications, 1980.

Challenging Problems in Algebra. by Alfred S. Posamentier, and Charles T. Salkind. Palo Alto, CA: Dale Seymour Publications, 1988.

Challenging Problems in Geometry. by Alfred S. Posamentier, and Charles T. Salkind. Palo Alto, CA: Dale Seymour Publications, 1988.

Chambers Science and Technology Dictionary. by Peter Walker, ed. Edinburgh, England: W & R Chambers, 1988.

Chaos, Fractals and Dynamics: Computer Experiments in Mathematics. by Robert L. Devaney. Menlo Park, CA: Addison-Wesley Innovative Learning Publications, 1990.

Chaos: Making a New Science. by James Gleick. New York: Penguin Books, 1987.

Charles Babbage and His Calculating Engines. by Phillip Morrison, and Emily Morrison, eds. New York: Dover Publications, 1961.

Charles Babbage, Father of the Computer. by Don Malacy. New York: Crowell-Collier Press, 1970.

Chinese Lattice Designs. by Daniel Sheets Dye. New York: Dover Publications, 1974.

Chinese Mathematics: A Concise History. by Li Yan, and Du Shiran. Oxford: Clarendon Press, 1987.

Classic Math: History Topics For the Classroom. by Art Johnson. Palo Alto, CA: Dale Seymour Publications, 1994.

Code Breakers. by David Kahn. New York: Macmillan, 1967.

Codes Galore. by Joseph Malkevitch. Arlington, MA: COMAP, 1990.

Codes, Puzzles, and Conspiracy. by Dennis Shasha. New York: W. H. Freeman, 1992.

Collected Logical Works. by George Boole. Peru, IL: Open Court, 1952.

Comparisons. by Diagram Group. New York: St. Martin's Press, 1980.

Complete Book of Fingermath. by Edwin M. Lieberthal. New York: McGraw-Hill, 1979.

Complete Handbook of Science Fair Projects. by Julianne Bochinski. New York: John Wiley & Sons, 1991.

Complete Origami. by Eric Kenneway. New York: St. Martin's Press, 1987.

Complete Strategist: Being a Primer on the Theory of Games of Strategy. by John D. Williams. New York: Dover Publications, 1986.

Computer from Pascal to von Neumann. by Herman H. Goldstine. Princeton, NJ: Princeton Univ. Press, 1972.

Computing and Mathematics. by James T. Fey, et al. Reston, VA: NCTM, 1984.

Concise History of Mathematics. 4th ed. by Dirk J. Struik. New York: Dover Publications, 1987.

Concise Science Dictionary. by Daintith Isaacs, and Martin Isaacs, eds. New York: Oxford Univ. Press, 1991.

Connections: The Geometric Bridge Between Art and Science. by Jay Kappraff. New York: McGraw-Hill, 1991.

Contemporary Motivated Mathematics. Book 1. by Stanley Bezuszka, Mary Farrey, and Margaret Kenney. Chestnut Hill, MA: Boston College Press, 1972.

Contemporary Motivated Mathematics. Book 2. by Stanley Bezuszka, Mary Farrey, and Margaret Kenney. Chestnut Hill, MA: Boston College Press, 1986.

Contemporary Motivated Mathematics. Book 3. by Stanley Bezuszka, Mary Farrey, and Margaret Kenney. Chestnut Hill, MA: Boston College Press, 1980.

Contemporary Motivated Mathematics. Book 4. by Stanley Bezuszka, Lou D'Angelo, and Margaret Kenney. Chestnut Hill, MA: Boston College Press, 1976.

Contemporary Motivated Mathematics. Book 9. by Stanley Bezuszka, Lou D'Angelo, and Margaret Kenney. Chestnut Hill, MA: Boston College Press, 1976.

Contemporary Motivated Mathematics. Book 12. by Margaret Kenney. Chestnut Hill, MA: Boston College Press, 1976.

Contemporary Motivated Mathematics. Book 13. by Stanley Bezuszka, Jeanne Cavanaugh, and Margaret Kenney. Chestnut Hill, MA: Boston College Press, 1984.

Continued Fractions. by C. D. Olds. Washington, D.C.: MAA, 1963.

Contributions to the Founding of the Theory of Transfinite Numbers. by Philip E. B. Jourdain, trans. New York: Dover Publications, 1955.

Convergence of Lives: Sofia Kovalerskaia: Scientist, Writer, Revolutionary. by Ann Hibner Koblitz. New Brunswick, NJ: Rutgers Univ. Press, 1993.

Create a Cube. by Margaret Smart, and Mary Laycock. Hayward, CA: Activity Resources Co., 1985.

Creating Escher-Type Drawings. by E. R. Ranucci, and J. L. Teeters. Oak Lawn, IL: Creative Publications, 1977.

Creative Constructions. by Dale Seymour, and Reuben Schadler. Oak Lawn, IL: Creative Publications, 1974.

Crescent Dictionary of Mathematics. by William Karush. Palo Alto, CA: Dale Seymour Publications, 1962.

Crest of the Peacock: Non-European Roots of Mathematics. by George Gheverghese Joseph. London: J. B. Tauris & Co., 1991.

Curve Stitching. by Jon Millington. Norfolk, England: Tarquin Publications, 1989.

Curves and Their Properties. by Robert C. Yates. Reston, VA: NCTM, 1952.

Curves of Life. by Theodore Andrea Cook. New York: Dover Publications, 1979.

Dancing Curves: A Dynamic Demonstration of Geometric Principles. by Merwin J. Lyng. Reston, VA: NCTM, 1978.

Decision Making and Math Models. by G. Surya Kumar. Arlington, MA: COMAP, 1989.

Decorative Art of the Southwestern Indians. by Dorothy Smith Sides. New York: Dover Publications, 1961.

Decorative Paper Snowflakes. by Brenda Lee Reed. New York: Dover Publications, 1987.

Deductive Systems: Finite and Non-Euclidean Geometries. by James R. Lockwood, and Garth E. Runion. Reston, VA: NCTM, 1978.

Design Motifs of Ancient Mexico. by Jorge Enciso. New York: Dover Publications, 1953.

Designs From Mathematical Patterns. by Linda Silvey, Stanley Bezuszka, and Margaret Kenney. Palo Alto, CA: Dale Seymour Publications, 1990.

Development of Mathematics in China and Japan. by Y. Mikami. New York: Chelsea, 1974.

Dictionary of Real Numbers. by Johnathan M. Borwein, and Peter B. Borwein. Belmont, CA: Wadsworth, 1990.

Did You Say Mathematics? by Y. Khurgin. Moscow: Mir Publishers, 1974.

Discovering Apple Logo. by David Thornburg. Menlo Park, CA: Addison Wesley Innovative Learning Publications, 1983.

Discovering Mathematics. Books 1 and 2. by Nigel R. Peace. London: Macmillan Education, 1987.

Discrete Mathematics Across the Curriculum K–12. by Margaret Kenney, and Christian Hirsch, eds. Reston, VA: NCTM, 1991.

Divine Proportion. by H. E. Huntley. New York: Dover Publications, 1970.

Doing Simple Math in Your Head. by W. J. Howard. Coos Bay, OR: Coast Publishing, 1992.

Dome. Books 1 and 2. by Lloyd Kahn, ed. Bolinas, CA: Pacific Domes, 1971.

Dymaxion World of Buckminister Fuller. by R. Buckminister Fuller, and Robert Marks. New York: Anchor Press/Doubleday, 1973.

Dynamic Programming: An Elegant Problem Solver. by William Sacco, Wayne Copes, Clifford Sloyer, and Robert Stark. Providence, RI: Janson Publications, 1987.

Education of T. C. MITS. by Lillian Lieber. New York: W. W. Norton, 1972.

Eighth Book of Tan: 700 Tangrams by Sam Loyd. by Sam Loyd. New York: Dover Publications, 1968.

Einstein: His Life and Times. by Phillip Frank. New York: Alfred A. Knopf, 1963.

Einstein: The Life and Times. by Ronald W. Clark. New York: World Publishing Co., 1971.

Elementary Cryptanalysis: A Mathematical Approach. by Abraham Sinkov. Washington, D.C.: MAA, 1966.

Elementary Number Theory. by U. Dudley. San Francisco: W. H. Freeman, 1978.

Elements of Non-Euclidean Geometry. by D. M. Y. Sommerville. New York: Dover Publications, 1958.

Emergence of Probability. by Ian Hacking. New York: Cambridge Univ. Press, 1975.

Emmy Noether, 1882–1935. by Auguste Dick. Cambridge, MA: Birkhäuser, 1981.

Encyclopedic Dictionary of Mathematics. by Shôkichi Tyanaga, and Yukiuosi Kawada, eds. Cambridge, MA: MIT Press, 1986.

Enjoyment of Mathematics. by Hans Rademacher. New York: Dover Publications, 1990.

Episodes from the Early History of Mathematics. by Asger Aaboe. Washington, D.C.: MAA, 1964.

Escher on Escher: Exploring the Infinite. by M. C. Escher. New York: Harry N. Abrams, 1986.

Every Number Is Special. by Boyd Henry. Palo Alto, CA: Dale Seymour Publications, 1985.

Excursions in Advanced Euclidean Geometry. by Alfred Posamentier. Menlo Park, CA: Addison-Wesley Innovative Learning Publications, 1984.

Experiments in Topology. by Stephen Barr. New York: Thomas Y. Crowell Co., 1964.

Experiments with Patterns in Mathematics. by Boyd Henry. Palo Alto, CA: Dale Seymour Publications, 1987.

Exploration of the Universe. by George O. Abell, David Morrison, and Sidney C. Wolff. Philadelpia, PA: Saunders College Publishing, 1991.

Explore Sorts. by Rochele Wilson Meyer. Arlington, MA: COMAP, 1990.

Exploring Calculus with a Graphing Calculator. by Charlene Beckman, and Theodore Sundstrom. Menlo Park, CA: Addison-Wesley Publishing Co., 1992.

Exploring Data. by James M. Landwehr, and Ann E. Watkins. Palo Alto, CA: Dale Seymour Publications, 1986.

Exploring Measurements. by Peter Barbella, James Kepner, and Richard Scheaffer. Palo Alto, CA: Dale Seymour Publications, 1994.

Exploring Probability. by Claire M. Newman, Thomas E. Obremski, and Richard Scheaffer. Palo Alto, CA: Dale Seymour Publications, 1987.

Exploring Statistics with the TI-81. by Gail Burrill, and Patrick Hopfensperger. Menlo Park, CA: Addison-Wesley Innovative Learning Publications, 1993.

Exploring Surveys and Information from Samples. by James M. Landwehr, Jim Swift, and Ann E. Watkins. Palo Alto, CA: Dale Seymour Publications, 1987.

Exploring the Sky. by Richard Moeschl. Chicago, IL: Independent Publishers Group, 1989.

Exploring with Squares and Cubes. by Ron Kremer. Palo Alto, CA: Dale Seymour Publications, 1989.

Facts on File Dictionary of Mathematics. by Carl Gibson, et al. New York: Facts on File, 1988.

Facts on File Dictionary of Numerical Allusions. by Lawrence Urdang. New York: Facts on File, 1986.

Fair Divisions: Getting Your Fair Share. by Sandi Bennett, et al. Arlington, MA: COMAP, 1986.

Fair Game. by Richard Guy. Arlington, MA: COMAP, 1989.

Famous Problems from Elementary Geometry. by Felix Klein. New York: Dover Publications, 1956.

Famous Problems of Mathematics. by Heinrich Tietze. New York: Graylock Press, 1965.

Fantasia Mathematica. by Clifton Fadiman. New York: Fireside Books, 1958.

Fascinating Fibonaccis. by Trudy Garland. Palo Alto, CA: Dale Seymour Publications, 1987.

Fascination of Groups. by F. J. Budden. New York: Cambridge Univ. Press, 1972.

Fermat's Last Theorem. by Harold Edwards. New York: Springer-Verlag, 1977.

Fibonacci and Lucas Numbers. by Verner E. Hoggatt. Santa Clara, CA: Fibonacci Association, 1969.

Fibonacci's Problem Book. by Marjorie Bicknell, and Vernon Hoggatt, eds. San Jose, CA: San Jose Univ. Fibonacci Assoc., 1974.

Figuring—The Joy of Numbers. by Shakuntala Devi. New York: Harper & Row, 1977.

Films in the Mathematics Classroom. by Barbara J. Bestgen, and Robert E. Reys. Reston, VA: NCTM, 1982.

First Concepts in Topology. by W. G. Chinn, and N. E. Steenrod. Washington, D.C.: MAA, 1966.

Flatland. by Edwin Abbott. New York: Dover Publications, 1952.

For All Practical Purposes. by Solomon Garfunkel, Lynn Steen, and Joseph Malkevich, et al. New York: W. H. Freeman, 1991.

Forever Undecided. by Raymond Smullyan. New York: Alfred A. Knopf, 1987.

Form, Function, and Design. by Paul Jacques Grillo. New York: Dover Publications, 1960.

Foundations of Higher Mathematics: Exploration and Proof. by D. Fendel, and D. Resek. Reading, MA: Addison-Wesley Publishing Co., 1990.

Foundations. by Stan Dolan, et al. New York: Cambridge Univ. Press, 1991.

Four-Color Problem. by Thomas L. Saaty, and Paul C. Kainen. New York: Dover Publications, 1986.

Four-Dimensional Geometry. by Adrien T. Hess. Reston, VA: NCTM, 1977.

Fourfield: Computers, Art, and the Fourth Dimension. by Tony Robbin. Boston: Bulfinch Press, 1992.

Fourth Dimension Simply Explained. by Henry P. Manning. New York: Dover Publications, 1960.

Fourth Dimension. by Rudyr Rucker. Boston: Houghton Mifflin Co., 1994.

Fourth-Dimension and Non-Euclidean Geometry in Modern Art. by Linda D. Henderson. Princeton, NJ: Princeton Univ. Press, 1983.

Fractal Geometry of Nature. by Benoit B. Mandelbrot. New York: W. H. Freeman, 1983.

Fractal Music, Hypercards, and More. by Martin Gardner. New York: W. H. Freeman, 1992.

Fractals for the Classroom. Vol. 1. by Heinz-Otto Peitgen, et al. New York: Springer-Verlag/NCTM, 1992.

Fractals for the Classroom. Vol. 2. by Heinz-Otto Peitgen, et al. New York: Springer-Verlag/NCTM, 1992.

Fractals: The Patterns of Chaos. by John Briggs. New York: Touchstone Books, 1992.

Fractals, Chaos, Power Laws. by Manfried Schroeder. New York: W. H. Freeman, 1991.

From Crystals to Kites: Exploring Three Dimensions. by Ron Kremer. Palo Alto, CA: Dale Seymour Publications, 1995.

From Home Runs to Housing Costs: Data Resource. by Gail Burrill, ed. Palo Alto, CA: Dale Seymour Publications, 1994.

From One to Zero: A Universal History of Numbers. by Georges Ifrah. New York: Viking Press, 1985.

From Pythagoras to Einstein. by K. O. Friedricks. Washington, D.C.: MAA, 1965.

From Zero to Infinity. 4th ed. by Constance Reid. Washington, D.C.: MAA, 1992.

Functions. by Stan Dolan, et al. New York: Cambridge Univ. Press, 1991.

Fundamentals of Logic. by James D. Carney, and Richard K. Scheer. New York: Macmillan, 1964.

Game Theory. by Bernadette Perham, and Arnold Perham. Menlo Park, CA: Addison-Wesley Innovative Learning Publications, 1993.

Game Theory: A Nontechnical Introduction. by Morton D. Davis. New York: Basic Books, 1970.

Gauss: A Biographical Study. by W. K. Bühler. New York: Springer-Verlag, 1981.

Genius of China. by Robert Temple. New York: Simon & Schuster, 1986.

Geodesic Math. by Hugh Kenner. Berkeley, CA: Univ. of California Press, 1976.

Geometric Concepts in Islamic Art. by Issam El-Said, and Ayse Parman. Palo Alto, CA: Dale Seymour Publications, 1976.

Geometric Design. by Dale Seymour. Palo Alto, CA: Dale Seymour Publications, 1988.

Geometric Etudes in Combinatorial Mathematics. by V. Boltyanski, and A. Soifer. Colorado Springs, CO: Center for Excellence in Mathematics Education, 1991.

Geometric Exercises in Paper Folding. by T. Sundara Row. New York: Dover Publications, 1966.

Geometric Patterns from Roman Mosaics and How to Draw Them. by Robert Field. Norfolk, England: Tarquin Publications, 1988.

Geometric Playthings. by Jean Pedersen, and Kent Pedersen. Palo Alto, CA: Dale Seymour Publications, 1973.

Geometric Transformations. by I. M. Yaglom. Washington, D.C.: MAA, 1979.

Geometric Transformations. by P. S. Moclenov, and A. S. Parkhomenko. New York: Academic Press, 1965.

Geometrical Foundation of Natural Structure. by Robert Williams. New York: Dover Publications, 1979.

Geometrical Investigations. by John Pottage. Reading, MA: Addison-Wesley Publishing Co., 1983.

Geometry and the Visual Arts. by Dan Pedoe. New York: Dover Publications, 1976.

Geometry in Architecture. by William Blackwell. Berkeley, CA: Key Curriculum Press, 1984.

Geometry in the Classroom: New Concepts and Methods. by H. A. Elliott, James R. MacLean, and Janet M. Jorden. Toronto: Holt, Rinehart and Winston of Canada, 1968.

Geometry of René Descartes. by David E. Smith, and Macia L. Latham, trans. New York: Dover Publications, 1954.

Geometry Revisited. by H. S. M. Coxeter, and S. L. Greitzer. Washington, D.C.: MAA, 1967.

Geometry, Relativity, and the Fourth Dimension. by Rudolf Rucker. New York: Dover Publications, 1977.

Geometry: Constructions and Transformations. by Iris Mack Dayoub, and Johnny W. Lott. Palo Alto, CA: Dale Seymour Publications, 1977.

Georg Cantor: His Mathematics and Philosophy of the Infinite. by Joseph Dauben. Cambridge, MA: Harvard Univ. Press, 1979.

George Boole: His Life and Work. by Desmond MacHale. Dublin: Boole Press, 1985.

George Pólya: Master of Discovery. by Harold Taylor, and Loretta Taylor. Palo Alto, CA: Dale Seymour Publications, 1993.

Gliding Flight. by John M. Collins. Berkeley, CA: Ten Speed Press, 1989.

Glyphs: Getting the Picture. by William Sacco, Wayne Copes, Clifford Sloyer, and Robert Stark. Providence, RI: Janson Publications, 1987.

Gödel, Escher, Bach: An Eternal Golden Braid. by Douglas R. Hofstadter. New York: Vintage Books, 1979.

Golden Section. by Garth E. Runion. Palo Alto, CA: Dale Seymour Publications, 1990.

Graph Theory. by Bernadette Perham, and Arnold Perham. Menlo Park, CA: Addison-Wesley Innovative Learning Publications, 1993.

Graph Theory: Euler's Rich Legacy. by William Sacco, Wayne Copes, Clifford Sloyer, and Robert Stark. Providence, RI: Janson Publications, 1987.

Graphic Work of M. C. Escher. by M. C. Escher. New York: Ballantine Books, 1960.

Graphing Calculator Activities. by Charles Lund, and Edwin Andersen. Menlo Park, CA: Addison-Wesley Innovative Learning Publications, 1992.

Graphs and Digraphs. by Gary Chartrand, and Linda Lesniak. Boston: Prindle, Weber and Schmidt, 1979.

Graphs and Their Uses. by Robin J. Wilson. Washington, D.C.: MAA, 1990.

Great American Buildings: Origami Cutouts. by Masahiro Chatani, and Keiko Nakazawa. New York: Kodansha International, 1991.

Great Architecture of the World. by John Norwich, et al. New York: Bonanza Books, 1975.

Great Mathematicians. by Herbert Westren Turnbull. New York: Simon & Schuster, 1962.

Great Scientists. by Jack Meadows. New York: Oxford Univ. Press, 1987.

Greek Geometry from Thales to Euclid. by G. J. Allman. New York: Arno Press, 1976.

Groups and Their Graphs. by Israel Grossman, and Magnus Wilhelm. Washington, D.C.: MAA, 1964

Guide to Metrics. by Terry Richardson. Ann Arbor, MI: Prakken Publications, 1978.

Guinness Book of Numbers. by Adrian Room. London: Guinness Publishing, 1989.

Handbook of Integer Sequences. by N. J. A. Sloane. New York: Academic Press, 1973.

Handbook of Ornament. by Franz Sales Meyer. New York: Dover Publications, 1957.

Handbook of Regular Patterns. by Peter S. Stevens. Cambridge, MA: MIT Press, 1984.

Height-O-Meters. by Cary Sneider, and Alan Gould. Berkeley, CA: Lawrence Hall of Science, 1988.

Hexaflexagons and Other Mathematical Diversions. by Martin Gardner. Chicago: Univ. of Chicago Press, 1988.

Historical Topics for the Mathematics Classroom. by J. Baumgart, et al. Reston, VA: NCTM, 1989.

Historical Topics in Algebra. by Arthur E. Hallenberg, et al. Reston, VA: NCTM, 1971.

History of Algebra. by B. L. Van Der Waerden. Berlin: Springer-Verlag, 1985.

History of Binary and Other Nondecimal Numeration. by Anton Glaser. Los Angeles: Tomash Publishing, 1981.

History of Computing Technology. by Michael R. Williams. Englewood Cliffs, NJ: Prentice Hall, 1993.

History of Greek Mathematics. by T. L. Heath. New York: Dover Publications, 1981.

History of Mathematics. 2d ed. by Carl B. Boyer. New York: John Wiley & Sons, 1991.

History of Mathematics. Vol. 1. by D. E. Smith. New York: Dover Publications, 1951.

History of Mathematics. Vol. 2. by D. E. Smith. New York: Dover Publications, 1951.

History of Non-Euclidean Geometry: Evolution of the Concept of a Geometric Space. by B. A. Rosenfeld. New York: Springer-Verlag, 1988.

History of Pi. by Petr Beckmann. New York: St. Martin's Press, 1971.

History of Statistics: The Measurement of Uncertainty Before 1900. by Stephen M. Stigler. Cambridge, MA: Harvard Univ. Press, 1986.

History of the Abacus. by J. M. Pullan. New York: Praeger Publishers, 1969.

Hornung's Handbook of Designs and Devices. by Clarence P. Hornung. New York: Dover Publications, 1946.

How Did We Find Out About Numbers? by Isaac Asimov. New York: Walker & Co., 1973.

How Does One Cut a Triangle? by Alexander Soifer. Colorado Springs, CO: Center for Excellence in Mathematics Education, 1990.

How Maps Are Made. by John Baynes. New York: Facts On File, 1987.

How Much and How Many? by Jeanne Bendick. New York: Franklin Watts, 1989.

How to Calculate Quickly. by Henry Sticker. New York: Dover Publications, 1955.

How to Draw a Straight Line. by A. B. Kempe. Reston, VA: NCTM, 1877.

How to Enrich Geometry Using String Designs. by Victoria Pohl. Reston, VA: NCTM, 1986.

How to Lie with Statistics. by Darrell Huff. New York: W. W. Norton, 1982.

How to Model It. by Anthony Stanfield, Karl Smith, and Andrew Bleloch. New York: McGraw-Hill, 1990.

How to Solve It. by George Pólya. Princeton, NJ: Princeton Univ. Press, 1973.

How to Think About Statistics. by John L. Phillips. New York: W. H. Freeman, 1988.

Hypatia Heritage. by Margaret Alic. Boston: Beacon Press, 1986.

I Am a Mathematician. by Norbert Wienen. Garden City, NY: Doubleday & Co., 1956.

I Want to Be Mathematician. by Paul R. Halmos. Washington, D.C.: MAA, 1985.

Incredible Pascal Triangle (Boston College Math Inst. Booklet 11). by Margaret Kenney. Chestnut Hill, MA: Boston College Press, 1976.

Index of the American Mathematical Monthly. by Kenneth O. May. Washington, D.C.: MAA, 1977.

Induction and Analogy in Mathematics. by George Pólya. Princeton, NJ: Princeton Univ. Press, 1954.

Infinite Sequences and Series. by K. Knopp. New York: Dover Publications, 1956.

Informal Geometry Explorations. by Margaret J. Kenney, Stanley J. Bezuszka, and Joan D. Mastin. Palo Alto, CA: Dale Seymour Publications, 1992.

Information Theory: Saving Bits. by William Sacco, Wayne Copes, Clifford Sloyer, and Robert Stark. Providence, RI: Janson Publications, 1987.

Innumeracy. by John Paulos. New York: Hill & Wang, 1988.

Instant Paper Airplanes. by E. Richard Churchill. New York: Sterling Publishing Co., 1988.

Intelligence Games. by Franco Agostini, and Nicola Alberto De Carlo. New York: Fireside Books, 1985.

Introduction to Difference Equations. by Samuel I. Goldberg. New York: John Wiley & Sons, 1958.

Introduction to Elementary Mathematical Logic. by Abram Aronovich Stolyar. New York: Dover Publications, 1970.

Introduction to Fibonacci Discovery. by Brother Alfred Brousseau. Santa Clara, CA: Fibonacci Assoc., 1965.

Introduction to Line Designs. by Dale Seymour. Palo Alto, CA: Dale Seymour Publications, 1992.

Introduction to Logic. 5th ed. by Irving M. Copi, and Keith Emerson Ballard. New York: Macmillan, 1978.

Introduction to Mathematical Reasoning. by Boris Iglewicz, and Judith Stoyle. New York: Macmillan, 1973.

Introduction to Operations Research. by Frederick S. Hillier. and Gerald J. Lieberman. New York: McGraw-Hill, 1980.

Introduction to Optical Art. by Cyril Barrett. New York: E. P. Dutton & Co., 1971.

Introduction to Tensegrity. by Anthony Pugh. Berkeley, CA: Univ. of California Press, 1976.

Introduction to Tessellations. by Dale Seymour, and Jill Britton. Palo Alto, CA: Dale Seymour Publications, 1989.

Introduction to the History of Mathematics. by Howard Eves. New York: Holt, Reinhart and Winston, 1964.

Introduction to the Theory of Numbers. by G. H. Hardy. and E. M. Wright. Oxford: Oxford Univ. Press, 1980.

Introductory Calculus. by Stan Dolan, et al. New York: Cambridge Univ. Press, 1990.

Inversions. by Scott Kim. New York: W. H. Freeman, 1989.

Investigating Mathematics with the TI-81. by David Williams, and Thomas Scott. Sunnyvale, CA: Stokes Publishing, 1993.

Invitation to Mathematics. by Norman Gowar. Oxford, England: Oxford Univ. Press, 1979.

Invitation to Number Theory. by Ore Oystein. Washington, D.C.: MAA, 1967.

Invitation to Statistics. by Gavin Kennedy. New York: Basil Blackwell, 1983.

Irascible Genius; the Life of Charles Babbage. by Mabeth Moseley. Chicago: Henry Regnery Co., 1964.

Islamic Patterns: An Analytical and Cosmological Approach. by Keith Critchlow. New York: Shocken Books, 1976.

Islands of Truth: A Mathematical Mystery Cruise. by Ivars Peterson. New York: W. H. Freeman, 1990.

It's All Done with Numbers. by Rose Wyler, and Gerald Ames. Garden City, NY: Doubleday & Co., 1979.

Japanese Abacus Explained. by Yozo Yoshino. New York: Dover Publications, 1963.

Japanese Optical and Geometric Art. by Hajime Ouchi. New York: Dover Publications, 1977.

Journey Through Genius: The Great Theorems of Mathematics. by William Dunham. New York: John Wiley & Sons, 1990.

Joy of Mathematics. by Theoni Pappas. San Carlos, CA: Wide World Publishing/Tetra, 1986.

Kaleidometrics. by Sheilah Shaw. Norfolk, England: Tarquin Publications, 1981.

Kaleidoscope Math. by Joe Kennedy, and Diane Thomas. Oak Lawn, IL: Creative Publications, 1978.

Kaleidoscopic Designs and How to Create Them. by Leslie Finkel. New York: Dover Publications, 1980.

Kites for Everyone. by Margaret Greger. Richmond, WA: M. Gregor, 1984.

Knotted Doughnuts and Other Mathematical Entertainments. by Martin Gardner. New York: W. H. Freeman, 1986.

Kusudama: Ball Origami. by Makato Yamaguchi. New York: Japan Publications, 1990.

Lady Luck: The Theory of Probability. by Warren Weaver. New York: Dover Publications, 1982.

Language of Pattern. by Keith Albarn, et al. New York: Harper & Row, 1974.

Learning by Discovery: A Lab Manual for Calculus. by Anita Solow, ed. Washington, D.C.: MAA, 1993.

Lesson in Mathematical Doodling (Boston College Math Inst. Booklet. 12). by Margaret Kenney. Chestnut Hill, MA: Boston College Press, 1976.

Letterforms and Illusion. by Scott Kim. New York: W. H. Freeman, 1989.

Life of Benjamin Banneker. by Silvio Bedini. New York: Charles Scribner & Sons, 1972.

Line Designs. by Dale Seymour, Joyce Snider, and Linda Silvey. Oak Lawn, IL: Creative Publications, 1974.

Linear Programming. by Bernadette Perham, and Arnold Perham. Menlo Park, CA: Addison-Wesley Innovative Learning Publications, 1993.

Little Book of Big Primes. by Paulo Ribenboim. New York: Springer-Verlag, 1991.

Living with Uncertainty. by Stan Dolan, et al. New York: Cambridge Univ. Press, 1991.

Logic and Boolean Algebra. by Kathleen Levitz, and Hilbert Levitz. Woodbury, NY: Barron's Educational Series, 1979.

Logic for Beginners. by Irving Adler. New York: John Day Co., 1964.

Logo and Models of Computation. by Michael Burke, and Roland Genise. Reading, MA: Addison-Wesley Publishing Co., 1987.

Long Way from Euclid. by Constance Reid. New York: T. Y. Crowell, 1963.

Lore of Large Numbers. by Philip Davis. Washington, D.C.: MAA, 1961.

Lure of the Integers. by Joe Roberts. Washington, D.C.: MAA, 1992.

M. C. Escher: Art and Science. by H. S. M. Coxeter, M. Emmer, R. Penrose, and M. L. Teuber, eds. New York: North-Holland, 1986.

Magic Cylinder Book. by Ivan Moscovich. Norfolk, England: Tarquin Publications, 1988.

Magic Mirror of M. C. Escher. by Bruno Ernst. Norfolk, England: Tarquin Publications, 1985.

Magic Mirror: An Antique Optical Toy. by McLoughlin Brothers staff. New York: Dover Publications, 1979.

Magic Numbers of Dr. Matrix. by Martin Gardner. Buffalo, NY: Prometheus Books, 1985.

Magic of Numbers. by Paul Emekwulu. Norman, OK: Novelty Books, 1993.

Magic Squares and Cubes. by W. S. Andrews. New York: Dover Publications, 1960.

Make Moving Patterns. by Tim Armstrong. Norfolk, England: Tarquin Publications, 1982.

Make Shapes. Books 1–3. by Gerald Jenkins, and Anne Wild. Norfolk, England: Tarquin Publications, 1990.

Making Connections with Mathematics. by John Egsgard, et al. Providence, RI: Janson Publications, 1988.

Making of Statisticians. by J. Gani. New York: Springer-Verlag, 1982.

Man and Number. by Donald Smeltzer. Buchanan, NY: Emerson Books, 1958.

Man and the Computer. by John G. Kemeny. New York: Charles Scribner & Sons, 1972.

Man Who Knew Infinity: Ramanujan. by Robert Kanigel. New York: Charles Scribner & Sons, 1991.

Manual of Greek Mathematics. by Thomas L. Heath. New York: Dover Publications, 1931.

Map-Coloring, Polyhedra, and the Four-Color Problem. by David Barnette. Washington, D.C.: MAA, 1983.

Markov Chain Theory. by Bernadette Perham, and Arnold Perham. Menlo Park, CA: Addison-Wesley Innovative Learning Publications, 1993.

Math and Music: Harmonius Connections. by Trudi Garland, and Charity Kahn. Palo Alto, CA: Dale Seymour Publications, 1994.

Math Art Posters. by Andria Troutman, and Sonia Forseth. Palo Alto, CA: Creative Publications, 1973.

Math Equals: Biographies of Women Mathematicians. by Teri Perl. Menlo Park, CA: Addison-Wesley Publishing Co., 1978.

Math Magic. by Scott Flansburg. New York: William Morrow & Co., 1993.

Math Projects for Young Scientists. by David A. Thomas. New York: Franklin Watts, 1988.

Math Space Mission. by Katherine Merseth, dir. Palo Alto, CA: Dale Seymour Publications, 1987.

Math-Computer Connection. by David A. Thomas. New York: Franklin Watts, 1986.

Mathemagics. by Arthur Benjamin, and Michael Shermer. Los Angeles: Lowell House, 1993.

Mathematical Career of Pierre de Fermat, 1601–1665. by Michael S. Mahoney. Princeton, NJ: Princeton Univ. Press, 1973.

Mathematical Carnival. by Martin Gardner. Washington, D. C.: MAA, 1989.

Mathematical Curiosities. Books 1–3. by Gerald Jenkins, and Anne Wild. Norfolk, England: Tarquin Publications, 1989.

Mathematical Discovery: On Understanding, Learning, and Teaching Problem Solving. by George Pólya. New York: John Wiley & Sons, 1981.

Mathematical Diversions. by J. A. H. Hunter, and Joseph S. Madachy. New York: Dover Publications, 1975.

Mathematical Experience. by Philip J. Davis, and Reuben Hirsh. Cambridge, MA: Birkhäuser, 1981.

Mathematical Fallacies and Paradoxes. by Bryan H. Bunch. New York: Van Nostrand Reinhold, 1982.

Mathematical Gems II. by Ross Honsberger. Washington, D.C.: MAA, 1976.

Mathematical Induction. by Leon Henkin. Washington, D.C.: MAA, Film.

Mathematical Investigations. Book 1. by Randall Souviney, et al. Palo Alto, CA: Dale Seymour Publications, 1990.

Mathematical Investigations. Book 2. by Randall Souviney, et al. Palo Alto, CA: Dale Seymour Publications, 1992.

Mathematical Investigations. Book 3. by Randall Souviney, et al. Palo Alto, CA: Dale Seymour Publications, 1992.

Mathematical Look at the Calendar. by Richard L. Francis. Arlington, MA: COMAP, 1988.

Mathematical Magic Show. by Martin Gardner. Washington, D.C.: MAA, 1990.

Mathematical Methods. by Stan Dolan, et al. New York: Cambridge Univ. Press, 1992.

Mathematical Models. by H. Martyn Cundy, and A. P. Rollett. New York: Oxford Univ. Press, 1961.

Mathematical Mystery Tour. by Mark Wahl. Tucson, AZ: Zephyr Press, 1988.

Mathematical Paradoxes. by Movshovitz-Hadar, and Webb. Dedham, MA: Janson Publications, 1994.

Mathematical People. by Donald J. Albers, and G. L. Alexanderson. Chicago: Contemporary Books, 1985.

Mathematical Principles. by Issac Newton. Berkeley, CA: Univ. of California Press, 1934. Translation.

Mathematical Proof: An Elementary Approach. by Arthur E. Hallerberg. New York: Hafner Press, 1974.

Mathematical Puzzles and Other Brain Twisters. by Anthony S. Filipiak. New York: Bell Publishing Co., 1942.

Mathematical Puzzling. by A. Gardiner. New York: Oxford Univ. Press, 1987.

Mathematical Recreations and Essays. by W. W. Rouse Ball, and H. S. M. Coxeter. Toronto, Canada: Univ. of Toronto Press, 1974.

Mathematical Scientists at Work. 1st & 2d eds. by MAA staff. Washington, D.C.: MAA, 1992.

Mathematical Snapshots. by M. Steinhaus. New York: Oxford Univ. Press, 1969.

Mathematical Theory of Elections. by Joseph Malkevitch, and Gary Froelich. Arlington, MA: COMAP, 1989.

Mathematical Thought from Ancient to Modern Times. 3 Vols. by Morris Kline. New York: Oxford Univ. Press, 1972.

Mathematical Topics for Computer Instruction. by Harris Schultz, and William Leonard. Palo Alto, CA: Dale Seymour Publications, 1990.

Mathematical Tourist. by Ivars Peterson. New York: W. H. Freeman, 1988.

Mathematical Visions. by Joan L. Richards. Boston: Academic Press, 1988.

Mathematician's Coloring Book. by Richard Francis. Arlington, MA: COMAP, 1989.

Mathematician's Delight. by W. W. Sawyer. Baltimore, MD: Penguin Books, 1943.

Mathematicians Are People, Too. Vol. 1. by Luetta Reimer, and Wilbert Reimer. Palo Alto, CA: Dale Seymour Publications, 1990.

Mathematicians Are People, Too. Vol. 2. by Luetta Reimer, and Wilbert Reimer. Palo Alto, CA: Dale Seymour Publications, 1994.

Mathematics. by David Bergamini. Alexandria, VA: Time-Life Books, 1980.

Mathematics and Measurement. by O. A. W. Dilke. Berkeley, CA: Univ. of California Press, 1987.

Mathematics and Medicine: How Serious Is the Injury? by William Sacco, et al. Providence, RI: Janson Publications, 1987.

Mathematics and Optimal Form. by Stefan Hildebrandt, and Anthony Tromba. New York: W. H. Freeman, 1985.

Mathematics and the Imagination. by Edward Kasner, and James R. Newman. Redmond, WA: Tempus Books, 1989.

Mathematics and the Search for Knowledge. by Morris Kline. Oxford, England: Oxford Univ. Press, 1985.

Mathematics Appreciation. by Theoni Pappas. San Carlos, CA: Wide World Publishing/Tetra, 1986.

Mathematics Books: Recommendations for High School and Public Libraries. by Lynn Arthur Steen, ed. Washington, D.C.: MAA, 1992.

Mathematics Dictionary and Handbook. by Eugene D. Nichols, and Sharon L. Schwartz. Hondale, PA: Nichols Schwartz Publishing Co., 1993.

Mathematics Dictionary. 5th ed. by Glenn James, and Robert James. New York: Van Nostrand Reinhold Co., 1992.

Mathematics Encyclopedia. by Max S. Shapiro, ed. Garden City, NY: Doubleday & Co., 1977.

Mathematics for the Millions. by Lancelot Hogben. New York: W. W. Norton, 1967.

Mathematics Illustrated Dictionary. by Jeanne Bendick, and Marcia Levin. New York: McGraw-Hill, 1965.

Mathematics in the Making. by Lancelot Hogben. New York: Doubleday & Co., 1960.

Mathematics in the Time of the Pharaohs. by Richard J. Gillings. Cambridge, MA: MIT Press, 1972.

Mathematics in Western Culture. by Morris Kline. Oxford, England: Oxford Univ. Press, 1978.

Mathematics Magazine: 50 Year Index. by J. Arthur Seebach, and Lynn Arthur Steen, eds. Washington, D.C.: MAA, 1978.

Mathematics of Choice or How to Count Without Counting. by Ivan M. Niven. Washington, D.C.: MAA, 1975.

Mathematics of Conflict. by Frank C. Zagare. Arlington, MA: COMAP, 1989.

Mathematics of Gambling. by Edward O. Thorp. Secaucus, NJ: Lyle Stuart, 1984.

Mathematics of Games and Gambling. by Edward Packel. Washington, D.C.: MAA, 1981.

Mathematics of Great Amateurs. by Julian Lowell Coolidge. New York: Dover Publications, 1963.

Mathematics of Sonya Kovalevskaya. by G. Cantor. New York: Springer-Verlag, 1984.

Mathematics Projects Handbook. by Adrien Hess, Glenn Allinger, and Lyle Andersen. Reston, VA: NCTM, 1989.

Mathematics Sampler: Topics for the Liberal Arts. by William Berlinghoff, and Kerry Grant. New York: Ardsley House, 1992.

Mathematics Teacher Resource Handbook. by Dan Dolan, ed. Millwood, NY: Kraus International Publications, 1993.

Mathematics Teacher: Cumulative Indices. by NCTM. Reston, VA: NCTM, 1984.

Mathematics Through Paper Folding. by Alton T. Olson. Reston, VA: NCTM, 1975.

Mathematics Today. by Lynn Arthur Steen, ed. New York: Springer-Verlag, 1978.

Mathematics with Applications in Management and Economics. by Earl K. Bowen, Gordon D. Prichett, and John C. Saber. Homewood, IL: Richard D. Irwin, 1987.

Mathematics, Magic, and Mystery. by Martin Gardner. New York: Dover Publications, 1956.

Mathematics: Ideas and Applications. by Daniel D. Benice. New York: Academic Press, 1978.

Mathematics: The New Golden Age. by Keith Devlin. London: Penguin Books, 1988.

Mathographics. by Robert Dixon. New York: Dover Publications, 1987.

Matrices. by Department of Mathematics and Computer Science. North Carolina School of Science and Mathematics. Reston, VA: NCTM, 1988.

Matrix Theory. by Bernadette Perham, and Arnold Perham. Menlo Park, CA: Addison-Wesley Innovative Learning Publications, 1993.

Measuring Earthquakes. by Nancy Cook. Menlo Park, CA: Addison-Wesley Innovative Learning Publications, 1994.

Memorabilia Mathematica: The Philomaths Quotation Book. by Robert O. Moritz. Washington, D.C.: MAA, 1942.

Men of Mathematics. by E. T. Bell. New York: Simon & Schuster, 1965.

Metamorphosis. by Lorraine Mottershead. Palo Alto, CA: Dale Seymour Publications, 1977.

Metric for Me. by Robert Shoemaker. South Beloit, IL: Blackhawk Publishing, 1993.

Metric Manual. by Lawrence Pedde, et al. Washington, D.C.: U.S. Government Printing Office, 1978.

Milestones in Geometry. by Jay Stepelman. New York: Macmillan, 1970.

Mind Benders: Games of Shape. by Ivan Moscovich. New York: Penguin Books, 1986.

Mind over Math. by Stanley Kogelman, and Joseph Warren. New York: McGraw-Hill, 1978.

Mind Sights. by Roger Shepard. New York: W. H. Freeman, 1990.

Mind Tools. by Rudy Rucker. Boston: Houghton Mifflin Co., 1987.

Mind's Eye: Imagery in Everyday Life. by Robert Sommer. Palo Alto, CA: Dale Seymour Publications, 1978.

Mindset for Math. by Judy Genshaft, and Jack Naglieri. Newton, MA: Education Development Center, 1987.

Mira Activities for High School. by Norm Gillespie. Toronto, CA: Mira Math Co., 1973.

Möbius and His Band: Mathematics and Astronomy in Nineteenth-Century Germany. by John Fauvel, Raymond Flood, and Robin Wilson. New York: Oxford Univ. Press, 1993.

Modeling with Circular Motion. by Stan Dolan, et al. New York: Cambridge Univ. Press, 1992.

Modeling with Force and Motion. by Stan Dolan, et al. New York: Cambridge Univ. Press, 1992.

Monte Carlo Methods. by J. M. Hammersly, and D. C. Handscomb. New York: John Wiley & Sons, 1964.

More Mathematical People. by D. Albers, G. Alexanderson, and C. Reid. San Diego, CA: Harcourt Brace Javanovich, 1990.

More Self-Working Card Tricks. by Karl Fulves. New York: Dover Publications, 1984.

Multicultural Mathematics. by David Nelson, George Joseph, and Julian Williams. New York: Oxford Univ. Press, 1993.

Multiculturism in Mathematics, Science, and Technology. by Thom Alcoze, et al. Menlo Park, CA: Addison-Wesley Publishing Co., 1993.

Mystery of Numbers. by Annemarie Schimmel. New York: Oxford Univ. Press, 1992.

Naive Set Theory. by Paul R. Halmos. New York: Springer-Verlag, 1974.

National Conference on Women in Math and the Sciences. by Sandra Keith, and Philip Keith. St. Cloud, MN: St. Cloud University, 1990.

Native American Mathematics. by M. F. Closs. Austin, TX: Univ. of Texas Press, 1986.

Navigation. by William Swart. Mt. Pleasant, MI: Tricon Mathematics, 1992.

NCEER Interim Bibliography of Earthquake Education Materials. by Kathryn Ross. Washington, D.C.: NSTA & FEMA, 1989.

Never at Rest: A Biography of Isaac Newton. by Richard S. Westfall. New York: Cambridge Univ. Press, 1983.

New Ambidextrous Universe. by Martin Gardner. New York: W. H. Freeman, 1990.

New Books of Puzzles: 101 Classic and Modern Puzzles to Make and Solve. by Jerry Slocum, and Jack Botermans. New York: W. H. Freeman, 1992.

New Origami. by Steve Biddle, and Megumi Biddle. New York: St. Martin's Press, 1993.

New Recreations with Magic Squares. by William H. Benson, and Oswald Jacoby. New York: Dover Publications, 1976.

Newton's Laws of Motion. by Stan Dolan, et al. New York: Cambridge Univ. Press, 1992.

Normal Distribution. by Stan Dolan, et al. New York: Cambridge Univ. Press, 1992.

Number Theory. by André Weil. Cambridge, MA: Birkhäuser, 1984.

Number Treasury. by Stanley Bezuszka, and Margaret Kenney. Palo Alto, CA: Dale Seymour Publications, 1982.

Number Words and Number Symbols: A Cultural History of Numbers. by Karl Menninger. Cambridge, MA: MIT Press, 1977.

Number: The History of Numbers and How They Shape Our Lives. by John McLeish. New York: Ballantine, 1991.

Numbers: Rational and Irrational. by Ivan Niven. Washington, D.C.: MAA, 1961.

Numbers: Their History and Meaning. by Graham Flegg. New York: Schocken Books, 1983.

150 Puzzles in Crypt-Arithmetic. by Maxey Brooke. New York: Dover Publications, 1969.

On the Shoulders of Giants. by Lynn A. Steen. Washington, D.C.: National Academy Press, 1990.

Op-Tricks: Creating Kinetic Art. by Mickey Klar Marks, and Edith Alberts. Philadelphia, PA: J. B. Lippincott Co., 1972.

Optical Designs in Motion with Moiré Overlays. by Carol Belanger Grafton. New York: Dover Publications, 1976.

Order in Space. by Keith Critchlow. New York: Viking Press, 1969.

Origami Boxes. by Tomoko Fusé. New York: Japan Publications, 1989.

Origami, Plain and Simple. by Robert Neale, and Thomas Hull. New York: St. Martin's Press, 1994.

Out of the Mouths of Mathematicians: A Quotation Book for Philomaths. by Rosemary Schmalz. Washington, D.C.: MAA, 1993.

Outstanding Women in Mathematics and Science. by National Women's History Project. Windsor, CA: National Women's History Project, 1991.

Ox. by Piers Anthony. New York: Avon, 1976.

Panorama of Numbers. by Robert J. Wisner. Glenview, IL: Scott, Foresman, & Co., 1970.

Paper and Scissors Polygons and More. by Linda Silvey, and Loretta Taylor. Palo Alto, CA: Dale Seymour Publications, 1995.

Paper Capers. by Jack Botermans. New York: Henry Holt & Co., 1986.

Paper Engineering for Pop-Up Books and Cards. by Mark Hiner. Norfolk, England: Tarquin Publications, 1985.

Paper Folding for Beginners. by William D. Murray, and Francis J. Rigney. New York: Dover Publications, 1960.

Paper Magic: Pop-Up Paper Craft. by Masahiro Chatani. Tokyo: Ondorisha Publishing, 1988.

Pascal's Triangle. by Thomas M. Green, and Charles L. Hamberg. Palo Alto, CA: Dale Seymour Publications, 1986.

Patterns in Nature. by Peter S. Stevens. Boston: Little, Brown & Co., 1974.

Patterns in Space. by Robert S. Beard. Palo Alto, CA: Creative Publications, 1973.

Patty Paper Geometry. by Michael Serra. Berkeley, CA: Key Curriculum Press, 1994.

Penguin Dictionary of Curious and Interesting Numbers. by David Wells. New York: Penguin Books, 1986.

Penrose Tiles to Trapdoor Ciphers. by Martin Gardner. New York: W. H. Freeman, 1989.

Perfect Numbers (Boston College Math Inst. Booklet 3). by Stanley Bezuszka, et al. Chestnut Hill, MA: Boston College Press, 1980.

Perfect Numbers. by Richard W. Shoemaker. Reston, VA: NCTM, 1973.

Perplexing Puzzles and Tantalizing Teasers. by Martin Gardner. New York: Dover Publications, 1969.

Perspective Drawing with the Geometer's Sketchpad. by Cathi Sanders. Berkeley, CA: Key Curriculum Press, 1995.

Perspective. by Alison Cole. New York: Dorling Kindersley, 1992.

Perspectives on Women and Mathematics. by Judith E. Jacobs, ed. Columbus, OH: Ohio State Univ., 1978.

Pi in the Sky. by Robert Pethoud. Tucson, AZ: Zephr Press, 1993.

Platonic Solids Activity Book. by Schmalzried Fetter, Eckert, Schattschneider, and Klotz. Berkeley, CA: Key Curriculum Press, 1991.

Playing with Infinity: Mathematical Explorations and Excursions. by Rózsa Péter. New York: Dover Publications, 1961.

Pólya Picture Album: Encounters of a Mathematician. by G. L. Alexanderson. Cambridge, MA: Birkhäuser, 1987.

Polyhedra Blocks. by Dale Seymour. Palo Alto, CA: Dale Seymour Publications, 1994.

Polyhedra Primer. by Peter Pearce. Palo Alto, CA: Dale Seymour Publications, 1978.

Polyhedra: A Visual Approach. by Anthony Pugh. Palo Alto, CA: Dale Seymour Publications, 1990.

Polyhedron Models. by Magnus J. Wenninger. New York: Cambridge Univ. Press, 1970.

Polyominoes. by Solomon W. Golomb. New York: Charles Scribner & Sons, 1965.

Polyominoes: A Guide to Puzzles and Problems in Tiling. by George E. Martin. Washington, D.C.: MAA, 1991.

Polysymetrics. by June Oliver. Norfolk, England: Tarquin Publications, 1979.

Pop-Up Greeting Cards. by Masahiro Chatani. New York: Ondorisha Publishing, 1986.

Portraits for Classroom Bulletin Boards Mathematicians. Book 1. by Susan Edeen, and John Edeen. Palo Alto, CA: Dale Seymour Publications, 1988.

Portraits for Classroom Bulletin Boards Mathematicians. Book 2. by Susan Edeen, and John Edeen. Palo Alto, CA: Dale Seymour Publications, 1988.

Portraits for Classroom Bulletin Boards Women Mathematicians. by Susan Edeen, and John Edeen. Palo Alto, CA: Dale Seymour Publications, 1990.

Power of Mathematics. by Moshe Flato. New York: McGraw-Hill, 1990.

Powers of Ten. by Philip Morrison, and Phylis Morrison. New York: W. H. Freeman, 1982.

Practical Conic Sections. by J. W. Downs. Palo Alto, CA: Dale Seymour Publications, 1993.

Prelude to Mathematics. by W. W. Sawyer. New York: Dover Publications, 1982.

Primer for the Fibonacci Numbers. by Marjorie Bicknell, and Verner E. Hoggatt. Santa Clara, CA: Fibonacci Assoc., 1972.

Probabilities in Everyday Life. by John D. McGervey. New York: Ivy Books, 1986.

Probability Without Tears: A Primer for Non-Mathematicians. by Derek Rowntree. New York: Charles Scribner & Sons, 1984.

Problem Solving Using Graphs. by Margaret B. Cozzens, and Richard D. Porter. Arlington, MA: COMAP, 1987.

Problem Solving with Ominoes. by Donald D. Paige. Palo Alto, CA: Dale Seymour Publications, 1987.

Problems of Mathematics. by Ian Stewart. New York: Oxford Univ. Press, 1992.

Programming the TI-81 & TI-85 Graphing Calculator to Explore Mathematics. by Brendan Kelly. Burlington, Ontario: Brendan Kelly Publishing, 1992.

Projects to Enrich School Mathematics: Level 2 and Level 3. by Leroy Sachs, ed. Reston, VA: NCTM, 1988.

Puzzle Craft. by Stewart T. Coffin. Lincoln, MA: Stewart T. Coffin, 1985.

Puzzle It Out: Cubes, Groups, and Puzzles. by John Ewing, and Czes Kosinowski. Cambridge, England: Univ. of Cambridge Press, 1982.

Puzzles Old and New. by Jerry Slocum, and Jack Boterman. Seattle, WA: Univ. of Washington Press, 1987.

Puzzling World of Polyhedral Dissections. by Stewart T. Coffin. New York: Oxford Univ. Press, 1991.

Pythagorean Proposition. by Elisha Scott Loomis. Reston, VA: NCTM, 1968.

Pythagorean Theorem: Eight Classic Proofs. by Sidney J. Kolpas. Palo Alto, CA: Dale Seymour Publications, 1992.

Queues: Will This Wait Never End! by William Sacco, Wayne Copes, Clifford Sloyer, and Robert Stark. Providence, RI: Janson Publications, 1987.

Ramanujan. by G. H. Hardy. New York: Chelsea Publishing Company, 1978.

Rapid Math Tricks and Tips. by Edward H. Julius. New York: John Wiley & Sons, 1992.

Rapid Math Without a Calculator. by A. Frederick Collins. Secaucus, NJ: Citadel Press, 1987.

Reading, Writing, and Doing Math Proofs: Advanced Math. by Daniel Solow. Palo Alto, CA: Dale Seymour Publications, 1984.

Reading, Writing, and Doing Math Proofs: Proof Techniques for Geometry. by Daniel Solow. Palo Alto, CA: Dale Seymour Publications, 1984.

Readings for Calculus. by Underwood Dudley, ed. Washington, D.C.: MAA, 1993.

Readings in Decision Analysis. by Simon French. New York: Chapman and Hall, 1989.

Realm of Numbers. by Isaac Asimov. Boston: Houghton Mifflin, 1959.

Recent Revolutions in Mathematics. by Albert Stwertk. New York: Franklin Watts, 1987.

Recreational Problems in Geometric Dissections & How to Solve Them. by Harry Lindgren. New York: Dover Publications, 1972.

Recurrence Relations: "Counting Backwards." by Margaret Cozzens, and Richard Porter. Arlington, MA: COMAP, 1989.

Regular Polytopes. by H. S. M. Coxeter. London: Methuen & Co., 1947.

Relativity and Common Sense. by H. Bondi. Garden City, NY: Doubleday & Co., 1964.

Renaissance Patterns for Lace, Embroidery, and Needlepoint. by Federico Vinciolo. New York: Dover Publications, 1971.

René's Place: Exploring Euclidean Geometry. by L. Roland Genise, Ronald Genise, and Michael E. Burke. Menlo Park, CA: Addison-Wesley Innovative Learning Publications, 1993.

Rhind Mathematical Papyrus. by A. B. Chace, ed. Reston, VA: NCTM, 1979.

Rhythmic Approach to Mathematics. by Edith L. Somerveil. Reston, VA: NCTM, 1906.

Riddles of the Sphinx and Other Mathematical Puzzle Tales. by Martin Gardner. Washington, D.C.: MAA, 1988.

Role of Mathematics in Science. by M. M. Schiffer, and L. Bowden. Washington, D.C.: MAA, 1984.

Rubik's Cube: The Ideal Solution. by Ideal Toy staff. Hollis, NY: Ideal Toy Corporation, 1980.

Sampler on Sampling. by Bill Williams. New York: John Wiley & Sons, 1978.

Science in Ancient China. by George Beshore. New York: Franklin Watts, 1988.

Science in Ancient Egypt. by Geraldine Woods. New York: Franklin Watts, 1988.

Science in Ancient Mesopotamia. by Carol Moss. New York: Franklin Watts, 1988.

Science of Moiré Patterns. by Gerald Oster. Barrington, NJ: Edmund Scientific Co., 1969.

Science of Soap Films and Soap Bubbles. by Cyril Isenberg. New York: Dover Publications, 1978.

Search for Pattern. by W. W. Sawyer. Baltimore, MD: Penguin Books, 1970.

Self-Working Number Magic. by Karl Fulves. New York: Dover Publications, 1983.

Sequences. by H. Halberstam, and K. F. Roth. New York: Springer-Verlag, 1983.

Sequencing and Scheduling. by Simon French. New York: John Wiley & Sons, 1982.

Shape of Space. by Jeffrey R. Weeks. New York: Marcel Dekker, 1985.

Shapes, Space, and Symmetry. by Alan Holden. New York: Columbia Univ. Press, 1971.

Short Account of the History of Mathematics. by W. W. Rouse Ball. New York: Dover Publications, 1980.

Short-Cut. by Gerard W. Kelly. New York: Dover Publications, 1984.

Silver Burdett Mathematical Dictionary. by R. E. Jason Abdelnoon. Morristown, NJ: Silver Burdett & Ginn, 1979.

Similarity. by Tom Apostal. Pasadena, CA: California Institute of Technology, 1990. Video and Guide.

Sines and Cosines. Parts I and II. by Tom Apostol. Reston, VA: NCTM. Video.

Sliding-Piece Puzzles: Recreations in Mathematics. by L. E. Hordern. New York: Oxford Univ. Press, 1986.

Snow Crystals: 2453 Illustrations. by W. A. Bentley, and W. J. Humphreys. New York: Dover Publications, 1931.

Soap Bubbles: Their Colors and the Forces That Mold Them. by C. V. Boys. New York: Dover Publications, 1959.

Some Prime Comparisons. by Stephen I. Brown. Reston, VA: NCTM, 1978.

Sonya Kovalevsky. by Carole Greenes. Providence, RI: Janson Publications, 1989.

Source Book of Problems for Geometry. by Mabel Sykes, 1912. Reprint, Palo Alto, CA: Dale Seymour Publications, 1994.

Space Mathematics: NASA. by Bernice Kastner. Palo Alto, CA: Dale Seymour Publications, 1987.

Sphereland. by Dionys Burger. New York: Harper & Row, 1965.

Spheres and Satellites. by William B. Martin. Arlington, MA: COMAP, 1988.

Spherical Models. by Magnus J. Wenninger. New York: Cambridge Univ. Press, 1979.

Spreadsheets in Math and Science Technology. by John Whitmer. Bowling Green, OH: School Science & Math Assoc., 1992.

Star Mosaics. by Jonathan Quintin. Palo Alto, CA: Dale Seymour Publications, 1993.

Statistical Abstract of the United States. by Glen King, et al. Washington, D.C.: U.S. Government Printing Office, 1993.

Statistical Thinking. 2d ed. by John L. Phillips Jr. New York: W. H. Freeman, 1982.

Statistics by Example: Weighing Chances. by Frederick Mosteller, et al. Menlo Park, CA: Addison-Wesley Innovative Learning Publications, 1973.

Statistics Without Tears: A Primer for Non-Mathematicians. by Derek Rowntree. New York: Charles Scribner & Sons, 1982.

Statistics: A Guide to the Unknown. by Judith Tanur, et al. Pacific Grove, CA: Wadsworth & Brooks/Cole, 1989.

Statistics: Concepts and Controversies. by David S. Moore. New York: W. H. Freeman, 1991.

Stella Octangula Activity Book. by Hilary Brest, et al. Berkeley, CA: Key Curriculum Press, 1991.

Story of Mathematics. by Lloyd Motz, and Jefferson Weaver. New York: Plenum Press, 1993.

Story of Pi. by Tom Apostol. Pasadena, CA: California Institute of Technology, 1989. Video.

String Figures and How to Make Them. by Caroline Furness Jayne. New York: Dover Publications, 1962.

String Sculpture. by John Winter. Oak Lawn, IL: Creative Publications, 1972.

Structure in Nature Is a Source for Design. by Peter Pearce. Cambridge, MA: MIT Press, 1978.

Student Poster Projects: Winners of the 1991–1992 ASA Competition. by the Center for Statistical Education, ASA. Palo Alto, CA: Dale Seymour Publications, 1994.

Student Research Projects in Calculus. by Marcus Cohen, et al. Washington, D.C.: MAA, 1991.

Super Sum (Boston College Math Inst. Booklet 10). by Margaret Kenney. Chestnut Hill, MA: Boston College Press, 1976.

Surface Plane. by Martha Boles, and Rochelle Newman. Bradford, MA: Pythagorean Press, 1992.

Surprise Attack in Mathematical Problems. by L. A. Graham. New York: Dover Publications, 1968.

Symbolic Logic. by Lewis Carroll. New York: Clarkson N. Potter Publishers, 1977.

Symmetries of Culture: Theory and Practice of Plane Pattern Analysis. by Dorothy K. Washburn, and Donald W. Crowe. Seattle, WA: Univ. of Washington Press, 1988.

Symmetry in Chaos. by Michael Field, and Martin Golubitsky. New York: Oxford Univ. Press, 1992.

Symmetry in Science and Art. by A. V. Shubnikov, et al. New York: Plenum, 1974.

Symmetry Patterns. by Alan Wiltshire. Norfolk, England: Tarquin Publications, 1989.

Symmetry, Rigid Motions, and Patterns. by Donald Crowe. Arlington, MA: COMAP, 1986.

Symmetry. by Hermann Weyl. Princeton, NJ: Princeton Univ. Press, 1980.

Symmography: Linear Thread Design. by Laura Sarff, and Jan Harem. Worcester, MA: Davis Publications, 1979.

Synergetics: Explorations in the Geometry of Thinking. by R. Buckminister Fuller. New York: Macmillan, 1975.

Tamari Balls. by Mary Wood. Tunbridge Wells, England: Search Press, 1991.

Tangramath. by Dale Seymour. Oak Lawn, IL: Creative Publications, 1971.

Tangrams. by Joost Elffers, and Michael Schuyt. New York: Abrams, 1979.

Tangrams: 330 Puzzles. by Ronald Read. New York: Dover Publications, 1965.

Teaching Tessellating Art. by Jill Britton, and Walter Britton. Palo Alto, CA: Dale Seymour Publications, 1992.

Techniques in Finite Differences. by Dale Seymour, and Peg Shedd. Palo Alto, CA: Dale Seymour Publications, 1973.

Tessellations Using Logo. by Margaret J. Kenney, and Stanley Bezuszka. Palo Alto, CA: Dale Seymour Publications, 1987.

Tessellations: The Geometry of Patterns. by Stanley Bezuszka, Margaret Kenney, and Linda Silvey. Oak Lawn, IL: Creative Publications, 1977.

Theorem of Pythagoras. by Tom Apostol. Pasadena, CA: California Institute of Technology, 1988. Video.

Thinking Physics. by Lewis Carol Epstein. San Francisco: Insight Press, 1992.

13 Books of Euclid's Elements. by Thomas L. Heath, trans. New York: Dover Publications, 1956.

Thirteen Lectures on Fermat's Last Theorem. by Paulo Ribenboim. New York: Springer-Verlag, 1979.

This Amazingly Symmetrical World. by L. Tarasov. Moscow: Mir Publishers, 1986.

This Book Is About Time. by Marilyn Burns. Boston, MA: Little, Brown & Co., 1978.

Those Amazing Reciprocals. by Boyd Henry. Palo Alto, CA: Dale Seymour Publications, 1992.

Tilings and Patterns. by Branko Grunbaum, and G. C. Shephard. New York: W. H. Freeman, 1987.

Time Travel and Other Mathematical Bewilderness. by Martin Gardner. New York: W. H. Freeman, 1988.

Tinkertoy Computer. by A. K. Dewdney. New York: W. H. Freeman, 1993.

Topics for Mathematics Clubs. by LeRoy Dalton, and Henry Snyder. Reston, VA: NCTM, 1988.

Topics in Recreational Mathematics. by J. H. Cadwell. New York: Cambridge Univ. Press, 1966.

Trachenberg Speed System of Mathematics. by Ann Cutler. Westport, CT: Greenwood Press, 1960.

Transformational Geometry. by Richard G. Brown. Palo Alto, CA: Dale Seymour Publications, 1973.

Transition to Chaos. by Robert L. Devaney. New York: Science Television, 1990.

Triad Optical Illusions and How to Design Them. by Harry Turner. New York: Dover Publications, 1978.

Trisection Problem. by Robert Yates. Reston, VA: NCTM, 1971.

Turbulent Mirror. by John Briggs, and David Peat. New York: Harper & Row, 1989.

Turntable Illusions: Kinetic Optical Illusions for Your Turntable. by John Kremer. Fairfield IA: Open Horizons Publishing, 1992.

Ultimate Paper Airplane. by Richard Kline. New York: Fireside Books, 1985.

Uniform Approach to Rate and Ratio Problems. by James R. Rogers. Arlington, MA: COMAP, 1989.

Unit Origami: Multidimensional Transformations. by Tomoko Fusé. New York: Japan Publications, 1990.

Universal Encyclopedia of Mathematics. by James R. Newman. New York: Simon & Schuster, 1964.

Universal Patterns. by Martha Boles, and Rochelle Newman. Bradford, MA: Pythagorean Press, 1980.

Uses of Infinity. by Leo Zippin. Washington, D.C.: MAA, 1962.

Using the TI-81 Graphing Calculator to Explore Functions. by Brendan Kelly. Burlington, Ontario: Brendan Kelly Publishing, 1991.

Using the TI-81 Graphing Calculator to Explore Statistics. by Brendan Kelly. Burlington, Ontario: Brendan Kelly Publishing, 1992.

Visions of Symmetry: Notebooks, Periodic Drawings, and Related Works of M. C. Escher. by Doris Schattschneider. New York: W. H. Freeman, 1990.

Visual Display of Quantitative Information. by Edward R. Tufse. Cheshire, CT: Graphics Press, 1983.

Visual Illusions: Their Causes, Characteristics, and Applications. by M. Luckiesh. New York: Dover Publications, 1965.

Visual Patterns in Pascal's Triangle. by Dale Seymour. Palo Alto, CA: Dale Seymour Publications, 1986.

VNR Concise Encyclopedia of Mathematics. 2d ed. by W. Gellert, M. Hellwich, H. Kastner, and H. Kustner, eds. New York: Van Nostrand Reinhold Co., 1989.

Was Pythagoras Chinese? by Frank J. Swetz, and T. I. Kao. Reston, VA: NCTM, 1977.

Webster's New World Dictionary of Mathematics. by William Karush. New York: Simon & Schuster, 1989.

What Do You See? An Optical Illusion Slide Show. by Theoni Pappas. San Carlos, CA: Wide World Publishing/Tetra, 1989.

What Is Calculus About? by W. W. Sawyer. Washington, D.C.: MAA, 1961.

What Is Mathematics? by Richard Courant, and Herbert Robbins. London: Oxford Univ. Press, 1941.

Wheels, Life, and Other Mathematical Amusements. by Martin Gardner. New York: W. H. Freeman, 1983.

When Are We Ever Gonna Have to Use This? 3d ed. by Hal Saunders. Palo Alto, CA: Dale Seymour Publications, 1988.

Why Buildings Stand Up. by Mario Salvadori. New York: McGraw-Hill, 1980.

Wings and Things: Origami That Flies. by Stephen Weiss. New York: St. Martin's Press, 1984.

Winning with Statistics. by Richard Runyon. Reading, MA: Addison-Wesley Publishing Co., 1977.

Winning Women into Mathematics. by Patricia Clark Kenchaft, ed. Washington, D.C.: MAA, 1991.

Women and Numbers. by Teri Perl. San Carlos, CA: Wide World Publishing/Tetra, 1993.

Women in Mathematics. by Lynn M. Osen. Cambridge, MA: MIT Press, 1974.

Women of Mathematics. by Louise S. Grinstein, and Paul J. Campbell, eds. Westport, CT: Greenwood Press, 1987.

Women, Numbers, and Dreams. by Teri Perl, and Joan Manning. Sant Rosa, CA: National Women's History Project, 1982.

Wonder Square (Boston College Math Inst. Booklet 2). by Stanley Bezuszka, Lou D'Angelo, and Margaret Kenney. Chestnut Hill, MA: Boston College Press, 1976.

Wonders of Magic Squares. by Jim Moran. New York: Vintage Books, 1981.

World of M. C. Escher. by J. L. Locker. New York: Harry N. Abrams, 1971.

World of Mathematics. 4 vols. by James R. Newman. Redmond, WA: Tempus Books, 1988.

World's Most Famous Math Problem, Is It Solved? by Marilyn Vos Savant. New York: St. Martin's Press, 1993.

"Abstract Parabola Fits the Concrete World." by Martin Gardner. *Scientific American* (August 1981): 16–27.

"Acoustics of Harpsichord." by Edward C. Kotlick, Thomas J. Hendrickson, and Kenneth D. Marshall. *Scientific American* (February 1991): 110–5.

"Acoustics of Violin Plates." by Carleen Maley Hutchins. *Scientific American* (September 1981): 171–86.

"Albert Dürer's Renaissance Connections Between Mathematics and Art." by Karen Doyle Walton. *Mathematics Teacher* (April 1994): 278–82.

"Algebra and a Super Card Trick." by Edward J. Davis, and Ed Middlebrooks. *Mathematics Teacher* (May 1983): 326–8.

"Allocation of Resources by Linear Programming." by Robert G. Bland. *Scientific American* (June 1981): 126–45.

"'Almost' Diophantine Equation." by Edward D. Gaughan. *Mathematics Teacher* (May 1980).

"Alternative Perspective on the Optical Property of Ellipses." by Kenzo Seo. *Mathematics Teacher* (November 1986).

"American's Pastime" by James O. Watson. *Mathematics Teacher* (September 1993): 450–1.

"Analysis of a Truck Driver's Square Root Algorithm." by Lowell Carmony. *Mathematics Teacher* (February 1981): 144–9.

"Analysis of Two Car-Buying Strategies." by Paul Bland, and Betty Givan. *Mathematics Teacher* (February 1983): 124–7.

"Analyzing Energy and Resource Problems." by Joseph Fishman. *Mathematics Teacher* (November 1993): 628–33.

"Anamorphic Pictures." by Jearl Walker. *Scientific American* (July 1981): 176–87.

"Ancient Babylonian Mathematics." by Evan M. Malestsky. *Mathematics Teacher* (April 1976): 295–8.

"'Ancient/Modern' Proof of Heron's Formula." by William Dunham. *Mathematics Teacher* (April 1985): 258–9.

"Ancient Problem." by Peter Flusser. *Mathematics Teacher* (May 1981): 389–90.

"Angles of Elevation of the Pyramids of Egypt." by Arthur Smith. *Mathematics Teacher* (February 1982): 124–7.

"Another Look at the Quadratic Formula." by Dean D. Obermeyer. *Mathematics Teacher* (February 1982): 146–52.

"Anyone Can Trisect an Angle." by Hardy C. Reyerson. *Mathematics Teacher* (April 1977): 319–21.

"Application of Clock Arithmetic." by Paul A. White. *Mathematics Teacher* (November 1973): 645–7.

"Application of Number Theory to Cryptology." by Joanne R. Snow. *Mathematics Teacher* (January 1989): 18–26.

"Application of Quadratic Equations to Baseball." by Milton P. Eisner, *Mathematics Teacher* (May 1986): 327–30.

"Applying the Technique of Archimedes to the 'Birdcage' Problem." by W. A. Stannard. *Mathematics Teacher* (January 1979): 58–60.

"Apportionment Examples: An Application of Decimal Ordering." by Bonnie Litwiller, and David Duncan. *Mathematics Teacher* (February 1983): 89–91.

"Apportionment—A Decennial Problem." by John J. Sullivan. *Mathematics Teacher* (January 1982): 20–5.

"Approximation of Area Under a Curve." by James M. Sconyers. *Mathematics Teacher* (February 1984): 92–3.

"Archimedes and Pi." by Thomas W. Shilgalis. *Mathematics Teacher* (March 1989): 204–6.

"Archimedes' Pi—An Introduction to Iteration." by Richard Cotspeich. *Mathematics Teacher* (March 1988): 208–10.

"Architecture of Christopher Wren." by Harold Dorn, and Robert Mark. *Scientific American* (July 1981): 160–75.

"Are Seven-Game Baseball Playoffs Fairer?" by E. Lee May. *Mathematics Teacher* (October 1992): 528–31.

"Are Triangles That Have the Same Area and the Same Perimeter Congruent?" by Robert Prielipp. *Mathematics Teacher* (February 1974): 157–9.

"Area = Perimeter." by Lee Merkowitz. *Mathematics Teacher* (March 1981): 222–3.

"Area and Perimeter Connections." by Jane B. Kennedy. *Mathematics Teacher* (March 1993): 218–21, 231–2.

"Artist as a Mathematician." by Norman Slawsky. *Mathematics Teacher* (April 1977): 298–308.

"Artist's View of Points and Lines." by Richard Millman, and Romona Speranza. *Mathematics Teacher* (February 1991): 133.

"Astounding Revelation on the History of Pi." by Alfred S. Posamentier, and Naom Gordan. *Mathematics Teacher* (January 1984): 52, 47.

"Aztec Arithmetic: Positional Notation and Area Calculation." by H. R. Harvey, and B. J. Williams. *Science* (October 1980): 499–505.

"Babylonian Quadratics." by Robert D. McMillan. *Mathematics Teacher* (January 1984): 63–5.

"Bank Shot." by Dan Byrne. *Mathematics Teacher* (September 1986): 429–30.

"Baseball Monte Carlo Style." by Larry H. Houser. *Mathematics Teacher* (May 1981): 340–1.

"Baseball Schedule: A Modest Proposal." by John F. Kurtzke. *Mathematics Teacher* (May 1990): 346–50.

"Baseball Statistics." by Edwin F. Bickenbach. *Mathematics Teacher* (May 1979): 35–52.

"Benjamin Banneker, Pioneer Negro Mathematician." by T. F. Mulcrone. *Mathematics Teacher* (February 1976): 155–60.

"Beyond Rubik's Cube: Spheres, Pyramids, Dodecahedrons, and God Knows What Else." by Douglas R. Hofstadter. *Scientific American* (July 1982): 16–31.

"Beyond the Usual Constructions." by Melfried Olson. *Mathematics Teacher* (May 1980): 361–4.

"Binomial Coefficients and the Partitioning of N-Dimensional Space." by Richard Crouse. *Mathematics Teacher* (November 1978): 698–701.

"Birthday Problem Again." by Kevin S. Jones. *Mathematics Teacher* (May 1993): 373–7.

"Boomerang! How to Make Them and Also How They Fly." by Jearl Walker. *Scientific American* (March 1979): 162–72.

"Box Plots: Basic and Advanced." by James Mullenex. *Mathematics Teacher* (February 1990): 108–12.

"Brief Look at the History of Probability and Statistics." by James E. Lightner. *Mathematics Teacher* (November 1991): 623–30.

"Buckytubes." by Phillip E. Ross. *Scientific American* (December 1991): 24.

"Buffon's Needle Problem on a Computer" by Ronald Carlson. *Mathematics Teacher* (November 1981): 638–40.

"Buffon's Needle Problem: An Exciting Application of Many Mathematical Concepts." by Lee L. Schroeder. *Mathematics Teacher* (February 1974): 183–6.

"Building Molecular Crystals." by Paul J. Fagan., and Michael D. Ward. *Scientific American* (July 1993): 48–55.

"Building the Cathedral in Florence." by Gustina Scaglia. *Scientific American* (January 1991): 66–76.

"Calculating Palindromic Sums by Computer." by Richard Donahue. *Mathematics Teacher* (April 1984): 269–71.

"Calculating the Distance to the Sun by Observing the Trail of a Meteor." by Jearl Walker. *Scientific American* (March 1987): 122–6.

"Camera Calculations." by George Fawcett. *Mathematics Teacher* (May 1981): 366–7, 398.

"Can a Purchaser Save Money by Financing?" by Donald Cohen. *Mathematics Teacher* (January 1993): 62–3.

"Casting Out Nines: An Explanation and Extensions." by Murray Lauber. *Mathematics Teacher* (November 1990): 661–5.

"Celebrating the Birthday Problem." by Neville Spencer. *Mathematics Teacher* (April 1977): 348–53.

"Chaos and Fractals in Human Physiology." by Ary L. Goldberger, David R. Rigney, and Bruce J. West. *Scientific American* (February 1990): 42–9.

"Check-Digit Schemes." by Mary L. Wheeler. *Mathematics Teacher* (April 1994): 228–30.

"Chinese Building Standards in the 12th Century." by Else Glahn. *Scientific American* (May 1981): 162–73.

"Chuck-a-Luck: Learning Probability Concepts with Games of Chance." by E. T. Noone Jr. *Mathematics Teacher* (February 1988): 121–3.

"Circles and Star Polygons." by Clark Kimberling. *Mathematics Teacher* (January 1985): 46–51, 54.

"Coloring of Unusual Maps Leads to Uncharted Territory." by Martin Gardner. *Scientific American* (February 1980): 14–9.

"Combinatorial Mathematics of Scheduling." by Ronald Graham. *Scientific American* (March 1978): 124–32.

"Combinatorial Scheduling." by Robert M. Dieffenbach. *Mathematics Teacher* (April 1990): 269–73.

"Complex Roots: The Bairstow-Hitchcock Method." by Clark Kimberling. *Mathematics Teacher* (April 1986): 278–82.

"Computer as a Musical Instrument." by Max V. Mathews, and John R. Pierce. *Scientific American* (February 1987): 126–33.

"Computer Poker." by Nicholas V. Finder. *Scientific American* (July 1978): 144–51.

"Computer Software for Information Management." by Michael Lesk. *Scientific American* (September 1984): 163–74.

"Computer Software in Science and Mathematics." by Stephen Wolfran. *Scientific American* (September 1984): 188–99.

"Computer's Impact on Mathematics: Numerical and Monte Carlo Methods." by Michael J. Flynn. *Mathematics Teacher* (May 1974): 458–60.

"Computer-Generated Magic Squares." by Antonio Pizarro. *Mathematics Teacher* (September 1986): 471–6.

"Computers and Architecture." by Donald P. Greenberg. *Scientific American* (February 1991): 104–9.

"Computers in Music." by Piene Boulez, and Andrew Gerzso. *Scientific American* (April 1988): 44–51.

"Concentration: A Winning Strategy." by Ian Stewart. *Scientific American* (October 1991): 126–8.

"Conics." by Clark Kimberling. *Mathematics Teacher* (May 1984): 363–8.

"Constructing and Trisecting Angles with Integer Angle Measures." by Joe Dan Austin, and Kathleen Ann Austin. *Mathematics Teacher* (April 1979): 290–3.

"Construction of a Slide Rule with Compass and Straightedge." by Jack R. Westwood. *Mathematics Teacher* (February 1973): 162–4.

"Construction with an Unmarked Protractor." by Joe Dan Austin. *Mathematics Teacher* (April 1982): 291–5.

"Conventional Cryptography." by Marie A. Wright. *Mathematics Teacher* (March 1993): 249–51.

"Convergence of Some Iteration Formulas and Solutions of Recurrence Formulas." by Avon Pinker. *Mathematics Teacher* (January 1972): 61–7.

"Coprimes and Randomness." by N. T. Gridgeman. *Mathematics Teacher* (November 1973): 663–4.

"Counting Using License Plates and Phone Numbers." by Edwin Landauer. *Mathematics Teacher* (March 1984): 183–7.

Cryptogram. Mundelein, IL: American Cryptogram Association.

"Crystal Palace." by Folke T. Kihlstedt. *Scientific American* (October 1984): 132–45.

"Crystals: Through the Looking Glass with Planes, Points, and Rotational Symmetries." by Carole J. Reesink. *Mathematics Teacher* (May 1987): 377–88.

"Cube Roots on a Calculator—Some More Thoughts." by Gregory K. Peterson. *Mathematics Teacher* (September 1979): 448–9.

"Curve-Stitching the Cardioid and Related Curves." by Peter Catranides. *Mathematics Teacher* (December 1978): 726–32.

"Data Structure and Algorithms." by Niklaus Wirth. *Scientific American* (September 1984): 60–9.

"David Copperfield's Orient Express Card Trick." by Sidney J. Kolpas. *Mathematics Teacher* (October 1992): 568–70.

"Decimals, Rounding, and Apportionment." by Kay I. Meeks. *Mathematics Teacher* (October 1992): 523–5.

"Demonstrating the Efficiency of Linear Programming." by Kil S. Lee, and Wayne Marx. *Mathematics Teacher* (December 1983): 664–6.

"Dense, Denser, Densest." by Richard A. Lamon. *Mathematics Teacher* (November 1976): 547–8.

"Determining Fuel Consumption—An Exercise in Applied Mathematics." by Clifford H. Wagner. *Mathematics Teacher* (February 1979): 134–6.

"Developing Mathematics on a Pool Table." by Thomas R. Harnel, and Ernest Woodward. *Mathematics Teacher* (February 1977): 154–63.

"Did Gauss Discover That, Too?" by Richard L. Francis. *Mathematics Teacher* (April 1986): 288–93.

"'Difference' in Babbage's Difference Equation." by Mary L. Crowley. *Mathematics Teacher* (May 1985): 366–72.

"Different Look at πR²." by William D. Jamski. *Mathematics Teacher* (April 1978): 273–4.

"Digital Sum Divisibility Tests." by Kenneth J. McCaffrey. *Mathematics Teacher* (December 1976): 670–4.

"Digits Count: Significant Digits and Calculators." by Joseph Brown. *Mathematics Teacher* (May 1991): 344–6.

"Direct Derivation of the Equations of the Conic Sections." by Duane DeTemple. *Mathematics Teacher* (March 1990): 190–3.

"Discover Pick's Theorem." by Douglas Wilcock. *Mathematics Teacher* (September 1992): 424–5.

"Discovering a Formula that Generates Even Perfect Numbers." by Giorgio Pasquali. *Mathematics Teacher* (October 1976): 469–70.

"Discovery Approach to the Cube Root Algorithm." by Elroy J. Bolduc, Jr. *Mathematics Teacher* (May 1976): 402–3.

"Discovery Involving Volume." by Frederick Eid. *Mathematics Teacher* (May 1984): 356–7.

"Discrete Analysis of 'Final Jeopardy.'" Jeffrey K. Floyd. *Mathematics Teacher* (May 1994): 328–31.

"Dr. Matrix, Like Dr. Holmes, Comes to an Untimely and Mysterious End." by Martin Gardner. *Scientific American* (September 1980): 20–4.

"Duplicating the Cube with a Mira." by George E. Martin. *Mathematics Teacher* (March 1979): 204–8.

"Easy-to-Paste Model of the Rhombic Dodecahedron." by M. Stoessel Wahl. *Mathematics Teacher* (November 1978): 689–93.

"Economics of Life and Death." by Amartya Sen. *Scientific American* (May 1993): 40–7.

"Efficiency of Algorithms." by Harry R. Lewis, and Chistos H. Papodimitrion. *Scientific American* (January 1978): 96–110.

"Electing a President in a Three-Candidate Race." by Andrew Sterrett. *Mathematics Teacher* (November 1980): 635.

"Election of a President." by John J. Sullivan. *Mathematics Teacher* (October 1972): 493–501.

"Emmy Noether, Greatest Woman Mathematician." by Clark Kimberling. *Mathematics Teacher* (March 1982): 246–9.

"Estimating the Volumes of Solid Figures with Curved Surfaces." by Donald Cohen. *Mathematics Teacher* (May 1991): 392–5.

"Euclid and Descartes: A Partnership." by Dorothy Wasclovich. *Mathematics Teacher* (December 1991): 706–9.

"Euclid and the Infinitude of Primes." by William Dunham. *Mathematics Teacher* (January 1987): 16–7.

"Euler, the Master Calculator." by Jerry Taylor. *Mathematics Teacher* (September 1983): 424–8.

"Eureka! Pythagorean Triples from the Multiplication Table." by Angelo DiDomenico. *Mathematics Teacher* (January 1983): 48–51.

"Examples of the Use of Statistics in Society." by Duane C. Hinders. *Mathematics Teacher* (February 1990): 136–41.

"Existence of Real Roots of a Radical Equation." by Goro Nagase. *Mathematics Teacher* (May 1987): 369–70.

"Exotic Horse-Race Wagering and Combinations." by Lynn A. Richbart. *Mathematics Teacher* (January 1984): 35–6.

"Expansion Rate and Size of the Universe." by Wendy L. Freeman. *Scientific American* (November 1992): 54–61.

"Expected Value and the Wheel of Fortune Game." by Ernest Woodward, and Marilyn Woodward. *Mathematics Teacher* (January 1994): 13–7.

"Exploring Baseball Data." by Alton T. Olson. *Mathematics Teacher* (October 1987): 565–9.

"Exploring Fractals . . . A Problem-Solving Adventure Using Mathematics and Logo." by Jane F. Kern, and Cherry C. Mauk. *Mathematics Teacher* (March 1990): 179–85; 244.

"Exploring Regression with a Graphing Calculator." by Edward C. Wallace. *Mathematics Teacher* (December 1993).

"Factorial!" by Robert Messer. *Mathematics Teacher* (January 1984): 50–1.

"Fast Brakes." by David S. Daniels. *Mathematics Teacher* (February 1989): 104–7, 111.

"Fermat's Last Theorem." by Charles Vanden Eynden. *Mathematics Teacher* (November 1989): 637–40.

"Fermat's Last Theorem." by Harold M. Edwards. *Scientific American* (October 1978): 104–22.

"Fibonacci Sequence and the Golden Ratio." by Vincent P. Schielack Jr. *Mathematics Teacher* (May 1987): 357–8.

"Figuring Out a Jigsaw Puzzle." by Ken Irby. *Mathematics Teacher* (April 1989): 260–3.

"Finance Charges on Credit Card Accounts." by Franklin Kost. *Mathematics Teacher* (November 1987): 624–30.

"Finding Areas Under Curves with Hand-Held Calculators." by Arthur A. Hiatt. *Scientific American* (May 1978): 420–3.

"Finding Chord Factors of Geodesic Domes." by Fred Blaisdell, and Art Indelicato. *Mathematics Teacher* (February 1977): 117–24.

"Finding Points of Intersection of Polar Coordinate Graphs." by Warren W. Esty. *Mathematics Teacher* (September 1991): 472–8.

"Four Labs to Introduce Quadratic Functions." by Jim Malone. *Mathematics Teacher* (November 1989): 601–4.

"Fractal Excursion." by Dane R. Camp. *Mathematics Teacher* (April 1991): 265–75.

"Fractals and Transformations." by Thomas J. Bannon. *Mathematics Teacher* (March 1991): 178–85.

"Fun with Repeating Decimals." by Sue S. Wagner. *Mathematics Teacher* (March 1979): 209–12.

"Galileo Affair." by Owen Gingerich. *Scientific American* (August 1982): 133–43.

"Galileo's Discovery of the Parabolic Trajectory." by S. Drake, and J. MacLachlan. *Scientific American* (March 1975): 102–10.

"Gambling, Casinos, and Game Simulation." by Robert L. Heiny. *Mathematics Teacher* (February 1981): 139–43.

"Game Theory: An Application of Probability." by Robert E. Rector. *Mathematics Teacher* (February 1987): 138–42.

"Gauss' Congruence Theory Was Mod as Early as 1801." by Martin Gardner. *Scientific American* (February 1981): 17–20.

"GCD, LCM, and Boolean Algebra." by Martin Cohen, and William A. Juraschek. *Mathematics Teacher* (November 1976): 602–5.

"Gears, Ratios, and the Bicycle." by Daniel T. Gerber. *Mathematics Teacher* (September 1989): 466–8.

"General Divisibility Test for Whole Numbers." by Walter Szetela. *Mathematics Teacher* (March 1980): 223–5.

"Generality of a Simple Area Formula." by Daniel J. Reinford. *Mathematics Teacher* (December 1993): 738–40.

"Generate Your Own Random Numbers." by Clark Kimberling. *Mathematics Teacher* (February 1984): 118–23.

"Generating Magic Squares Whose Orders Are Multipiles of Four." by Antonio Pizarro. *Mathematics Teacher* (March 1989): 216–21.

"Generating Random Numbers Using Modular Arithmetic." by Arthur Indelicato. *Mathematics Teacher* (May 1969): 385–91.

"Geodesic Domes by Euclidean Construction." by Magnus J. Wenninger. *Mathematics Teacher* (October 1978): 582.

"Geography of U.S. Presidential Elections." by J. Clark Archer, et al. *Scientific American* (July 1988): 44–53.

"Geomegy or Geolotry: What Happens When Geology Visits Geometry Class?" by Carole J. Reesink. *Mathematics Teacher* (September 1982): 454–61.

"Geometric Constructions Using Hinged Mirrors." by Jack M. Robertson. *Mathematics Teacher* (May 1986): 380–6.

"Geometric Interpretation of Series." by John Van Beynen, and Robert L. McGinty. *Mathematics Teacher* (March 1981): 218–21.

"Geometrical Approach to the Six Trigonometric Ratios." by Martin V. Bonsangue. *Mathematics Teacher* (September 1993): 496–8.

"Geometry of Microwave Antennas." by William Parzynski. *Mathematics Teacher* (April 1984): 294–6.

"Geometry of Soap Films and Soap Bubbles." by Frederick J. Almgren, and Jean E. Taylor. *Scientific American* (July 1976): 82–93.

"Geometry of Tennis." by Jay Graening. *Mathematics Teacher* (November 1982): 658–63.

"Georg Cantor and the Origins of Transfinite Set Theory." by Joseph W. Dauben. *Scientific American* (June 1983): 122.

"Get Away from the Table! Make Interest More Interesting." by M. Jane Carr. *Mathematics Teacher* (December 1986): 703–5.

"Get the Message? Cryptographs, Mathematics, and Computers." by James Reagan. *Mathematics Teacher* (October 1986): 547–53.

"Getting to the Roots of the Problem." by Joseph F. Aieta. *Mathematics Teacher* (May 1978): 414–7.

"Giving Geometry Students an Added Edge." by Allan Gibb. *Mathematics Teacher* (April 1982): 296–301.

"Golden Ratio: A Golden Opportunity to Investigate Multiple Representations of a Problem." by Edwin M. Dickey. *Mathematics Teacher* (October 1993): 554–7.

"Golden Section and Conic Sections." by Ralph Verno. *Mathematics Teacher* (April 1974): 361–3.

"Gothic Structural Experimentation." by Robert Mark, and William W. Clark. *Scientific American* (November 1984): 176–85.

"Graphical Properties of Sequences and Equations." by Robert D. Alexander, et al. *Mathematics Teacher* (November 1977): 665–72.

"Graphing Powers and Roots of Complex Numbers." by Charles Vonder Embse. *Mathematics Teacher* (October 1993): 589–97.

"Graphs That Can Help Cannibals, Missionaries, Wolves, Goats, and Cabbages Get There from Here." by Martin Gardner. *Scientific American* (March 1980): 24–38.

"Growing Human Population." by Nathan Keyfitz. *Scientific American* (September 1989): 118–27.

"Harmonic Mean as a Factor in Currency Conversion." by Joseph Ercolano. *Mathematics Teacher* (February 1979): 146–8.

"Harmonic Mean: A Nomograph and Some Problems." by Akiva Skidell. *Mathematics Teacher* (January 1977): 30–4.

"Harmonic Series Revisited." by Gerald Beimler. *Mathematics Teacher* (March 1983): 178–9.

"Hawaiian Number Systems." by Barnabas Hughes. *Mathematics Teacher* (March 1982): 253–6.

"History of Census Tabulation." by Keith S. Reid-Green. *Scientific American* (February 1989): 98–103.

"History of Discovery of Amicable Numbers." by Elvin J. Lee, and Joseph Madachy. *Journal of Recreational Math* Vol. 5.

"How Is Area Related to Perimeter?" by Betty Clayton Lyon. *Mathematics Teacher* (May 1983): 360–3.

"How Many Games in a Tournament?" by Ernest Woodward. *Mathematics Teacher* (May 1989): 332–5.

"How to Build a Simple Seismograph to Record Earthquake Waves at Home." by Jearl Walker. *Scientific American* (July 1979): 152–9.

"How to Draw Tessellations of the Escher Type." by Joseph L. Teeters. *Mathematics Teacher* (April 1974): 307–10.

"How to Measure the Size of the Earth with Only a Foot Rule or a Stopwatch." by Jearl Walker. *Scientific American* (May 1979): 172–82.

"How to Pan for Primes in Numerical Gravel." by A. K. Dewdney. *Scientific American* (July 1988): 120–3.

"Illustrating the Euler Line." by James M. Rubillo. *Mathematics Teacher* (May 1987): 389–93.

"Imaginableness of the Imaginary Numbers." by Martin Gardner. *Scientific American* (August 1979): 18–24.

"Imagination Meets Geometry in the Crystalline Realm of Latticeworms." by A. K. Dewdney. *Scientific American* (June 1988): 120–3.

"Impact of the Black Death (1348–1405) on World Population: Then and Now." by Michael G. Gonzales, and William J. Carr. *Mathematics Teacher* (February 1986): 92–4.

"Implementing the Discrete Mathematics Standards: Focusing on Recursion." by Stanley J. Bezuszka, and Margaret Kenney. *Mathematics Teacher* (November 1993): 676–80.

"Improvement of a Historic Construction." by Kim Iles, and Lester S. Wilson. *Mathematics Teacher* (January 1980): 32–4.

"In Celebration: Newton's Principia, 1687–1987." by Dorothy Goldberg. *Mathematics Teacher* (December 1987): 711–4.

"In Which a Mathematical Aesthetic Is Applied to Modern Minimal Art." by Martin Gardner. *Scientific American* (November 1978): 22.

"In Which Players of Ticktacktoe are Taught to Hunt Bigger Game." by Martin Gardner. *Scientific American* (April 1979): 18–28.

"Inching Our Way Towards the Metric System." by Gerardus Vervoort. *Mathematics Teacher* (April 1973): 297–302.

"Incredible Shrinking Can: Mathematics of Diminishing Returns Revealed." by Frank J. Swetz. *Mathematics Teacher* (November 1993): 642–4.

"Infinity: The Twilight Zone of Mathematics." by William P. Love. *Mathematics Teacher* (April 1989): 284–92.

"Instant Insanity: That Ubiquitous Baffler." by Dewey C. Duncan. *Mathematics Teacher* (February 1972): 131–5.

"Interest in Interest." by Joseph C. Tisdale III. *Mathematics Teacher* (February 1989): 126–7.

"Interest in Mathematics—It's in the Cards." by Catherine Herr Mulligan. *Mathematics Teacher* (February 1989): 100–3.

"Internal Rhythms in Bird Migration." by Eberhard Gwinner. *Scientific American* (April 1986).

"Introducing the Musha." by Jearl Walker. *Scientific American* (February 1978): 156–61.

"Invertable Points of Time." by Boonchai Kuekiatngam Stensholt, and Eivind Stensholt. *Mathematics Teacher* (April 1988): 304–5.

"Investigating Circles and Spirals with a Graphing Calculator." by Stuart Moskowitz. *Mathematics Teacher* (April 1994): 240–3.

"Is Nature Supersymmetric?" by Howard E. Haber, and Gordon L. Kane. *Scientific American* (June 1986): 52–75.

"Island Epidemics." by Andrew Cliff, and Peter Haggett. *Scientific American* (May 1984): 138–47.

"Iterative for Computing Solutions to Equations Using a Calculator." by Bert K. Waits, and James E. Schultz. *Mathematics Teacher* (December 1979): 685–9.

"Kaleidoscopes and Mathematics." by S. Orans. *Arithmetic Teacher* (1973): 576–9.

"Ladies' Diary . . . Cira 1700." by Teri Perl. *Mathematics Teacher* (April 1977): 354–8.

"Language of Fractals." by Hartmut Jürgens, Dietmar Saupe, and Heinz-Otto Peitgen. *Scientific American* (August 1990): 60–7.

"Lessons Learned While Approximating Pi." by James E. Beamer. *Mathematics Teacher* (February 1987): 154–9.

"Life-Expectancy and Population Growth in the Third World." by Davidson R. Gwatkin, and Sarah K. Brandel. *Scientific American* (May 1982): 57–65.

"Line Reflections in the Complex Plane—A Billiards Player's Delight." by Gary L. Musser. *Mathematics Teacher* (January 1978): 60–4.

"Linear Measurement U.S. Square Measurement; or, Why the Queen Used Two Pi R." by Margaret W. Maxfield. *Mathematics Teacher* (January 1988): 51–3.

"Logo in the Mathematics Curriculum." by Tom Addicks. *Mathematics Teacher* (September 1986): 424–8.

"Logorithmic Spiral." by Eli Maor. *Mathematics Teacher* (April 1974): 321–7.

"Magic Cube's Cubies are Twiddled by Cubes and Solved by Cubemeisters." by Douglas R. Hofstradter. *Scientific American* (March 1981): 20–39.

"Magic Cubes: A Total Experience." by Aviv and Rachlin. *Mathematics Teacher* (September 1981): 464–72.

"Magic of Mathematics." by John L. Morgan, and John L. Ginther. *Mathematics Teacher* (March 1994): 150–3.

"Magic Squares of All Orders." by Judson McCranie. *Mathematics Teacher* (November 1988): 674–8.

"Making a Barometer That Works with Water in Place of Mercury." by Jearl Walker. *Scientific American* (April 1987): 122–7.

"Map-Coloring Algorithm." by David Keeports. *Mathematics Teacher* (December 1991): 759–63.

"Mapping to Preserve a Watershed." by Karen Jescauage-Bernard, and Anders Crofoot. *Scientific American* (May 1993): 134.

"Maps: Geometry in Geography." by Thomas W. Shilgalis. *Mathematics Teacher* (May 1977): 400–4.

"Mass Extinctions in the Ocean." by Steven M. Stanley. *Scientific American* (June 1984): 64–83.

"Master of Tessellations: M. C. Escher, 1898–1972." by Ernest R. Ranucci. *Mathematics Teacher* (April 1974): 299–306.

"Mathematical Aspects of a Lunar Shuttle Landing." by Bill Anderson, and John Lamb. *Mathematics Teacher* (October 1981): 549–53.

"Mathematical Connections with a Spirograph®." by Alfino Flores. *Mathematics Teacher* (February 1992): 129–38.

"Mathematical Induction: A Focus on the Conceptual Framework." by N. Mooshovitz-Hadar. *School Science & Math Journal* (December 1993): 408–17.

"Mathematical Iteration Through Computer Programming." by Mary Kim Pritchard. *Mathematics Teacher* (February 1993): 150–6.

"Mathematical Model for the Height of a Satellite." by Sharon Thoemke, and Pam Shriver. *Mathematics Teacher* (October 1993): 563–5.

"Mathematical Modeling and the Presidential Election." by Joseph C. Witkowski. *Mathematics Teacher* (October 1992): 520–1.

"Mathematical Modeling in a Feast of Rabbits." by Graham Jones. *Mathematics Teacher* (December 1989): 770–3.

"Mathematical Modeling: Lemonade from Lemons." by David S. Daniels. *Mathematics Teacher* (October 1989): 516–9.

"Mathematician's Repertoire of Means." by Eli Maor. *Mathematics Teacher* (January 1977): 20–5.

"Mathematics and Medical Indexes: A Life-Saving Connection." by Richard J. Crouse, and Clifford W. Sloyer. *Mathematics Teacher* (November 1993): 624–6.

"Mathematics and Meteorology." by Eric F. Wood. *Mathematics Teacher* (November 1986): 602–3.

"Mathematics Expressed in Trademarks." by Woodward and Tolleson. *Mathematics Teacher* (September 1981): 437–9.

"Mathematics in Ancient Egypt: A Checklist." by L. Guggenbuhl. *Mathematics Teacher* (November 1965): 630–4.

"Mathematics in Baseball." by Michael T. Battista. *Mathematics Teacher* (April 1993): 336–42.

"Mathematics in Photography." by Neil J. Jeffrey. *Mathematics Teacher* (December 1980): 657–62.

"Mathematics of Buying a Car: A Basic Skills Unit." by Mary Jo Doebling. *Mathematics Teacher* (March 1981): 184–6, 238.

"Mathematics of Elections." by Martin Gardner. *Scientific American* (October 1980): 16–26.

"Mathematics of Genetics." by Joe Dan Austin. *Mathematics Teacher* (November 1977): 685–90.

"Mathematics of Public-Key Cryptography." by Martin E. Hellman. *Scientific American* (August 1979): 146–57.

"Mathematics of Sight." by George Knill, and George Fawcett. *Mathematics Teacher* (November 1981): 636–7.

"Mathematics of Three-Dimensional Manifolds." by William P. Thorsfon, and Jeffrey R. Weeks. *Scientific American* (July 1984): 108–21.

"Matrix Method for Generating Pythagorean Triples." by Phylis Lefton. *Mathematics Teacher* (February 1987): 103–8.

"Maya Arithmetic." by J. B. Lambert, et. al. *American Scientist* (1980): 249–55.

"Mayan Arithmetic." by James K. Bidwell. *Mathematics Teacher* (November 1967): 762–8.

"Method of Centroids in Plane Geometry." by Aron Pinker. *Mathematics Teacher* (May 1980): 378–85.

"Method of Finite Differences: Some Applications." by Henry P. Guilotte. *Mathematics Teacher* (September 1986): 466–70.

"Methods and Optics of Perceiving Color in Black-and-White Grating." by Jearl Walker. *Scientific American* (March 1986): 112–8.

"Microcomputer Unit: Generating Random Numbers." by William E. Haigh. *Mathematics Teacher* (February 1986): 132–6.

"Minimal Surfaces Revisited." by Rita M. Ehrmann. *Mathematics Teacher* (February 1976): 146–52.

"Mirror Images." by David Emil Thomas. *Scientific American* (December 1980): 206–30.

"Möbius Band." by Martin Gardner. *Scientific American* (August 1978): 18–25.

"Modeling the Cost of Homeownership." by Floyd Vest. *Mathematics Teacher* (November 1986): 610–3.

"Modulo Systems: One More Step." by Nathaniel Mann III. *Mathematics Teacher* (March 1972): 207–9.

"Modulo-Seven Arithmetic—A Perfect Example of Field Properties." by Boyd Henry. *Mathematics Teacher* (October 1972): 525–8.

"Moiré Effects, the Kaleidoscope, and Other Victorian Diversions." by Jearl Walker. *Scientific American* (December 1978): 182–8.

"Monte Carlo Method: A Fresh Approach to Teaching Probabilistic Concepts." by Kenneth J. Travers, and Kenneth G. Gray. *Mathematics Teacher* (May 1981): 327–34.

"Monte Carlo, Probability, Algebra, and Pi." by Duane C. Hinders. *Mathematics Teacher* (May 1981): 335–9.

"More about Triangles with the Same Area and the Same Perimeter." by Donovan R. Lichtenberg. *Mathematics Teacher* (November 1974): 659–60.

"Move to Metric: Some Considerations." by Donald H. Firl. *Mathematics Teacher* (November 1974): 581–5.

"Murder at Ghastleigh Grange (Networks)." by Ian Stewart. *Scientific American* (October 1992): 118–20.

"Music and Ammonia Vapor Excite the Color Pattern of Soap Film." by Jearl Walker. *Scientific American* (August 1987): 104–7.

"Mysticism and Magic in Number Squares of Old China." by Frank Swetz. *Mathematics Teacher* (January 1978): 50–6.

"Nearly Isosceles Pythagorean Triples—Once More." by Hermann Hering. *Mathematics Teacher* (December 1986): 724–5.

"Nested Platonic Solids: A Class Project in Solid Geometry." by Ronald B. Hopley. *Mathematics Teacher* (May 1994): 312–8.

"Networks." by Vinton G. Cerf. *Scientific American* (September 1991): 72–85.

"New Angle for Constructing Pentagons." by John Benson, and Debra Borkovitz. *Mathematics Teacher* (April 1982): 288–90.

"New Look, Pythagoras!" by Carol A. Thornton. *Mathematics Teacher* (February 1981): 98–100.

"Newton's Apple and Galileo's Dialogue." by Stillman Drake. *Scientific American* (August 1980): 150–7.

"Newton's Discovery of Gravity." by I. Bernard Cohen. *Scientific American* (March 1981): 166–81.

"Nine-Point Circle on a Geoboard." by Robert L. Jones. *Mathematics Teacher* (February 1976): 141–4.

"Novel Way to Factor Quadratic Polynomials." by Malanie Ann Autrey, and Joe Dan Austin. *Mathematics Teacher* (February 1979): 127–8.

"Now and Then: From Cashier to Scan Coordinator." by Sue Barnes. *Mathematics Teaching in the Middle School* (April 1994): 59–64.

"Number Systems of the North American Indian." by W. C. Eels. *American Mathematical Monthly* (1913): 263–72, 293–9.

"Number Theory and Public-Key Cryptography." by Phyllis Lefton. *Mathematics Teacher* (January 1991): 34–62.

"Number Theory for Secondary Schools?" by David L. Pagni. *Mathematics Teacher* (January 1979): 20–2.

"Number Tricks Explained with Algebra." by Eddie Escultura. *Mathematics Teacher* (January 1983): 20–1.

"Numbers and Measures in the Earliest Written Records." by Jöran Friberg. *Scientific American* (February 1984): 110–9.

"Numeration Systems with Unusual Bases." by David Ballew. *Mathematics Teacher* (May 1974): 413–5.

"Oliver Heaviside." by Paul J. Nahin. *Scientific American* (June 1990).

"On Altering the Past, Delaying the Future, and Other Ways of Tampering with Time." by Martin Gardner. *Scientific American* (March 1979): 21–30.

"On Ancient Chinese Mathematics." by D. J. Struik. *Mathematics Teacher* (October 1963): 424–32.

"On Archimedean Solids." by Tom Boag, Charles Boberg, and Lyn Hughes. *Mathematics Teacher* (May 1979): 371–6.

"On Population and Resources." by Steven Schwartzman. *Mathematics Teacher* (November 1983): 605–8.

"One Checker Jumping, the Amazon Game, Weird Dice, Card Tricks, and Other Playful Pastimes." by Martin Gardner. *Scientific American* (February 1978): 19–33.

"Operating Systems." by Peter J. Denning, and Robert C. Brown. *Scientific American* (September 1984): 94–106.

"Packing of Spheres." by N. J. A. Sloane. *Scientific American* (January 1984): 116–25.

"Paradoxes in Averages." by John Mitchen. *Mathematics Teacher* (April 1989): 250–3.

"Pascal Pyramid." by John Staib, and Larry Staib. *Mathematics Teacher* (September 1978): 505–10.

"Pascal's Triangle and Fibonacci Numbers." by James Varnadore. *Mathematics Teacher* (April 1991): 314–6.

"Pascal's Triangle: Some Recent References." by Louise S. Grinstein. *Mathematics Teacher* (September 1981): 449–50.

"Pattern Discovery with Binary Trees." by Andy Parker. *Mathematics Teacher* (May 1979): 337.

"Patterned Ground." by William B. Krantz, Kevin J. Gleason, and Nelson Caine. *Scientific American* (December 1988): 68–77.

"Patterns in Powers of Digits." by Richard W. Shoemaker. *Mathematics Teacher* (April 1988): 294–8.

"People, People, People." by Samuel L. Dunn, et al. *Mathematics Teacher* (April 1978): 283–91.

"Perfect Numbers, Abundant Numbers, and Deficient Numbers." by Robert W. Prielipp. *Mathematics Teacher* (December 1970): 692–6.

"Periodic Pictures." by Ray S. Nowak. *Mathematics Teacher* (February 1987): 126–33.

"Perplexed by Hexed® (Pentominoes)." by Caroline Hollingsworth. *Mathematics Teacher* (October 1984): 560–2.

"Physics of Somersaulting and Twisting." by Cliff Frohlich. *Scientific American* (March 1980): 154–65.

"Physics of the Follow, the Draw, and the Massé." by Jearl Walker. *Scientific American* (July 1983): 124–35.

"Physics of the Patterns of Frost on a Window, Plus an Easy-to-Read Sundial." by Jearl Walker. *Scientific American* (December 1980): 231–8.

"Pick's Theorem Extended and Generalized." by Christopher Polis. *Mathematics Teacher* (May 1991): 399.

"'Piling up of Squares' in Ancient China." by Frank Swetz. *Mathematics Teacher* (January 1977): 72–9.

"Playoff Series and Pascal's Triangle." by Bonnie H. Litwiller, and David R. Duncan. *Mathematics Teacher* (October 1992): 532–5.

"Pleasures and Perils of Iteration." by Lawrence O. Cannon, and Joe Elich. *Mathematics Teacher* (March 1993): 233–9.

"Poker Probabilities: A New Setting." by Bonnie H. Litwiller, and David R. Duncan. *Mathematics Teacher* (December 1977): 766–71.

"Polygonal Numbers and Recursion." by William A. Miller. *Mathematics Teacher* (October 1990): 555–62.

"Popular Measures of Central Tendency." by Robert G. Mogall. *Mathematics Teacher* (December 1990): 744–6.

"Population Explosion: An Activity Lesson." by Donald T. Piele. *Mathematics Teacher* (October 1974): 496–502.

"Population of China." by Nathan Keyfitz. *Scientific American* (February 1984): 38–47.

"Power of Maps." by Denis Wood. *Scientific American* (May 1993): 85–93.

"Practical Geometry Problems: The Case of the Ritzville Pyramids." by Donald Nowlin. *Mathematics Teacher* (March 1993): 198–200.

"Predicting Chemistry from Topology." by Dennis H. Rouvray. *Scientific American* (September 1986): 40–7.

"Prime Numbers—A Locust's View." by James M. Sconyers. *Mathematics Teacher* (February 1981): 105–8.

"Primes." by Clark Kimberling. *Mathematics Teacher* (September 1983): 434–7.

"Probability and Basketball." by Don Serba. *Mathematics Teacher* (November 1981): 624–7.

"Probability of Winning Dice Games." by Bonnie H. Litwiller, and David R. Duncan. *Mathematics Teacher* (September 1979): 458–61.

"Probability Simulation in Middle School." by Glenda Lappan, and M. J. Winter. *Mathematics Teacher* (September 1980): 446–9.

"Problem of Galaxa: Infinite Area Versus Finite Volume." by James McKim. *Mathematics Teacher* (April 1981): 294–6.

"Problem Solving with Simulation." by Dwayne E. Channell. *Mathematics Teacher* (December 1989): 713.

"Program for Rotating Hypercubes Includes Four-Dimensional Dementia." by A. K. Dewey. *Scientific American* (April 1986): 14–23.

"Program to Simulate the Galton Quincunx." by Joseph Hilsenrath, and Bruce Field. *Mathematics Teacher* (November 1983): 571–3.

"Pythagorean Curiosity." by M. M. Marche. *Mathematics Teacher* (November 1984): 611–3.

"Pythagorean Dissection Puzzles." by William A. Miller, and Linda Wagner. *Mathematics Teacher* (April 1993): 302–8.

"Pythagorean Theorem on an Isometric Geoboard." by James Hirstein. J., and Sidney L. Rachlin. *Mathematics Teacher* (February 1980): 141–4.

"Pythagorean Triples from the Addition Table." by Angelo S. DiDomencio. *Mathematics Teacher* (May 1985): 346–8.

"Pythagorean Triples." by Alvin Tirman. *Mathematics Teacher* (November 1986): 652–5.

"Quadratic Formula: A Historic Approach." by K. R. S. Sastry. *Mathematics Teacher* (November 1988): 670.

"Quadratic Formulas." by Yves Nievergelt. *Mathematics Teacher* (September 1992): 461–5.

"Quadratic Formula—An Enrichment Approach." by Kenneth Stilwell. *Mathematics Teacher* (May 1972): 472–3.

"Quantum Cryptography." by Charles H. Bennett, Gilles Blassard, and Arthur K. Ekert. *Scientific American* (October 1993): 50–7.

"Random Number Omega Bids Fair to Hold the Mysteries of the Universe." by Martin Gardner. *Scientific American* (November 1979): 20–34.

"Randomness in Physics and Mathematics." by Joseph A. Troccolo. *Mathematics Teacher* (December 1977): 772–4.

"Rapidly Converging Recursive Approach to Pi." by Joseph B. Dence, and Thomas P. Dence. *Mathematics Teacher* (February 1993): 121–4.

"Rasmanujan and Pi." by Jonathan M. Borein, and Peter B. Borwein. *Scientific American* (February 1988): 112–7.

"Rates and Taxes." by Warren W. Esty. *Mathematics Teacher* (May 1992): 376–9

"Rational Collective Choice." by Douglas H. Blair, and Robert A. Pollack. *Scientific American* (August 1983): 88–95.

"Recognizing Quadratic Equations with No Real Roots." by Betty Perham. *Mathematics Teacher* (March 1979): 195–6.

"Recursion Mathematics." by Alton T. Olson. *Mathematics Teacher* (October 1989): 571–2, 576.

"Recursive Approach to the Construction of the Deltahedra." by William E. McGowan. *Mathematics Teacher* (March 1978): 204–10.

"Reflection Borders for Patchwork Quilts." by Duane DeTemple. *Mathematics Teacher* (February 1986): 138–43.

"Renaissance Intarsia: The Art of Geometry." by Alan Tormey, and Judith Farr Tormey. *Scientific American* (July 1982): 136.

"Repeating Decimals: Geometric Patterns and Open-Ended Questions." by Robert McGinty, and William Mutch. *Mathematics Teacher* (October 1982): 600–2.

"Riemann's Rearrangement Theorem." by Stewart Galanor. *Mathematics Teacher* (November 1987): 675–81.

"Rise and Fall of the Lunar M-Pire." by Ian Stewart. *Scientific American* (April 1993): 120–1.

"Rolling Curves." by Stanley A. Smith. *Mathematics Teacher* (March 1974): 239–42.

"Roman Aqueduct of Nines." by George F. W. Hauck. *Scientific American* (March 1989): 98–105.

"Roman Numeral Puzzle." by Robert Spieler. *Mathematics Teacher* (February 1980): 108, 156.

"Round Robin Schedules." by Michael A. Tannone. *Mathematics Teacher* (March 1983): 194–5.

"Rule of 78: A Rule That Outlived Its Useful Life." by Alonza F. Johnson. *Mathematics Teacher* (September 1988): 450–3; 480.

"Search for Prime Numbers." by Carl Pomerance. *Scientific American* (December 1982): 136–47.

"Secret Codes with Matrices." by Dane R. Camp. *Mathematics Teacher* (December 1985): 676–80.

"Self-Checking Codes—An Application of Modular Arithmetic." by Eric F. Wood. *Mathematics Teacher* (April 1987): 312–6.

"Semiregular Polyhedra." by Rick N. Blake, and Charles Verhille, *Mathematics Teacher* (October 1982): 577–81.

"Shape of a Baseball Field." by Milton P. Eisner. *Mathematics Teacher* (May 1993): 366–71.

"Shipboard Weather Observation." by Richard J. Palmaccio. *Mathematics Teacher* (March 1983): 165–8.

"Short Life of Évariste Galois." by Tony Rothman. *Scientific American* (April 1982): 136–49.

"Short Trek to Infinity." by Ian Stewart. *Scientific American* (December 1991): 144–7.

"Sierpiński Triangle: Deterministic Versus Random Models." by Margaret Cibes. *Mathematics Teacher* (November 1990): 617–21.

"Simple Constructions for the Regular Pentagon and Heptadecagon." by Duane W. DeTemple. *Mathematics Teacher* (May 1989): 361–5.

"Smart Soap Bubbles Can Do Calculus." by Dale T. Hoffman. *Mathematics Teacher* (May 1979): 377–85.

"Soma Cubes." by George S. Carson. *Mathematics Teacher* (November 1973): 583–92.

"Some Irrational Results with Irrational Numbers." by Daniel T. Dolan. *Mathematics Teacher* (April 1981): 258–61.

"Some Little-Known Rules and Why They Work." by Steven Schwartzman. *Mathematics Teacher* (October 1985): 554–8.

"Some Mathematical Applications of Pari-Mutual Wagering." by Frank P. Soler. *Mathematics Teacher* (May 1987): 394–9.

"Some Packing Problems That Cannot Be Solved by Sitting on the Suitcase." by Martin Gardner. *Scientific American* (October 1979): 18–26.

"Some Properties of the Calculator Square Root Function." by Carl Dorn, and Samuel Councilman. *Mathematics Teacher* (March 1980): 218–21.

"Some Surprising Probabilities from Bingo." by Joseph O. Mercer. *Mathematics Teacher* (December 1993): 726–31.

"Some Unusual Tests of Divisibility." by Najib Yazbak. *Mathematics Teacher* (December 1976): 667–8.

"Some Variations on a Mathematical Card Trick." by Lee Markowitz. *Mathematics Teacher* (November 1983): 618–9.

"Spherical Geodesics." by William D. Janski. *Mathematics Teacher* (March 1981): 227–8; 236.

"Spirolaterals." by Frank C. Odds. *Mathematics Teacher* (February 1973): 121–4.

"Spirolaterals." by Richard Brannan, and Scott McFadden. *Mathematics Teacher* (April 1981): 279–82.

"Spirolaterals: An Advanced Investigation from an Elementary Standpoint." by Alice Kaseberg Schwandt. *Mathematics Teacher* (March 1979): 166–9.

"Square Root and Cube Root Extraction in 1788." by Viggo P. Hansen. *Mathematics Teacher* (February 1968): 175–6.

"Square Roots from Anywhere." by Terry A. Goodman, and John Bernard. *Mathematics Teacher* (May 1979): 344–5.

"Strip of Wallpaper." by Joseph A. Troccolo. *Mathematics Teacher* (January 1977): 55–8.

"Structure of Quasicrystals." by Peter W. Stephens, and Alan I. Goldman. *Scientific American* (April 1991): 44–53.

"Studying Decimal Fractions with Microcomputers." by Ruth Ann Meyer, and James E. Riley. *Mathematics Teacher* (February 1987): 144–8.

"Surprising Fact About Pythagorean Triples." by Susan A. Brown. *Mathematics Teacher* (October 1985): 540–1.

"*t* in *i* = *prt*." by Alonzo F. Johnson. *Mathematics Teacher* (October 1982): 595–7.

"Tale of a Kite." by J. E. Beamer. *Arithmetic Teacher* (1975): 382–6.

"Teaching Quadratic Problem Solving." by Donald W. Stover. *Mathematics Teacher* (January 1978): 13–6.

"Teaching the Square Root Algorithm by the Discovery Approach." by Edward C. Tarte. *Mathematics Teacher* (April 1974): 317–9.

"Techniques of Fractions in Ancient Eygpt and Greece." by W. Knorr. *Historia Mathematica* (1982): 133–71.

"Technology, Linear Equations, and Buying a Car." by James T. Sandefur. *Mathematics Teacher* (October 1992): 562–7.

"Thinking About Physics While Scared to Death." by Jearl Walker. *Scientific American* (October 1983): 163.

"Thinking the Unthinkable: The Story of Complex Numbers." by Israel Kleiner. *Mathematics Teacher* (October 1988): 583–92.

"Tinkertoy Computer That Plays Tic-Tac-Toe." by A. K. Dewdney. *Scientific American* (October 1989): 120–3.

"Tonka® Toy Truck Does the Trick." by Victoria A. Borlaug. *Mathematics Teacher* (April 1993): 282–7.

"Topology of Knots." by Martin Gardner. *Scientific American* (September 1983): 18–28.

"Triangles of Equal Area and Perimeter and Inscribed Circles." by Jeane E. Kilmer. *Mathematics Teacher* (January 1988): 65–70.

"Triangular Numbers: The Building Blocks of Figurate Numbers." by Melfried Olson, Gerald K. Goff, and Murray Blose. *Mathematics Teacher* (November 1983): 624–5.

"Trisecting an Angle—Almost." by John F. Lamb. *Mathematics Teacher* (March 1988): 220–2.

"Truck Driver Looks at Square Roots." by John Risoen, and Jane Stanzel. *Arithmetic Teacher* (November 1978).

"Turning Landslides into Cliffhangers: An Analysis of Presidential Election Returns." by David R. Duncan, and Bonnie H. Litwiller. *Mathematics Teacher* (November 1986): 605–8.

"Turning Turtle Gives One a View of Geometry from the Inside Out." by Brian Hayes. *Scientific American* (February 1984): 14–20.

"Two Eygptian Construction Tools." by John F. Lamb. *Mathematics Teacher* (February 1993): 166–7.

"252/7: A Divisibility Pattern." by Gary Schatzman. *Mathematics Teacher* (October 1986): 542–6.

"Two Meanings of Algorithmic Mathematics." by Stephen B. Maurer. *Mathematics Teacher* (September 1984): 430–5.

"Two Problems That Illustrate the Technique of Computer Simulation." by Pearl W. Brazier, and Joseph E. Chance. *Mathematics Teacher* (December 1986): 726–31.

"Two Proofs that Only Five Regular Polyhedra Exist." by Peter L. Glidden, and Erin K. Fry. *Mathematics Teacher* (November 1993): 657–61.

"Understanding the AIDS Pandemic." by Roy M. Anderson, and Robert M. Mey. *Scientific American* (May 1992): 58–69.

"Understanding the Birthday Problem." by Frederick Mosteller. *Mathematics Teacher* (May 1962): 322–5.

"Using a Calculator to Find Rational Roots." by Bert K. Waits. *Mathematics Teacher* (May 1978): 418–9.

"Using a Microcomputer to Simulate the Birthday Coincidence Problems." by John Ginther, and William Ewbank. *Mathematics Teacher* (December 1982): 769–75.

"Using Logarithms to Explore Power and Exponential Functions." by James R. Rahn, and Barry A. Berndes. *Mathematics Teacher* (March 1994): 161–8.

"Using Puzzles to Teach the Pythagorean Theorem." by James E. Beamer. *Mathematics Teacher* (May 1989): 336–41.

"Using the Monochord: The Mathematics of Musical Scales." by Sheila Haak. *Mathematics Teacher* (March 1982): 238–44.

"Using the TI-81 to Analyze Sports Data." by Robert Plummer, Maita Levine, and Raymond H. Rolwing. *Mathematics Teacher* (November 1993): 636–41.

"Variations on a Theme by Pólya." by Raymond Dacey. *Mathematics Teacher* (November 1973): 598–9.

"Volume of a Cone." by Boris Lavric. *Mathematics Teacher* (May 1993): 384–5.

"What Are My Car Payments Going to Be?" by Donald Nowlin. *Mathematics Teacher* (April 1993): 299–300.

"What Can Be Done with a Mira?" by Johnny Lott, and Iris Mack Dayoub. *Mathematics Teacher* (May 1977): 394–9.

"What Do We Mean by Area and Perimeter?" by Virginia C. Stimpson. *Mathematics Teacher* (May 1989): 342–4.

"What in Heaven Is a Digital Sundial?" by Ian Stewart. *Scientific American* (August 1991): 104–6.

"What Is Data Analysis?" by Richard Scheaffer. *Mathematics Teacher* (February 1990): 90–3.

"What Is There So Mathematical About Music?" by Eli Maor. *Mathematics Teacher* (September 1979): 414–22.

"Wheel of Aristotle." by David W. Ballew. *Mathematics Teacher* (October 1972): 507.

"When and How Can We Use Modeling?" by Frank Swetz. *Mathematics Teacher* (December 1989): 722–6.

"When Are Logarithms Used?" by Charles Kluepfel. *Mathematics Teacher* (April 1981): 250–3.

"When Are We Ever Gonna Have to Use This?" by Hal Saunders. *Mathematics Teacher* (January 1980): 7–16.

"When Did Euclid Live? An Answer Plus a Short History of Geometry." by Gail H. Adele. *Mathematics Teacher* (September 1989): 460–3.

"When Melting and Freezing Points Are Not the Same." by R. Stephen Berry. *Scientific American* (August 1990): 68–74.

"Where Is the Ball Going?" by Jack A. Ott, and Anthony Contento. *Mathematics Teacher* (September 1986): 456–60.

"Which Mean Do You Mean?" by André Michelle Lubecke. *Mathematics Teacher* (January 1991): 24.

"Who Killed the Cook?" by James J. Corbet, and J. Susan Milton. *Mathematics Teacher* (April 1978): 263–6.

"Who's Going to Win the Playoff?" by Jack A. Ott. *Mathematics Teacher* (October 1985): 559–63.

"Why American's Bridges Are Crumbling." by Kenneth F. Dunker, and Basile G. Rabbat. *Scientific American* (March 1993): 66–73.

"Why Women Succeed in Mathematics." by M. Fabricant, S. Svitak, and C. Kenschaft. *Mathematics Teacher* (February 1990): 150–4.

"World of Buckminister Fuller." by Ernest R. Ranucci. *Mathematics Teacher* (October 1978): 568–77.

"Yin and Yang: Recursion and Iteration, the Tower of Hanoi, and the Chinese Rings." by A. K. Dewdney. *Scientific American* (November 1984): 19–28.

Publisher Addresses

Abrams, Harry N. Inc.
100 Fifth Avenue
New York, NY 10011

Academic Press
1250 Sixth Avenue
San Diego, CA 92101

Activities for Learning
Route 4, Box 34
Hutchinson, MN 55350

Activity Resources Co.,
Inc.
P. O. Box 4875
20655 Hathaway Avenue
Hayward, CA 94541

Addison-Wesley
Publishing Co., Inc.
Route 128
Reading, MA 01867

Alfred A. Knopf
Subsidiary of Random
House, Inc.
201 East 50th Street
New York, NY 10022

American Cryptogram
Association
ARACHNE
18789 West Hickory Street
Mundelein, IL 60060

Anchor Press/Doubleday
& Co., Inc.
666 Fifth Avenue
New York, NY 10103

Archon Books
Imprint of Shoe String
Press, Inc.
P. O. Box 4327
Hamden, CT 06514

Ardsley House Publishing,
Inc.
320 Central Park West
New York, NY 10025

Arno Press
Imprint of Ayer Co.
Publishers, Inc.
P. O. Box 958
Salem, NH 03079

Avon Books
1350 Avenue of the
Americas, 2nd Floor
New York, NY 10019

Ballantine Books, Inc.
201 East 50th Street
New York, NY 10022

Barron's Educational
Series, Inc.
P. O. Box 8040
250 Wireless Blvd.
Hauppauge, NY 11788

Basic Books, Inc.
10 East 53rd Street
New York, NY 10022

Beacon Press
25 Beacon Street
Boston, MA 02108

Bell Publishing
15 Surry Lane
East Brunswick, NJ 08816

Birkhäuser Boston
675 Massachusetts Avenue
Cambridge, MA 02139

Blackhawk Publishing, Inc.
P. O. Box 543
South Beloit, IL 61080

Blackwell, Basil, Inc.
Cambridge Center
Cambridge, MA 02142

Blaisdell Publications
Division of Random
House
210 East 50th Street, 31st
Floor
New York, NY 10022

Bonanza Books
Division of Crown
Publishers
One Park Avenue
New York, NY 10016

Boole Press
26 Temple Lane
Dublin 2
Ireland

Boston College Press
Boston College
Mathematics Institute
Boston College
Chestnut Hill, MA 02167

Brendan Kelly Publications
2122 Highview Drive
Burlington, Ontario
L7R 3X4
Canada

Brooks/Cole Publishing
Co.
511 Forest Lodge Road
Pacific Grove, CA 93950-
5098

Bulfinch Press
Division of Little, Brown
& Co.
34 Beacon Street
Boston, MA 02108

California Institute of
Technology
Bookstore
1201 East California Blvd.
Pasadena, CA 91125

California State University,
Northridge
Instructional Media Center
18111 Nordoff Street
Northridge, CA 91330

Cambridge University
Press
40 West 20th Street
New York, NY 10011

Center for Excellence in
Mathematics Education
885 Red Mesa Drive
Colorado Springs, CO
80906

Chapman and Hall
29 West 35th Street
New York, NY 10001-
2291

Charles E. Tuttle, Co., Inc.
77 Central Street
Boston, MA 02109

Charles Scribner & Sons
Division of Macmillan
Publishing Co., Inc.
866 Third Avenue
New York, NY 10022

Chelsea Publishing Co.
15 East 26th Street
New York, NY 10010

Chicago Review Press, Inc.
814 North Franklin Street
Chicago, IL 60610

Citadel Press
Imprint of Carol
Publishing Group
600 Madison Avenue,
11th Floor
New York, NY 10022

Clarendon Press
Imprint of Oxford
University Press
200 Madison Avenue
New York, NY 10016

Clarkson N. Potter, Inc.,
Publishers
Division of Crown
Publications, a division of
Random House
201 East 50th Street
New York, NY 10022

Coast Publishing
P. O. Box 3399
Coos Bay, OR 97420

Columbia University Press
562 West 113th Street
New York, NY 10025

COMAP, Inc.
(Consortium for
Mathematics and Its
Applications)
Suite 210
57 Bedford Street
Lexington, MA 02173

Contemporary Books, Inc.
180 North Michigan
Avenue
Chicago, IL 60601

Creative Publications
5040 West 11th Street
Oak Lawn, IL 60453

Critical Thinking Press
Midwest Publications
P. O. Box 448
Pacific Grove, CA 93950

Crossroad Publishing Co.
370 Lexington Avenue
New York, NY 10017

Crowell-Collier Press
Imprint of Macmillan
Publishing Co.
866 Third Avenue
New York, NY 10022

Dale Seymour Publications
P. O. Box 10888
Palo Alto, CA 94303

Davis Publications, Inc.
50 Portland Street
Worcester, MA 01608

DeCapo Press
Subsidiary of Plenum
Publishing Corporation
233 Spring Street
New York, NY 10013

Dorling Kindersley, Inc.
232 Madison Avenue,
Suite 1206
New York, NY 10016

Dorrance and Company
643 Smithfield Street
Pittsburgh, PA 15222

Doubleday & Co., Inc.
Division of Bantam
Doubleday Dell
666 Fifth Avenue
New York, NY 10103

Dover Publications, Inc.
31 East Second Street
Mineola, NY 11501

E. P. Dutton & Co.
201 Park Avenue South
New York, NY 10003

Edmund Scientific Co.
101 East Gloucester Pike
Barrington, NJ 08007

Education Development
Center
55 Chapel Street
Newton, MA 02160

Emerson Books, Inc.
121 North Hampton
Drive
White Plains, NY 10603

Facts on File, Inc.
460 Park Avenue South
New York, NY 10016

Fibonacci Associates
Santa Clara University
500 El Camino Real
Santa Clara, CA 95052

Fireside Books
8356 Olive Blvd.
St. Louis, MO 63132

Foundation for
Architecture
One Penn Center at
Suburban Station
No. 1665
Philadelphia, PA 19103

Franklin Watts
Subsidiary of Grolier, Inc.
387 Park Avenue South,
4th Floor
New York, NY 10016

Gardner Press, Inc.
19 Union Square West
New York, NY 10003

Graphics Press
3017 Santa Monica Blvd.,
Suite 406
Santa Monica, CA 90404

Graylock Press
5130 Rickett
Bethesda, MD 20814

Greenwood Press
Imprint of Greenwood
Publishing Group, Inc.
88 Post Road, West
P. O. Box 5007
Westport, CT 06881

Grosset & Dunlap
Imprint of Putnam
Publishing Group
200 Madison Avenue
New York, NY 10016

Guinness Publishers, Ltd.
33 London Road
Enfield, Middlesex,
England
Distributed by Sterling
Publishing Co.
387 Park Avenue South
New York, NY 10016-
8810

Hafner Press
Division of Macmillian
Publishing Co., Inc.
866 Third Avenue
New York, NY 10022

Harcourt Brace Jovanovich
1250 Sixth Avenue
San Diego, CA 92101

Harper & Row
Now HarperCollins
Publishers
10 East 53rd Street
New York, NY 10022

Harry N. Abrams, Inc.
See Abrams, Harry N., Inc.

Harvard University Press
79 Garden Street
Cambridge, MA 02138

Henry Holt & Co.
115 West 18th Street
New York, NY 10011

Henry Regnery Co.
Now Regnery Publishing
422 First Street, S.E.,
Suite 300
Washington, DC 20003

Hill & Wang
19 Union Square West
New York, NY 10003

Holt, Rinehart & Winston
of Canada
55 Horner Avenue
Toronto, Ontario,
M8Z 4X6
Canada

Holt, Rinehart &
Winston, Inc.
Division of Harcourt Brace
Jovanovich, Inc.
301 Commerce Street,
Suite 3700
Ft. Worth, TX 76102

Houghton Mifflin Co.
1 Beacon Street
Boston, MA 02108

Howard W. Sams Co., Inc.
2647 Waterfront Parkway
East Drive
Indianapolis, IN 46214

I. B. Tauris & Co., Ltd.
Imprint of St. Martin's
Press, Inc.
175 Fifth Avenue
New York, NY 10010

Ideal Toy Corporation
184–10 Jamaica Avenue
Hollis, NY 11423

Independent Publishers
Group
814 North Franklin
Chicago, IL 60610

Insight Press
614 Vermont Street
San Francisco, CA 94107

Ivy Books
201 East 50th Street
New York, NY 10022

J. B. Lippincott Co.
227 East Washington
Square
Philadelphia, PA 19106-
3780

Janson Publications
222 Richmond Street
Providence, RI 02903

Japan Publications, Inc.
45 Hawthorn Place
Briarcliff Manor, NY
10510

Jeremy P. Tarcher
5858 Wilshire Blvd., Suite
200
Los Angeles, CA 90036

John Day Co.
62 West 45th Street
New York, NY 10036

John Murray, Ltd.
Imprint of Heinemann
Educational Books, Inc.
361 Hanover Street
Portsmouth, NH 03801-
3959

John Wiley & Sons, Inc.
605 Third Avenue
New York, NY 10158-
0012

Journal of Recreational
Math
See National Council of
Teachers of Mathematics

Key Curriculum Press
P. O. Box 2304
Berkeley, CA 94702

Kodansha International
U.S.A., Ltd.
114 Fifth Avenue, 18th
Floor
New York, NY 10011

Kraus International
Publications
Route 100
Millwood, NY 10546

Lawrence Hall of Science
University of California,
Berkeley
Berkeley, CA 94720

Little, Brown & Co.
34 Beacon Street
Boston, MA 02108

Lowell House
1875 Century Park East,
#220
Los Angeles, CA 90067

Lyle Stuart
Division of Carol
Publishing Group
600 Madison Avenue,
11th Floor
New York, NY 10022

Macmillan Publishing
Company
866 Third Avenue
New York, NY 10022

Marcel Dekker
270 Madison Avenue
New York, NY 10016

Mathematical Association
of America
1529 18th Street, N.W.
Washington, DC 20036

McGraw-Hill Publishing
Co.
1221 Avenue of the
Americas
New York, NY 10020

Methuen & Co.
Imprint of Heinemann
Educational Books, Inc.
361 Hanover Street
Portsmouth, NH 03801-
3959

Mills College
5000 MacArthur Blvd.
Oakland, CA 94613

Mir Publishers
Distributed by Imported
Publications, Inc.
320 West Ohio Street
Chicago, IL 60610-4175

Mira Math Co.
2883 Rainbow Crescent
Mississauga, Ontario,
L5L 2H7
Canada

MIT Press
77 Massachusetts Avenue,
Room 9-234
Cambridge, MA 02139

National Academy Press
2101 Constitutional
Avenue, N.W.
Washington, DC 20418

National Council of
Teachers of Mathematics
1906 Association Drive
Reston, VA 22091

National Women's History
Project
7738 Bell Road
Windsor, CA 95492-8518

Nichols Schwartz
Publishing Co.
315 Fifteenth Street
Hondale, PA 18431-2019

North-Holland
Imprint of Elsevier Science
Publishing Co., Inc.
P. O. Box 882
Madison Square Garden
Station
New York, NY 10159

Novelty Books
P. O. Box 2482
Norman, OK 73070-2482

NSTA & FEMA
National Science Teachers
Association
5110 Roanoke Place, Suite
101
College Park, MD 20740

Ohio State University Press
1070 Carmack Road
Pressey Hall, Room 108
Columbus, OH 43210-
1002

Ondorisha Publishing
Distributed in the U.S. by
Kodansha America Inc.
Farrar, Straus, & Giroux
19 Union Square West
New York, NY 10003

Open Court Publishing
Co.
315 Fifth Street
Peru, IL 61354

Open Horizons Publishing
Co.
P. O. Box 105
Fairfield, IA 52556-0205

Oxford University Press,
Inc.
200 Madison Avenue
New York, NY 10016

Pacific Domes
Box 219
Bolinas, CA 94924

Penguin Books
375 Hudson Street
New York, NY 10014-
3657

Phaidon Publishers
Imprint of Chronicle
Books
275 Fifth Street
San Francisco, CA 94103

Plenum Press
Imprint of Plenum
Publishing Corporation
233 Spring Street
New York, NY 10013-
1578

Praeger Pubishers
Imprint of Greenwood
Publishing Group, Inc.
88 Post Road West
Box 5007
Westport, CT 06881

Prakken Publications, Inc.
416 Longshore Drive
Ann Arbor, MI 48107

Prentice Hall
Division of Simon &
Schuster, Inc.
15 Columbus Circle
New York, NY 10023

Princeton University Press
41 William Street
Princeton, NJ 08540

Prindle, Weber and
Schmidt
Imprint of PWS-KENT
Publishing Co.
20 Park Plaza
Boston, MA 02116

Prometheus Books
700 East Amherst Street
Buffalo, NY 14215

Pythagorean Press
P. O. Box 162
Bradford, MA 01835

Richard D. Irwin, Inc.
1818 Ridge Road
Homewood, IL 60430

Rutgers University Press
109 Church Street
New Brunswick, NJ 08901

Saunders College
Publishing
Division of Harcourt Brace
Jovanovich, Inc.
465 South Lincoln Drive
Troy, MO 63379

Schocken Books
Now Pantheon/Schocken
Books
Division of Random
House
201 East 50th Street, 31st
Floor
New York, NY 10022

School Science and
Mathematics Association,
Inc.
Bowling Green State
University
126 Life Science Building
Bowling Green, OH
43403-0256

Science Television
P. O. Box 2498
Times Square Station
New York, NY 10108

Scientific American
Library
Distributed by W. H.
Freeman and Co.
41 Madison Avenue
New York, NY 10010

Scott, Foresman & Co.
1900 East Lake Avenue
Glenview, IL 60025

Silver Burdett & Ginn,
Inc.
250 James Street
Morristown, NJ 07960

Simon & Schuster
1230 Avenue of the
Americas
New York, NY 10020

Springer-Verlag New York,
Inc.
175 Fifth Avenue
New York, NY 10010

St. Cloud University
720 Fourth Avenue, South
St. Cloud, MN 56301-
4498

St. Martin's Press, Inc.
175 Fifth Avenue
New York, NY 10010

Stewart T. Coffin
79 Old Sudbury Road
Lincoln, MA 01773

Stokes Publishing Co.
1125 Robin Way, Suite E.
Sunnyvale, CA 94087

Strawberry Press
Imprint of Electric
Strawberry Enterprises
7911 West Road
Houston, TX 77064

T. Y. Crowell Junior Books
Imprint of HarperCollins
Children's Books
10 East 53rd Street
New York, NY 10022

Tarquin
Distributed by Parkwest
Publications, Inc.
238 West 72nd Street
New York, NY 10023

Tempus Books
Imprint of Microsoft Press
1 Microsoft Way
Redmond, WA 98052-
6399

Ten Speed Press
P. O. Box 7123
Berkeley, CA 94707

Thames & Hudson
500 Fifth Avenue
New York, NY 10110

Thomas Y. Crowell Co.
See Crowell-Collier Press

Time-Life Books
Division of Time Warner
Publishing
777 Duke Street
Alexandria, VA 22314

Touchstone Books
Imprint of Simon &
Schuster Trade
1230 Avenue of the
Americas
New York, NY 10020

Tricon Mathematics
P. O. Box 146
Mt. Pleasant, MI 48804

U.S. Government Printing
Office
USGPO Stop SSMR
Washington, DC 20402

University of California
Press
2120 Berkeley Way
Berkeley, CA 94720

University of Chicago
Press
5801 Ellis Avenue, 4th
Floor
Chicago, IL 60637

University of Texas Press
Austin, TX 78712

University of Washington
Press
P. O. Box 50096
Seattle, WA 98145-5096

University of Toronto Press
340 Nagel Drive
Cheektowaga, NY 14225

Van Nostrand Reinhold
115 Fifth Avenue
New York, NY 10003

Viking Press
Division of Penguin
375 Hudson Street
New York, NY 10014-
3657

Vintage Books
Division of Random House
201 East 50th Street, 31st
Floor
New York, NY 10022

W&R Chambers
43–45 Annandale Street
Edinburgh EH7 4AZ
England

W. H. Freeman & Co.
41 Madison Avenue
East 26th, 35th Floor
New York, NY 10010

W. W. Norton & Co., Inc.
500 Fifth Avenue
New York, NY 10110

Wadsworth Publishing Co.
10 Davis Drive
Belmont, CA 94002

Walker and Co.
720 Fifth Avenue
New York, NY 10019

Wide World
Publishing/Tetra
P. O. Box 476
San Carlos, CA 94070

Wiley
See John Wiley & Sons,
Inc.

William Morrow & Co.,
Inc.
1350 Avenue of the
Americas
New York, NY 10019

World Publishing Co.
P. O. Box 301
Antioch, TN 37011
OR: 3223 LuAnn Dr.
Antioch, TN 37013

Zephyr Press
P. O. Box 13448
Tucson, AZ 85732-3448